Gabriel Hebert's Liturgy and Society is an important book, however its influence has not been fully recognised in contemporary Anglican ecclesiology. In this book, Andrew Bishop addresses that oversight. He engages with Hebert's text in order to explore the place and function of the church in today's world; he enriches our understanding of personhood, worship and mission. By echoing Hebert's non-anxious and generous spirit, this offers a vision of discipleship and witness rooted in the Eucharist whilst remaining attentive to the world.

Julie Gittoes, Residentiary Canon at Guildford Cathedral, UK

In this study Andrew Bishop re-reads Gabriel Hebert's writings, and, marshalling a range of conversation partners, persuasively argues that a church that is able to participate in the missio dei is a church that is first shaped by worship, and that a church that is shaped by worship is a church that is both in and for the world.

Christopher Irvine, Canon Librarian and Director of Education,
Canterbury Cathedral, UK

Eucharist Shaping and Hebert's *Liturgy and Society*

The contemporary Church of England is wrestling with issues around the relationship between its worship and mission and relating both to wider society. Much of this hinges on an understanding of the nature of the Church. Gabriel Hebert's seminal book *Liturgy and Society* (1935) took as its subtitle, *The Function of the Church in the Modern World*. For many this book inspired engagement with Eucharistic worship, with new patterns emerging, paving the way for further liturgical reform in the second half of the twentieth century.

Eucharist Shaping and Hebert's Liturgy and Society re-examines Hebert's work, doing so uniquely in the light of the current dialogue about Church, liturgy and mission. Andrew Bishop argues that Hebert's contribution has been overlooked latterly and that a re-appreciation opens up fruitful ways of thinking and acting, making this book a distinctive contribution to a lively debate. If the options are reaction or novelty, *Eucharist Shaping and Hebert's* Liturgy and Society shows how Hebert's thinking subtly undermines both.

Andrew Bishop is a priest of the Church of England. He has served in parishes in London and Basingstoke over 15 years. Andrew obtained an MTh in Pastoral Theology from Heythrop College, London and DThMin from King's College, London. He is currently a Residentiary Canon of Guildford Cathedral and Anglican and Coordinating Chaplain to the University of Surrey. He is a member of the Alcuin Club and Society for Liturgical Study.

Liturgy, Worship and Society

Series Editors

Dave Leal
Brasenose College, Oxford, UK

Bryan Spinks and Teresa Berger
Yale Divinity School, USA

Paul Bradshaw
University of Notre Dame, USA

Phillip Tovey
Ripon College Cuddesdon, UK

Eucharist Shaping and Hebert's *Liturgy and Society*

Church, Mission and Personhood

Andrew Bishop

Routledge
Taylor & Francis Group

LONDON AND NEW YORK

First published 2016
by Routledge

2 Park Square, Milton Park, Abingdon, Oxfordshire OX14 4RN
52 Vanderbilt Avenue, New York, NY 10017

Routledge is an imprint of the Taylor & Francis Group, an informa business

First issued in paperback 2020

British Library Cataloguing in Publication Data
A catalogue record for this book is available from the British Library

Library of Congress Cataloging-in-Publication Data
Names: Bishop, Andrew (Canon)
Title: Eucharist shaping and Hebert's Liturgy and society : church,
   mission, and personhood / by Andrew Bishop.
Description: Burlington : Ashgate, 2016. | Series: Liturgy, worship, and
   society series | Includes bibliographical references and index.
Identifiers: LCCN 2015035582| ISBN 9781472463289 (hardcover) |
   ISBN 9781472463296 (ebook) | ISBN 9781472463302 (epub)
Subjects: LCSH: Hebert, A. G. (Arthur Gabriel), 1886–1963. Liturgy
   and society. | Church. | Worship. | Apologetics.
Classification: LCC BV178.H43 B57 2016 | DDC 264/.03—dc23
LC record available at http://lccn.loc.gov/2015035582

ISBN: 978-1-4724-6328-9 (hbk)
ISBN: 978-0-367-59686-6 (pbk)

Typeset in Bembo
by Apex CoVantage, LLC

In thanksgiving for the life and ministry of Graham Johnson, priest.

For Alice, Edmund, Charles, Hugh and Beatrice.

Contents

Preface

The Smell of Incense and the Smell of Toast

An 11-year-old boy from a mixed Anglican and Nonconformist family background. The boy's father a Scottish Presbyterian, who, in exile in England, has found a home in the United Reformed Church (URC); the boy's mother the daughter of an Anglican priest of what might be called a 'Low Church' background. The family worship together at the URC, where Sunday school teaching tells the foundational stories of the Old and New Testaments. The father's greatest desire is to have a son who will be both a Presbyterian and a rugby player for Scotland. One problem: the local rugby club junior training begins at 10.30 on a Sunday morning – exactly the same time as the morning service at the URC. A solution: the boy goes with his Anglican mother to the parish church whose morning service, a 'Parish Eucharist', begins at 9.30 a.m. So the boy can play rugby and go to church, because the latter really matters to the family. The outcome: the boy is lost to Presbyterianism and to Scottish rugby. The boy's heart has been 'strangely warmed' in what he has apprehended, expressed in the two distinctive smells: the smell of incense and the smell of toast. Incense: he has fallen in love with the beauty of holiness expressed in worship, music, ceremony, preaching. Toast: he is making new and meaningful friendships with other children, and with adults, over a shared breakfast at the end of the service.

During the recessional hymn at Holy Cross Church, Daventry, in the early 1980s and for many years before, the smell of incense really did give way to the smell of toast as the parish breakfast was prepared in the church gallery where many of the congregation gathered after the service for toast and marmalade and, at Easter, a boiled egg. This was typical of what had become known as the Parish Communion. In my own experience it both celebrated the worship of the Church and was profoundly incarnational. Wider society became a locus of liturgy; I had been formed as *homo eucharisticus*.[1] It encouraged me to do door-to-door collections for Christian Aid, visiting a blind old lady on my way home from church; spending time in Bangladesh as a volunteer working in a rehabilitation of the paralysed and pondering a vocation to ordination.

The Parish Communion had 'worked' for me. My experience can be juxtaposed with the two following statements of Gabriel Hebert: 'The Holy Eucharist is the central act of the worship of the Church, the People of God, God's universal spiritual family';[2] and, 'In England, in well-to-do districts, where the Sunday Breakfast is firmly established, present a problem of a special difficulty, which may in some cases be solved by the institution of a communal breakfast in the Parish Room.'[3]

My own formation as a Christian was rooted in a parish that, in hindsight, Arthur Gabriel Hebert, known most commonly as Gabriel, would have recognised and of which he would have, no doubt, approved. Indeed a previous incumbent of Daventry, of living memory, trained for ordination at Kelham, the home of Hebert's order, the Society of the Sacred Mission. History does not relate a direct connection between the two men, but it is personally appealing to speculate on a version of Apostolic Succession (something which, incidentally, Hebert clearly values but sees can become lopsided!).[4]

The aroma of incense and toast is the *starting point* for an opportunity to research the roots and relevance of that tradition; to interrogate, critique and evaluate it in the light of how the Church functions in the modern world today. Whilst the Parish Communion is the starting point for, and hinterland of, this book it is not its sole focus. In particular it is not a description of the liturgical practices of the Parish Communion. On the publication of *The Parish Communion* (1937) Hebert was clear that he and his fellow contributors were not writing a book about how the Sunday service was to be arranged.[5] As Donald Gray notes, Hebert was 'anxious that the movement for the establishment of the Parish Communion should not be side-tracked by being made into some sort of new ritualistic movement'.[6] In *Liturgy and Society* Hebert most assuredly avoids that. He sees first that liturgy is participation in the common life of the Church, the Mystical Body of Christ, and also what shapes Christians in their day-to-day lives. It connects the incense of the sanctuary and the toast, or daily bread, of society, and shows that the Christian must engage in both so as to be shaped by the Church's worship and that the Church's worship must be shaped such that it is focused towards God but enables participation by everyone. The liturgy – primarily, but not exclusively the Sunday Eucharist – is where Church and world connect and each informs the other. This is why *Liturgy and Society* is not a piece of liturgical or ecclesiological archaeology but a vibrant call to a pastoral-missional ecclesiology rooted in worship.

Gabriel Hebert's *Liturgy and Society: The Function of the Church in the Modern World* offers a continuing contribution to theological endeavour, practical ecclesiology and ways of Christian discipleship and engagement in Church and society today. This book identifies and explores three key themes emerging from *Liturgy and Society* which all contribute to Hebert's central proposition that liturgy, principally the Eucharist, shapes Christian identity. The first theme is ecclesiology. This is significant because for Hebert the Church is indispensable in mission and her dogma is embodied in liturgy. The second theme is mission. Hebert's examination of the function of the Church in the modern world has a missional character. The third theme is personhood. This theme comes from Hebert's conception of what shapes persons through liturgy. I propose the notion of 'liturgical anthropology' as a way of articulating Hebert's idea of personhood.

I will set Hebert in context historically and theologically within the 'Parish Communion Movement' and twentieth-century Anglican theology. Furthermore I will take Hebert beyond his original setting by analysing his work alongside contemporary writers on the three themes, demonstrating that he can be set in relation to contemporary writers in the fields of ecclesiology, mission and liturgical anthropology. In each area Hebert is a fruitful conversation partner in which his thought is elucidated by and resonates with other writers.

Whilst the influence of the Parish Communion Movement is still current in the Church of England, Hebert's approach is not uncontested in the contemporary Church. However Hebert's rejection of individualism, his recognition of the intimate relationship between mission and Church and his vision of the liturgical grounding of the practical and ethical consequences of the function of the Church in the modern world speak powerfully today. I write both as a recipient of the implementation of the Parish Communion, but also more significantly as a fieldworker, as it were, and priest-theologian called upon constantly to interpret *plausibly* the lived experience of the Church, her liturgy, doctrine and mission. The challenge for me is to be clear about the essentials not aesthetics – the smell of toast or incense – of the Parish Communion Movement or *Liturgy and Society* and how that might continue to shape lives within the Church.

Notes

1 Rowan D. Williams, *Faith in the Public Square* (London: Continuum, 2012), 96.
2 Arthur Gabriel Hebert, *Liturgy and Society: The Function of the Church in the Modern World* (London: Faber, 1935), 3.
3 Hebert, *Liturgy and Society*, 5.
4 Arthur Gabriel Hebert, *Apostle and Bishop: A Study of the Gospel, Ministry and the Church Community* (London: Faber, 1963), 70.
5 Arthur Gabriel Hebert, ed., *The Parish Communion*, (London: SPCK, 1937).
6 Donald Gray, *Earth and Altar: The Evolution of the Parish Communion in the Church of England to 1945* (Norwich: Alcuin Club Canterbury Press, 1986), 206.

Acknowledgements

This book grew out of a doctoral thesis, and I am grateful to Dr James Steven and Professor Peter Ward for their supervision at different stages of the project.

I have been very fortunate to have friends and colleagues who provided much encouragement while I was working on the project and for their continued interest and conversation. My thanks to colleagues past and present at Guildford Cathedral, particularly Victor Stock and Nicholas Thistlethwaite for their support and encouragement. I am also grateful to Christopher Irvine for conversations in the very early stages of my study.

My special thanks is to my friend and colleague Julie Gittoes who has read drafts and discussed the book with me. Her insights, challenges and questions have been invaluable.

This project would never have started had not I been generously supported by Penny Potter during my doctoral studies at King's College, London. I am deeply grateful for her support and interest.

I have benefited spiritually and intellectually from those who I have served and with whom I have worshipped and celebrated the Eucharist at St Stephen's Rochester Row, Westminster, St Mary Abbots, Kensington, St Mary's, Old Basing and Lychpit. They have contributed to this book in ways they will never know. I give thanks to God for all who worship and minister in the parishes of the Church of England.

I am deeply grateful to Alice, my wife, and Edmund, Charles, Hugh and Beatrice my children. Their patience and love continues to be the most wonderful support.

1   Issues

Participation in a Common Life

The way in which the Church functions in the modern world was of profound concern to Gabriel Hebert. It is the pivotal feature of *Liturgy and Society* and its subtitle, *The Function of the Church in the Modern World.* His reflection upon it had both an impact at the time and is of value to the contemporary Church in her self-reflection and engagement with contemporary society. Three key principles guide the trajectory of this book. First, that the influence of the Parish Communion Movement is at worst anonymous and at best understated in contemporary Anglican ecclesiology and missiology, and that this is a weakness. Secondly, that in *Liturgy and Society* Hebert articulates an essential voice which helps to reframe current debate about the nature of the Church and mission because of his approach to Church, mission and personhood. Thirdly, in reappraising Hebert, contemporary resonant voices that show affinity with his work in the key areas of liturgy, mission and personhood. This not only illustrates Hebert's enduring value but also how theological discourse informs, and is informed by, liturgical and missional practice as the function of the Church, disciples of Jesus Christ, in the world continues to be reflected upon.

So *Liturgy and Society* will be set in 'conversation' with contemporary writers, notably with Daniel W. Hardy (ecclesiology); Andrew Walker (mission); Paul Roberts (liturgy and worship); and Samuel Wells, James K.A. Smith and William Cavanaugh (Church in society). Engagement with the novel *Saturday* by Ian McEwan will also bring a dissonant, and yet necessary, voice because McEwan's account of identity and the secular 'liturgies' that form it is inevitably at variants from a theological one, Hebert's included. The interplay between the conversation partners will enable the construction of a plausible pastoral theology of worship, Church and mission that situates Hebert's work as substantive, vibrant and informative to the contemporary Church engaging with the modern world.

Liturgy and Society has lasting credibility in offering a robust but irenic challenge to contemporary theological discourse. It is a book of its time in many ways. To consider it today is not a nostalgic or inward-looking pursuit because the issues in Church and society that Hebert addresses are perennial. None of these themes – Church, mission and liturgy – are introspective. Hebert's constant eye to the function of the Church in the modern world turns his thinking outwards. This continues to be essential for the Church today so that she does not become self-serving and thereby have little to contribute to the world in which she is set. A Church that does not consider her public dimension does not function adequately in the modern world however aesthetically attractive liturgically.

It is important to note at the outset that Hebert was an Anglican. When the term 'Church' is used it sometimes means the Church of England, but most frequently the rather more nebulous and less specific sense of the Western Church in general. Reference will be made clear to which is being referred. This (lack of) definition honours Hebert since he was a creature of the wider Anglican Communion and not exclusively the Church of England: he spent time ministering in Australia and South Africa. Moreover he knew, and had an affinity with, the Lutheran Churches especially in Sweden and the continental Roman Catholic Church, whose own liturgical movement cannot be disregarded as being formative to Hebert too. Hebert is a catholic figure.

Hebert's ecclesiology is central to his approach both to the Church's worship and life in wider society is also dependent on what is meant by 'Church'. Hebert is not clear what he means. When, for instance, he refers to 'the Church and her dogma' he is not apparently specific about which Church he is speaking. His use of the term 'Church' sometimes means the Church of England but more often appears to be referring to the Western Church more generally, and even then this is nuanced.[1] Hebert's ecumenical heart often assumed the Church as the Mystical Body of Christ, and as such not fractured by denominationalism.

Nevertheless Hebert has a distinctively Anglican contribution to make. Yet that contribution is not uncontested today. Furthermore it does not address ecumenical sensibilities. So there are disconnects in Hebert's work. Nicholas Healy's account of ways describing the 'concrete Church', drawing on Barth and Bonhoeffer, highlights this and is apposite to these disconnections.[2] Healy calls for a description of the Church that engages critically with disciplines that account for 'the complexities and confusions of human activity' and is 'thoroughly catholic (i.e. ecumenical)'. Hebert contributes to this 'ecclesial bricolage' as the Church seeks her identity in a pluralist society.[3] Hebert can have the aroma of an idealist. Although, countering that sense, Critchton notes that Hebert served in parish centres in South Africa where he designed and built a church.[4] Theologically his work on initiation rites make a pastorally connected liturgical provision for baptism of infants and, significantly, for adults.[5] Healy's appeal for consistency of theological statements about the Church in relation to the observable life of individual Christians is apposite.

Liturgy is the embodied expression of a Church's normative ecclesiology and therefore, according to Hebert, it matters: the way in which that is expressed enables a judgement to be made if the Church is a social body or a collection of individuals. This is the challenge to Christians who associate in different ways. Liturgy is performative ecclesiology: is it though a participation in a common life? The way the Church of England, and other 'liturgical Churches', express this is by maintaining an authorised liturgy. That is to say liturgy that has norms, albeit diverse in practice. Liturgy also has the capacity to express the relational character of the Church which reaches beyond any one congregation. Hebert's approach is not simply theoretical but it flows from a theological conviction about the nature of the Church as what can be named when those baptised gather to worship, corporately, in the name of the Trinity in their task of engagement with the world. Furthermore that their worship is in some way shaped and informed by what they understand the nature of the Church to be. Hebert sought to address the lived life of the Church in all its variety, and touches aesthetics, as well as the social and political dimension in its task of functioning in the modern world.

Liturgy has a transformative effect, and in as much as it affects and shapes persons Hebert has a *liturgical anthropology*; a conception of being human, shaped and defined by liturgy. This is not an ideological imperative but one that Hebert fashions with thought and imagination. At its best liturgy opens up possibilities of Christian living and does not close them down. If human persons conceive of themselves as atomised individuals and live as such, society as a whole becomes selfish. Hebert posits that the task of the Church is to face down individualism and to shape individuals into social persons who embody the social worth of the Church to society. This opens persons to God and to one another and is deeply missiological. Liturgy shapes and defines who persons are because, and only because, it places them, in the power of the Spirit, before the Father in the name of the Word–made–flesh. The person is at stake in this as much as the Church.

It is not simply Hebert's conclusions that are of value, it is his method too. He is both patient and attentive to the 'inherited Church' and at the same time radical and traditional. The terms 'radical' and 'traditional' are not contradictory; they are used in their proper senses: radical, being rooted, and traditional, having received what is handed on. From this base he explores what all this might mean to the Church and society of his own day. Along the way Hebert is very hard to pin down to any one ecclesiastical party, which is itself refreshing and important because it raises the issues at hand above the polemics of the contemporary Church and the vagaries of passing pressures.

Issues: The Contemporary Impact of *Liturgy and Society*

This critical reading and evaluation of Hebert today is, of necessity, set within a wider contemporary debate which is of direct relevance and interest to the Church of England today (and it should be noted the Methodist Church too in its interest ecumenically in 'Fresh Expressions'). A call to the Church of England in 'deepening conversation in generosity' has been made that seeks to engage those who seek to prioritise the missionary calling of the Church, and to seek evermore creative and imaginary ways of engaging in that task, and those who affirm the place of inherited patterns and structures that cannot be simply discarded and that still have life left in them.[6] As a response to this call Hebert's approach and method, patient and attentive as it is, will be set out, navigating between the twin poles of the Church of England report *Mission-shaped Church*[7] and critiques of Fresh Expressions, such as *For the Parish*.[8] To situate *Liturgy and Society* in this way is not to misuse it as either unrelated or anachronistic. Rather, Hebert's work is invaluable in responding to the call to 'deepening conversation in generosity'. Even more than that, *Liturgy and Society* opens up new contributions to contemporary debate and theological pursuit by resetting some priorities.

An example of this contribution is the treatment of 'place'. This becomes most clear in ecclesiological and missional terms in the current discussion of the 'parish system' in the Church of England.[9] The discussion can be caricatured as an 'either or' question: either parishes or no parishes. For some the parish is a 'unit of mission' conceived as an organisational convenience and a nostalgic notion belonging to the era of Christendom; for others it is a way in which place, and the real localities in which people live are taken seriously. Re-engaging with Hebert aids a reassessment of the language used, for instance, of place. The significance of place becomes diminished by functionality illustrated by the phrase the 'parochial *system*'. Theologically the question is not about a particular system but the valuing of the places where people live and love, where they share their lives with other people, where they play and are renewed and where they worship. To reflect on place also prompts the Church to reflect on presence and what it means to be present.[10] So for instance, *Mission-shaped Church* frames its language in terms of function and the 'strategy to deliver incarnational mission'.[11] In contrast, John Milbank sees 'the logic of parish organization [as] simply the logic of ecclesiology itself'.[12] Hebert is not confined to polarities, and *Liturgy and Society* creatively and generously engages with what *matters* about places and locations, the built environment and aesthetics of buildings domestic, public and ecclesiastical, albeit in a somewhat patrician style. This is what the Parish Communion Movement brought and *Liturgy and Society* continues to articulate.

In missiology Hebert proposes patience and what might be termed the 'long game'. His is an organic approach to mission. This is encapsulated, as shall be noted again, in his quoting T.S. Eliot: 'take no thought of the harvest / but only of the proper sowing'.[13] Such an approach can be a threat to those who conceive mission in terms of the imperative for rapid, unrelenting growth. Furthermore it exposes what might be termed 'anxiety driven mission'. Conversely it can also be a gift, especially in how liturgy and mission can relate in a non-rivalistic, mutually nourishing and non-utilitarian way. Such a hermeneutic resists the commercial/transactional language of production, results and yield in mission.[14]

A similar approach can be identified in relation to liturgy and the function of the Church in the modern world. This is potentially problematic in a culture that is becoming increasingly unfamiliar with Christian liturgy and language, whilst still having discernible roots in it.[15] This is also a challenge to Christians who do not associate with 'historic Christianity'. Hebert was writing in a time when it was assumed that at the very least Christian liturgy was understood as significant, even if not totally understood. Liturgy today is not widely familiar, let alone understood, outside the Churches. Matthew Guest et al. juxtapose this contemporary cultural change with that of the changes in the Churches. So, for instance, in the Church of England, the *Alternative Service Book 1980* and *Common Worship* (2000) 'prioritize accessibility and choice over the nurturing of a common language rooted in British history'.[16] That is not a value-judgement but an acknowledgement of a changing landscape. It is also the case that within Churches the sense of common association with a deeper tradition is tenuous, and:

> the label 'Christian' has acquired a life of its own as a preferred identity for those wishing to distance themselves from the trappings of denominational Church structures, and as a symbolic marker for a constellation of ethnic, cultural and moral, rather than, religious values.[17]

The sociological issues are sharper today, but Hebert unpicks similar questions that he faced. He does this principally in relation to how theology is 'not reaching the mind of the modern man [sic]' and that it, and the Church and Bible are not rejected as untrue, but 'set aside as irrelevant'.[18]

This reassessment of *Liturgy and Society* will invite the Church to face the questions of Church growth, the relevance of Christian belief and practice, in the light of reflection on the function of the Church in the modern world.

That function is shaped by patient and faithful attention to the liturgy, principally the Eucharist, in the way that it shapes the corporate and individual life of the Church and her members. This engages the Church as a society within and to wider society as well as to God.

A recurring theme through this book is that ecclesiology, missiology and liturgy are inseparable; distinctive but interconnected. The enduring and significant contribution of *Liturgy and Society* diminishes in value if it is simply part of a self-referencing conversation. Peter Ward is alert to a very present danger when there is a 'disconnection between what we say doctrinally about the Church and the experience of life in a local parish'.[19] It is possible to assert a relationship between theory and practice without ever making the connections that make such a relationship either meaningful or plausible. Hebert shares that concern such that he is able to make that relationship credible.

Ward's warning about the earthing of any study of the Church is salutary. It helps to frame and drive the argument of Hebert's enduring value by challenging Hebert where he is nostalgic and perhaps attractive on aesthetic grounds but not specific on how grace is mediated. To that end connections directly from the lived experience of parochial ministry in the Church of England will be made. This is to demonstrate 'the correspondence between the theological representation of the Church and the lived social reality of Christian communities'.[20] That demands the resistance of any desire to 'base whole arguments on anecdote and the selective treatment of experience',[21] but rather to give a sense of what provoked a prolonged investigation into *Liturgy and Society*. Nevertheless, as Healy suggests, no one worshipping community, or even series of communities, can encompass socially, demographically or culturally the whole of the Church's experience in worship and mission.

The primary original move of this book is to position Hebert in *Liturgy and Society* as an interlocutor in the discourse on the nature and purpose of the Church and mission. Hebert's relative anonymity and consequent lack of visibility and audibility demands an assessment of his work today. It is not that he is absent from contemporary discourse. For instance, Paul Roberts writing on liturgy and mission invokes Hebert's legacy. Furthermore this book takes the analysis of Hebert's work beyond previous studies.[22] Such studies are invaluable background to Hebert and his age. Christopher Irvine's work is primarily descriptive and historical, whilst sketching out theological themes. Gray and others set him emphatically within the Parish Communion milieu. This book focuses on and develops in an intentional way the three key strands of *Liturgy and Society*: ecclesiology, missiology and liturgiology. This task sets Hebert's work in the context of the corporate nature of worship and the place of the Eucharist within that. More particularly it explores the place and nature of Sunday worship; the nature of mission; the way in which liturgy shapes individual lives and the corporate life of the Church. The proposition of this book is that Hebert does this as a practical theologian.[23]

The secondary move is to identify and draw from Hebert a renewed impulse to extrospection through the formation of the individual Christian. Hebert's own originality, and the reason he captured the minds of clergy and congregations in his day, was not in liturgical tinkering but in how he brought to bear his ecclesiology into a substantial renegotiation of the 'Sunday contract' for churchgoers: *if our ecclesiology looks like this, then our liturgy must look like this, and if our liturgy looks like this, then our missiology must look like this, for this is the persons we are called to be.* Hebert's epistemology frames a significant question for the Church and congregations today, and one that will be developed. This is a key element of the argument that proposes that Hebert's work can be set within the life of the contemporary Church which enables connections to be made with other theologians.

The Historical and Theological Milieu of Gabriel Hebert

Gabriel Hebert is a name known to few contemporary Anglicans; whereas, for example, George Herbert is known to significantly more. Indeed to refer simply to Hebert often elicits the response, 'Don't you mean *Herbert?*' The name of George Herbert is often credited with the legacy of the classical Anglican parochial model, despite the fact that he probably represented more of the exception than the rule of the pattern of parochial ministry in the Church of England of his day.[24] However in the second half of the twentieth century Gabriel Hebert has been more formative to Anglican parochial ministry, ecclesiology and missiology than George Herbert. Hebert, most especially in *Liturgy and Society* and in his shared enterprise editing *The Parish Communion*, has been deeply influential on a past and present generation of Anglican clergy and through them the continuing shape of the worship and ministry of the Church of England.[25]

Hebert is often 'pigeonholed' as a writer about liturgy, but that is not his sole concern.[26] Irvine surveys his wider corpus and describes the breadth of his work, which embraces biblical theology, ecclesiology, episcopacy and Church union.[27] Use of some of these works will demonstrate his wider theological hinterland.[28] As such *Liturgy and Society* sets the practice of the Parish Communion in a rich and subtle context. Yet novelty is something that cannot be ascribed to Hebert. The Parish Communion was a phenomenon that pre-existed Hebert. This is not to confuse the Parish Communion with the Tractarian and later Ritualist emphasis on the Eucharist. Gray notes that 'despite Hebert's anxiety to place his advocacy of the Parish Communion in the fullest possible setting, reviewers . . . fastened on to that part of the book which was about the introduction of a particular form of service called "The Parish Communion"'.[29] Gray suggests that it was what many were waiting for, a theological rationale for the practice that was spreading. This 'theological rationale' for his understanding of liturgy came first from his ecclesiology from which flowed his missiology, all of which is bound into his conception of the human person.

So the practice predates the theology in this instance. Throughout *Liturgy and Society* Hebert quotes examples of practice. He does not claim to be inaugurating something new, but elucidating and finding the theological, ecclesiological and missional merit in what already exists. Despite the title of *Liturgy and Society* Hebert was not, as might be supposed, a liturgical archaeologist. Rather he sought to engage in reflection upon how the normative life of the Church in her worship and teaching (he prefers the word 'dogma') is sustainable in the modern world. It is more than that too. Hebert's conception of the Church is not of inward-looking sustainability but the Church as agent of the gospel in society. That compels public worship.

Regardless of his significance, Hebert is too often overlooked in contemporary Anglican thinking on ecclesiology, missiology and what constitutes being human. He is sometimes misrepresented or simplistically caricatured: the introduction of the offertory procession, the flight from Matins, a folksy communitarianism and the time of Divine Service.[30] Hebert is a pivotal figure in the Parish Communion Movement and the twentieth-century Church of England; so why is he overlooked? Perhaps his work has become regarded as dated, or that he was all too implausible as a writer, being a 'posh monk' who spent significant times abroad. These perceptions will be challenged. The only other figure of his generation to have made such an impact was his friend Dom Gregory Dix, most notably in *The Shape of the Liturgy*.[31] Dix, another monastic, has retained a place in the popular imagination in a way that Hebert has not. It is typical that books about Anglicanism will reflect this, having Dix and Herbert in their index but not Hebert.[32] Whilst Dix's work marked a new way of thinking of liturgical theology, his work is now feeling the effects of time.[33] Hebert's impact was less stellar and less obviously innovative, but certainly more enduring.

Hebert is an eclectic writer. *The Guardian* review of *Liturgy and Society* drew attention to the many streams which had fertilised 'this remarkable book'.[34] Gray sees the wider roots of the Parish Communion Movement in Christian Socialism, and Hebert is also clearly influenced by the thinking of F.D. Maurice. Gray also notes that in its genesis the Parish Communion Movement shows little evidence of 'any detectable borrowing from the comparable Roman Catholic Liturgical Movement which was developing on the

Continent of Europe'.[35] As will be shown below, this is not true of Hebert. With extensive overseas and ecumenical experience, Hebert also translated works of theology, particularly Scandinavian in origin, most notably, from a liturgical and ecclesiological point of view, of Yngve Brilioth.[36] Theirs was a mutually generative relationship. Brilioth acknowledges his debt to the Society of the Sacred Mission in general and Hebert in particular, and 'the fuller sacramental life of the English Church' which, he says, 'has helped more than anything to open my eyes to the hidden, half-forgotten riches of my own Church'.[37] In return Hebert was similarly indebted to Brilioth, who hoped that his book, and its translation by Hebert, 'may bear witness to the reality of this spiritual *commercium*'.[38] Hebert brought to bear many influences on the Parish Communion Movement and nurtured it in the distinctive *terroir* of the Church of England. The Parish Communion was not a uniquely English phenomenon since it mirrored and mutually enriched the continental Liturgical Movement and the first signs of the Parish Communion can be traced to the 1890s, as Gray does.[39] Nevertheless the seminal *Liturgy and Society* anticipated much of the liturgical reform in the Church of England and of the Second Vatican Council. That in itself was a huge achievement and could only be born out of a rediscovered and renewed ecclesiology.

George Guiver describes the Parish Communion Movement as, 'a movement for a participatory Eucharist with general communion suitable for all ages, and held at a time when most could come . . . It was to have an enormous success into our own day.'[40] The place of the Parish Communion today is not as secure as it has been, and this is not about liturgical fashion or taste *per se*. It is ecclesiological too. More significant is the perception that the participatory Eucharist envisaged by Hebert no longer fits with the prevailing ecclesiology and missiology articulated in *Mission-Shaped Church*.[41] Despite having been widely embraced *Mission-Shaped Church* and the 'Fresh Expressions' that flow from it have not been received entirely uncritically.[42] That is why revisiting Hebert enables a significant understanding of the Church and her function in society.

Hebert is a figure of substance who, as Peter Hinchliff comments, 'made his contemporaries and the subsequent generations do some serious thinking'.[43] This book is a contribution to that thinking. *Liturgy and Society* is worthy of fresh attention. This is for two principal reasons. First, because historically it infused the Church of England afresh with a pastoral-liturgical and missional vision; and, secondly, because the fundamental issue it addresses has not gone away: the function of the Church in the modern world which relates to ecclesiology and understanding of society. As already noted, this is a contested area currently in the Church of England.[44] In this, and in the field of pastoral liturgy, *Liturgy and Society* has the advantage of not being associated with any contemporary polemic. It opens up a way in which the Eucharist shapes the Church and the Church the Eucharist. Furthermore, as shall be demonstrated, *Liturgy and Society* invites reflection on the function of the Church in the modern world – whether that of 1936 or of 2015 – in such a way that mission and being human are integral to his vision. The 'serious thinking' that Hinchliff says Hebert's work calls for is engaging and recalibrates ecclesiological, missional and anthropological discourse.

Liturgy and Society: **Beyond Polemic**

The Church of England today would be unrecognisable to Hebert, not simply with the passing of time. Much of what has preoccupied the Church of England in recent years has been precisely about one of Hebert's concerns, that of Church order: the nature of Holy Orders, ordained ministry (the sex and sexuality of bishops, priests and deacons), concern for mission and the deployment of ministry (Pioneer Ministers) and episcopal jurisdiction (Alternative Episcopal Oversight, Bishops' Mission Orders and Women in the Episcopate) loom large in Anglican ecclesiology. There is a wealth of contemporary writing on ecclesiology, missiology, liturgy and personhood into which Hebert's work can speak. Very often those fields are treated as discrete areas, yet at times they are brought together.[45] Other works engage this approach and illuminate its ethical and political dimension.[46] Hebert is within that company: he sees that his theology of worship cannot be divorced from that of the Church, and that as such his theology has also to understand the personhood of the Christian. This is consonant with Hebert's understanding of the relational character of being human: the human person is created for relationship. For Hebert this is always true of worship, Church and mission. In worship we never worship truly alone. Within the Church each is a member one of another (Romans 12.4). Mission is always relational since it involves communication, of one sort or another. In an unrecognisable Church there are recognisable features and the enduring challenge of identifying and living out the function of the Church and the Christian in the modern world. This offering of a fresh articulation of Hebert's theology holds the Church faithful to the relational charism of being human and being a member of the Church, a Christian. The impact is to counter tendencies to see worship either as a commodity, an end in itself, or something divorced from expressing who and what the Church is called to be.[47] For Hebert relationality is paramount: related to God; related to one another.

There is another challenge too: the credibility of liturgical worship itself is under scrutiny in the Church of England today. For example, Graham Cray can write that it is easy for Christians, 'who become so used to reciting the creeds, and hearing their lectionary passages read out, that their missionary implications are ignored'.[48] Writing from his experience as Archbishop of Canterbury, Rowan Williams notes:

> there are many varieties of Christian practice spreading in the world at present in which eucharistic practice is not obviously central, and eucharistic theology is very thin. There are parts of my own Communion . . . in which eucharistic theology seems to have slipped away from a prime position.[49]

He goes on to suggest that 'we need to understand better why it is that some apparently very popular forms of Christianity do not seem to find the Eucharist central to their practice'.[50] *Liturgy and Society* asserts the primacy of liturgy, and specifically the Eucharist, in that it relates at a profound level both mission and personal meaning. In that sense it provides a rejoinder to those who assume liturgical worship to be formulaic, restrictive and not generative of mission or personal commitment: it is often wrongly caricatured as static and ossified, wrongly because it both receives and generates the fruits of mission. This recasts how liturgical worship is perceived and sets Hebert as a necessary voice within Anglican ecclesiological and missional identity – characterised by *Mission-shaped Church* and *For the Parish* – not as a fluffy *via media* but a robust, yet irenic, reframing of the debate.

Notes

1 I will follow his lead in being unspecific, except where I particularly mean to be specific. This will honour the influence of the wider Anglican Communion, notably South Africa and Australia; the Lutheran Churches of Northern Europe, especially Sweden; and the Roman Catholic Church, whose own Liturgical Movement cannot be disregarded as being formative to Hebert too.

2 Nicholas Healy, *Church, World and the Christian Life: Practical-Prophetic Ecclesiology* (Cambridge: Cambridge University Press, 2000), 4–7.

3 Healy, *Church, World and the Christian Life*, 109.

4 J.D. Critchton, *Lights in the Darkness: Fore-Runners of the Liturgical Movement* (Dublin: Columba Press, 1996), 88.

5 Arthur Gabriel Hebert, *An Essay in Baptismal Regeneration* (Westminster: Dacre Press, 1947), 70.

6 Julie Gittoes, Brutus Green and James Heard, eds, *Generous Ecclesiology: Church, World and the Kingdom of God* (London: SCM Press, 2013), 14.

7 The Archbishops' Council, *Mission-Shaped Church: Church Planting and Fresh Expressions of Church in a Changing Context* (London: Church House, 2004).

8 Andrew Davison and Alison Milbank, *For the Parish: A Critique of Fresh Expressions* (London: SCM Press, 2010).

9 Steven Croft, ed., *The Future of the Parish System: Shaping the Church of England for the 21st Century* (London: Church House, 2006).

10 Ben Quash, 'The Anglican Church as a Polity of Presence', in *Anglicanism: The Answer to Modernity*, eds Duncan Dormer, Jack McDonald and Jeremy Caddick (London: Continuum, 2003), 38–57.

11 Archbishops' Council, *Mission-shaped Church*, xi.

12 John Milbank, 'Stale Expressions: The Management-Shaped Church', *Studies in Christian Ethics* 21/1 (2008): 125.

13 Hebert, *Liturgy and Society*, 260.

14 Robert Skidelsky and Edward Skidelsky, *How Much is Enough? Money and the Good Life* (London: Penguin, 2012). The Skidelskys critique such a notion of growth in the financial world. They give an ethical and faith-based rationale for their conclusions.

15 Matthew Guest, Elizabeth Olsen and John Wolffe, 'Christianity: The Loss of Monopoly', in *Religion and Change in Modern Britain*, eds Linda Woodhead and Rebecca Catto, 57–78 (London: Routledge, 2012), 67.

16 Guest et al, 'Christianity: The Loss of Monopoly', 67.

17 Guest et al, 'Christianity: The Loss of Monopoly', 61.

18 Hebert, *Liturgy and Society*, 163.

19 Peter Ward, *Perspectives on Ecclesiology and Ethnography* (Grand Rapids MI: Eerdmans, 2012), 4.

20 Ward, *Perspectives on Ecclesiology and Ethnography*, 5.

21 Ward, *Perspectives on Ecclesiology and Ethnography*, 4.

22 Most notably in Donald Gray, *Earth and Altar: The Evolution of the Parish Communion in the Church of England to 1945* (Norwich: Alcuin Club Canterbury Press, 1986) and Christopher Irvine, *Worship, Church and Society: An Exposition of the Work of Arthur Gabriel Hebert to Mark the Centenary of the Society of the Sacred Mission of Which He Was a Member* (Norwich: Canterbury Press, 1993).

23 Helen Cameron, Philip Richter, Douglas Davies and Frances Ward, 'How to Study the Local Church', in *Studying Local Churches: A Handbook*, eds Cameron et al. (London: SCM Press, 2005), 17–18.

24 Justin Lewis-Anthony, *If You Meet George Herbert on the Road, Kill Him: Radically Re-thinking Priestly Ministry* (London: Mowbray, 2009), 1–65.

25 Irvine, *Worship, Church and Society*, 151.

26 Critchton, *Lights in the Darkness*, 88–94 and Christopher Irvine, *They Shaped our Worship: Essays on Anglican Liturgists* (London: SPCK, 1998).

27 Irvine, *Worship, Church and Society*, 157–8.

28 In this study we will draw on some of Hebert's other works, primarily *The Parish Communion* (1937), *The Form of the Church* (1944, revised edition 1954) and *God's Kingdom and Ours* (1959).

29 Gray, *Earth and Altar*, 203.

30 G. J. Cumming, *A History of Anglican Liturgy* (London: Macmillan, 1969), 248 and John Fenwick, J, 'These Holy Mysteries', in *Anglo-Catholic Worship: An Evangelical Appreciation after 150 Years*, ed. Colin Buchanan (Bramcote: Grove, 1983), 9–16. Gray, *Earth and Altar*, also details the debate over the optimum time of the Parish Communion that was centred not on practical issues for worshippers but on the notion of a divine hour.

31 Simon Bailey, *A Tactful God: Gregory Dix Priest, Monk and Scholar* (Leominster: Gracewing, 1995), 256.

32 For instance, Ian Bunting, *Celebrating the Anglican Way* (London: Hodder & Stoughton, 1996) and Kenneth Hylson-Smith, *The Churches in England from Elizabeth I to Elizabeth II (Volume III) 1833–1998* (London: SCM Press, 1998).

33 Simon Jones, introduction to *The Shape of the Liturgy* by Gregory Dix (London: Continuum, 1945, 2005), xi.

34 Gray, *Earth and Altar*, 203.

35 Gray, *Earth and Altar*, 5.

36 Yngve Brilioth, *Eucharistic Faith and Practice: Evangelical and Catholic*, trans. Arthur Gabriel Hebert (London: SPCK, 1930).

37 Brilioth, *Eucharistic Faith and Practice*, viii.

38 Brilioth, *Eucharistic Faith and Practice*, viii. A *commercium*, a word left untranslated by Hebert, is 'a traditional academic feast known at universities in most Central and Northern European countries'. http://en.wikipedia.org/wiki/Commercium [accessed 9 June 2012].

39 Gray, *Earth and Altar*, 153–63.

40 George Guiver, *Vision upon Vision: Processes of Change and Renewal in Christian Worship* (Norwich: Canterbury Press, 2009), 145.

41 Archbishops' Council. *Mission-shaped Church*.

42 Works such as Paul Bayes and Tim Sledge, *Mission-shaped Parish: Traditional Church in a Changing Context* (London: Church House, 2006); Steven Croft and Ian Mobsby, eds, *Fresh Expressions in the Sacramental Tradition* (Norwich: Canterbury Press, 2009); and Davison and Milbank, *For the Parish*.

43 Epilogue in Irvine, *Worship, Church and Society*, 152.

44 It can be broadly caricatured between the proponents of Davison and Milbank's *For the Parish* and *Mission-shaped Church*.

45 David Ford, *Self and Salvation: Being Transformed* (Cambridge: Cambridge University Press, 1999) and David Ford and Daniel Hardy, *Living in Praise: Worshipping and Knowing God* (London: Darton, Longman, Todd, 2005).

46 Samuel Wells, *God's Companions: Reimagining Christian Ethics* (Oxford: Blackwell, 2006); Stanley Hauerwas and Samuel Wells, eds, *The Blackwell Companion to Christian Ethics* (Oxford: Blackwell, 2004); William Cavanaugh, *Torture and Eucharist: Theology, Politics and the Body of Christ* (Oxford: Blackwell, 1998).

47 Bryan D. Spinks, *The Worship Mall: Contemporary Responses to Contemporary Culture* (London: SPCK, 2010), xxiii.

48 Graham Cray, 'Focusing Church life on a Theology of Mission', in *The Future of the Parish System: Shaping the Church of England for the Twenty-First Century*, ed. Steven Croft (London: Church House, 2006), 61.

49 Rowan D. Williams, 'Archbishop's Address at 50th Anniversary of PCPCU [Pontifical Council for Promoting Christian Unity]' (Vatican City, 17 November 2010), http//www.archbishopofcanterbury.org/3078#top [accessed 29 November 2010].

50 'Archbishop's Address at 50th Anniversary of PCPCU'.

2   What I Learnt in the House of God

Liturgy and Society contains a distinctive and highly personal section which gives an insight into Gabriel Hebert the man. It gives a way in to beginning to understand *Liturgy and Society* and its implications. Such a personal disclosure is rare in a work of theology. The threads of key themes are woven together and can be clearly identified. Biographical details and theological influences, such as that of Frederick Denison Maurice, set Hebert in context. This chapter will set what formed Hebert alongside *Liturgy and Society* to give a wider historical-theological context. A detailed contextual analysis of the personal, confessional, section of *Liturgy and Society* will be given and which will define the capacity that the liturgical experience has in shaping lives in general and how it shaped Hebert's in particular.

A significant contribution that Hebert gives to the contemporary Church is reflection on how the individual worshipper always worships in company with others: his relational priority. Christian worshippers are shaped and formed by liturgy to be equipped to live and engage in the modern world; but more than that, in the act of worshipping, the Church models the way that she is called to live. The relational priority shapes Hebert's 'liturgical anthropology': this is an understanding of being human, and the human being, primarily as the one who worships.[1] It is within this liturgical anthropology that Hebert and *Liturgy and Society* are best understood. It is not aesthetics, nostalgia and the like, but the projection of the Church beyond herself into relationship with the world.

Gabriel Hebert: The Man

It is important to establish something of Hebert the man. His personality and experience weave together in the theologian he became. Eric Mascall gives a pen portrait of Hebert in his memoirs.[2] Set alongside Gregory Dix, Lionel Thornton and Charles Hutchinson, Hebert is described as one of 'Four Outstanding Priests'.[3] Mascall gives a good starting point for a brief biographical sketch and review of Hebert. Mascall's portrait of Hebert begins with the setting of Kelham, the central house of the Society of the Sacred Mission of which Hebert was a member from 1915 until his death in 1963. For Mascall the significance of Kelham was, 'its central house, its theological seminary and the great square chapel dominated by Jagger's realistic rood, which was looked on by many Anglicans as embodying the ideal setting for the liturgy'.[4]

The house, seminary and chapel speak of Hebert's life in community, his teaching, especially the formation of priests, and his pastoral liturgical heart. Indeed, for Mascall, it was Hebert's concern with ordinands that gave his theology a 'markedly pastoral orientation'.[5] He connects this directly to the lack of recognition of Hebert in England as a theologian as opposed to in Scotland, where he was awarded an honorary doctorate, because 'the concept of theology as the science of God and of other beings in relation to God has suffered less erosion'.[6] Hebert's theology exemplifies that relationship because he is unabashed in speaking of the importance of a personal engagement with God, in prayer, in the sacraments and through the Church. Mascall also gives a lovely personal insight into Hebert, 'with his tall, slightly bending figure, his beaked profile, his eager gait and his high-pitched faintly slobbering cackle, he always reminded me of a large and purposeful, but wholly benevolent, vulture'.[7]

Mascall describes *Liturgy and Society* as 'an enlightening and inspiring work, in spite of some idiosyncrasies'.[8] He does not identify or elucidate the idiosyncrasies, but it may be that he has in his sights Hebert's moving, but now for many quite remote, poetic interlude, 'What I learnt in the House of God'.[9] This is the poem that is one of the hermeneutic keys for unlocking an understanding of Hebert and *Liturgy and Society*, despite its idiosyncratic style.

Irvine's comprehensive description of the contours of Hebert's life and interests does not need a thorough recapitulation here.[10] However it is important to note key themes. Irvine's chapter headings point to those interests. First he describes Hebert as 'A Catholic Character': to describe him as such should not be seen within the confines of 'catholic' as a denominational label. Rather it describes his catholic sense of interest and enquiry in a broad range of ecclesiastical and intellectual pursuits. Whilst thoroughly Anglican and eschewing party labels, Hebert does describe himself in his preface to Brilioth's *Eucharistic Faith and Practice*: 'I write as an Anglo-Catholic'.[11] He follows that with a balanced account of what being a Catholic or Protestant might mean.

Secondly, 'The Scandinavian Connection' highlights Hebert's great admiration for the Swedish Archbishop Nathan Söderblom from which flowed his translations, first of Söderblom's work, from Swedish into English. More significantly it was as part of these contacts that Hebert began to critique the Anglo-Catholic movement within the Church of England. He could praise its most significant achievement, 'to recall the Church of England to the sacramental basis of its life and worship', and be excoriating about its partisan attitude.[12] It is within this context that Irvine traces Hebert's first signs of the desirability of having a weekly communicating parish Eucharist as the chief Sunday service; the nascent idea of the Parish Communion. This reflection on the nature of the Church was informed further in his reflection on the nature of catholicity and apostolicity with direct reference to the Swedish Church. This theme is picked up further in his *Apostle and Bishop* (1963) and *The Form of the Church* (1944).

The third chapter, 'Ecumenism and Worship', highlights Hebert's abiding interest in the reunion of the Church. The sticking point, as far as Hebert was concerned, was articulated by the 1930 Lambeth Conference that intercommunion 'should be the goal of, rather than a means to, the restoration of communion'.[13] The challenge for Hebert is that reunion 'would be ultimately related to the Church's corporate and sacramental worship'.[14] This reveals again Hebert's ecclesiological conviction that, in Irvine's words, 'when the people of God gather for worship, the Church is clearly seen to be the Church'.[15]

Fourthly, on the subject of 'Liturgical Renewal' it is clear that Hebert was not greatly interested in texts and words for their own sake. That said, he did engage in the debates around the 1927/28 Prayer Book revision and expressed views on epiclesis, the moment of consecration and other 'technical' liturgical issues. His *An Essay in Baptismal Revision* (1947) is primarily a pastoral work and not a work of liturgical archaeology in the manner of Dix. Irvine sees *Liturgy and Society* as breaking the impasse that followed the ructions over the Prayer Book revision. This is an important observation as it illustrates Hebert's ability to reach beyond diverse positions through fundamental theology.

Finally, in 'Bible and Worship' Irvine notes Hebert's interest in and reputation for biblical studies. This is manifested first in *The Throne of David* (1941) and more fully in *The Authority of the Old Testament* (1947). Mascall somewhat quixotically relates the way in which Hebert would distinguish between different parts of the Old Testament and the application given to it, suggesting that some of the Old Testament was 'good clean fun for the long winter evenings'.[16] More seriously, he sees in Hebert's biblical theology the use of 'typology', including the judicious use of 'the great prophetic types recorded in the writings of the Ancient Dispensation [that] are fulfilled in Christ and in his Church and mediated in the Sacraments'.[17] It is too much to claim *Liturgy and Society* as the book that draws together all Hebert's thinking, but it does unite the themes Irvine describes. Many of them come to the fore at different points.

Liturgy and Society: Hebert's Aims

Hebert sets two priorities. The first is that 'this book is an appeal to the authority of the Church'.[18] At first sight this statement is deeply conservative, and there is arguably an underlying authoritarianism and paternalism in Hebert's practical ecclesiology. There is a sense in which Hebert knows what is good for his readers: he does acknowledge he is writing to those inclined to agree.[19] His second priority marks a change of tone, as he suggests that its appeal is to those inside the Church and the thinking person outside. This reveals the creative tension of the issues that Hebert deals with as he negotiates the relationship between what are often seen as polar opposites, such as individualism and corporatism, Church and society, liturgy and reform.

With those two priorities, Hebert sets out three clear aims of *Liturgy and Society* which give it a place in dialogue with contemporary Anglican missiology and ecclesiology because all three aims can be situated in the relationship of the individual to the Church as a body. These aims encapsulate his whole project. It is reflection on those aims that enables a consideration of the mode of theological voice in which he writes. His first aim, which will be explored in depth in the next chapter, is that the Church should be seen as 'not merely an organisation to bring together a number of religious individuals'.[20] The Church is the mystical Body of Christ, and not simply 'militant here in earth'.[21] Individualism is the problem to be addressed by the Church through both her inner and exterior life in eucharistic worship that shapes the life of the Church. This aim underlies all that Hebert will say about the nature of the Eucharist and what he sees the Parish Communion as achieving both as a liturgical act and the way in which it shapes those who attend. In this way liturgy shapes the eucharistic parish.[22] The expression of individual opinion becomes problematic within the individualistic reactionary dogmatism of liberal theologians. Finally, in the paralysing individualism of many forms of piety Hebert identifies an introspective individualism that is debilitating and contrary to the possibilities of the life of the gospel and the action of the Holy Spirit. The Parish Communion is not simply a convenient gathering point but rather seminal in the life of many Churches.

Secondly, *Liturgy and Society* endeavours to aid 'an escape from corrupting influence of Liberalism in the theological region'.[23] Liberalism is not understood by Hebert to be either a woolly, wishy-washy theology or disregard for truth in theology, and certainly not as a party point. He writes approvingly of the 'virtues' of 'the Liberal theologians' in their desire 'to be honest, open minded and to love the truth'.[24] It is important to note that Hebert makes no attempt to deny that he himself held 'liberal' views, but he suggests that like him others want to make that escape. His primary criticism of liberal theologians is not simply their implied individualism, something he develops further through *Liturgy and Society*, but a 'reactionary dogmatism of their own'.[25]

The third aim combines the first two points somewhat and sets out the dangers of individualism in a missiological framework. The missiological crisis for Hebert is that 'Christians are still in danger of suffering from an inferiority complex owing very largely to our habit of regarding Christianity as a way of religion for the individual; about our personal piety we have naturally a certain shyness.'[26] Hebert's sense of tradition does not preclude the development of rites. Development also enables the Church's tradition to be responsive and germane to the modern world which underlies his aims and whole project. The danger in such responsiveness is the accusation of an attempt at relevance. The word 'relevant' developed unfortunate connotations in the Church after Hebert's time when it and trendiness were seen to be appropriate responses to societal shifts. Societal and cultural mores are theologically inadequate when appropriated uncritically by the Church. Therefore if cafés are places of sociability Hebert prompts the question of how theologically and critically churches engage with them. One strategy is that of serving coffee after the service; another is to make the liturgy in the style of a café. *Liturgy and Society* prompts the thought that neither is fully adequate. One is bolting on and the other replicating: neither addresses how Christians function in the modern world.

Hebert could give the impression of undertaking the rebranding of old dogma and practice, endeavouring to make it appear relevant to the modern world. He urges that Christianity should not be viewed as a product: 'it is commonly believed that the Churches are organisations which provide religion for those who want it; religion of various brands'.[27] Thus despite writing in the first part of the twentieth century Hebert is perfectly aware of consumerism, something which developed further later in the century.[28] The human person is not for Hebert a consumer, but he is very attentive to what might be called the post-Enlightenment person who in all things including, or especially, matters of religion, sees himself as autonomous.

Liturgy and Society in Its Theological and Historical Setting

Ronald Jasper situates Hebert within the ferment of the middle decades of the twentieth century and the pressures for liturgical change.[29] His account echoes clearly what Hebert says of himself in *Liturgy and Society*. The challenge for theologians was to 'look again at what the Bible had to say about God and his dealings with humanity'.[30] This was prompted by a number of developments, most fundamentally the loss of confidence in Theological Liberalism presaged by the First World War. Furthermore there was the burgeoning influence of Karl Barth and his neo-orthodoxy and *The Epistle to the Romans*. At this stage Hebert's reputation was that of biblical theologian, with *The Throne of David* (1941) being a key work. Jasper sees the re-evaluation of the nature of the Church and 'its central place in Christian faith and practice as the mystical Body of Christ' as a direct result of that biblical theology.[31] This hints at what was to become for Hebert an interest in the nature of the Church in engagement with modern thought.

Michael Ramsey and Lionel Thornton began to work out not only the implications of incorporation into the Body of Christ through baptism but also the activity of the Church in its liturgical, evangelical and corporate aspects.[32] Such a trajectory includes *Liturgy and Society*. Hebert can legitimately be placed both as a writer of his time and within the broad sweep of theology in the middle years of the twentieth century. From another direction, Hebert was part of the growing interest in and hope for Church reunion. Hebert's *Intercommunion* (1932) was part of that, combining principles of eucharistic sacrifice with an approach that saw in Anglicanism a synthesis forming a 'middle way' that could be both catholic and evangelical.[33] This should not be surprising since Hebert's translation of Brilioth has the insightful title *Eucharistic Faith and Practice: Evangelical and Catholic* (1930), in which the eucharistic sacrifice is addressed. Indeed, Jasper comments on that translation as it gave, for the first time, a comparative study of Anglican, Lutheran and Reformed liturgical history. More significantly, the strands on the Body of Christ, participation and sacrifice came together as Hebert's thought developed. The themes of participation and incorporation are further elucidated by Hebert in his essay on baptismal regeneration which, whilst not mentioned by Jasper, can again be situated within his survey of the way in which initiation could not be isolated from eucharistic theology.[34] This relationship continues to be stressed in current Anglican liturgical material, which is where the understated influence of the Parish Communion Movement is to be found.[35] It further states the sacramental principle of the mediation of grace in the two dominical sacraments which are at the heart of the Church.[36]

Jasper suggests that *Liturgy and Society* is 'the most significant English work on the Liturgical Movement'.[37] Previous works that were foundational to the Liturgical Movement on the continent included Friedrich Heiler's *The Spirit of Worship*, in which he surveys Guéranger, Herwegen, Casel, Otto, Monod and others: all, with the exception of Monod, significant and influential names that occur in *Liturgy and Society*. However for Jasper, which reinforces Irvine's point, Hebert's contribution 'raised the whole discussion of liturgy above party and academic interests; and in the light of world affairs, it was now shown to have a new sense of urgency – was truly a liturgiology of crisis'.[38] In 1936, the year after *Liturgy and Society* was published, three books appeared that Jasper sees as part of the continuum in which *Liturgy and Society* stood. Evelyn Underhill's *Worship*, the Free Church symposium's *Christian Worship* and W.D. Maxwell's *An Outline of Christian Worship*. The most explicit connection he makes is with Underhill. She recognised, like Hebert, that 'the Christian is required to use the whole of his existence as sacramental material . . . bringing the imperfect human creature and his changing experience into direct and conscious relation with God the Perfect and reminding him of the supernatural aim of human life'.[39] Since Underhill quotes *Liturgy and Society*, it is fair to judge that it made a direct impact on her too.[40]

The other significant liturgical work post-*Liturgy and Society* was *The Shape of the Liturgy*.[41] In it Gregory Dix wanted to go beyond Walter Frere's assertion that there was one unifying primitive eucharistic rite and suggest its Jewish origins. Dix's classic fourfold 'shape' of the liturgy – taking, blessing, breaking and giving – caught the imagination of liturgists and clergy. In addition, as Jasper notes, Dix also deeply related the Eucharist to humanity.[42] Hebert and Dix are different writers, just as *Liturgy and Society* and *The Shape of the Liturgy* are different works. With the exception of his baptismal rite, Hebert seemed little interested with the detail of liturgical reform and fundamental liturgical change. His concern was in one sense about recovery of primitive forms, primarily that the Eucharist was the central act of worship. This contrasts with Dix's interest, which suggested that antiquity gave validity to liturgy. Despite some affinity, it is primarily in this sense that he and Dix differed.

Liturgy and Society

In the preface Hebert describes the planning of *Liturgy and Society: The Function of the Church in the Modern World*. His original intention was to write about the Liturgical Movement. He quickly discovered that more was at stake than simply a description of 'the treasures of the liturgy'.[43] Such an enterprise would have echoed the earlier work of Romano Guardini.[44] It would have been essentially introspective and would not make the connection between liturgy and society: Hebert saw the need to go further.[45] In doing so, freed from pieties, he gave a richer work with which to engage. This move by Hebert positions *Liturgy and Society* as an essential voice that helps contribute to a vibrant ecclesiological and missional theological evaluation of contemporary discourse.

Hebert prefaces his interest in the continental and, by implication, Roman Catholic Liturgical Movement by stating, 'I write as an Anglican'.[46] Of his Anglicanism, Irvine comments: 'If St Paul could claim to be a Hebrew born of Hebrews, Arthur Gabriel Hebert could claim to be an Anglican born of Anglicans.'[47] Hebert's Anglicanism gives a distinctive tone to his writing, although in an intriguing way. The Church of England as a discrete subject occupies 15 of the 260 pages of *Liturgy and Society*. He draws on the Lambeth-Chicago Quadrilateral, primarily as grounds for ecumenical rapprochement and reunion (one of his passions). His account of the post-Reformation Church of England bears a distinctively catholic Anglican flavour of continuity and not disruption. Hebert's narrative reflects the sense that his standpoint was beginning to hold the day in the Church of England, if it did not already. Hebert's monastic background in the Society of the Sacred Mission may account for this in part, but also a dramatically altered terrain in the priority of mission in the Church of England. Hebert assumes a doxological priority from which flows pastoral care and mission. Nonetheless Hebert clearly has a social concern and conscience which is typical of his age and influences, which meant a work of liturgical piety was unsustainable.

It is clear in reading Hebert that he wants to appeal to the mind as much as the heart: in other words in rational argument as much as in credal formulae and liturgical text. The opening chapters reflect a concern for 'modern man' that assumes that doctrinal clarification will result in people seeing the light and returning to the fellowship of the life of the Church. In that way Hebert reflects what has become caricatured as a Christendom model of mission: everyone is essentially a Christian; those who do not attend are lapsed and are therefore ripe for drawing into the life of the Church. His assumption is that people do not simply reject the Christian faith but reject the fellowship of the Church. Whilst it is a characteristically modern outlook, this is not to say that Hebert is purely a rationalist who sees no merit in liturgical expressions of faith. On the contrary; he is emphatic that worship, especially eucharistic worship, is the means by which the individual is drawn into and shaped in his life and faith. In his thought modern people are inclined to celebrate faith autonomously rather than corporately in the Church. That assumption pressed further means each person becomes his own authority. That assumes the authority of the individual mind as if relationality is somehow irrational. Hebert sees living in relationship as not only rational but also about accountability, and therefore not about individual autonomy.

So what could have been a pious or devotional exposition of the Church's liturgy becomes something quite different. Perhaps it was the social conscience of his Anglicanism influenced by Maurice and Christian Socialism that led Hebert to a different style of book:

> Thus I began to plan a book that would show how Christian dogma
> finds its typical expression in worship, and how Christian religion is not
> merely a way of piety for the individual soul, but is in the first place a
> participation in a common life.[48]

This definitive statement encapsulates Hebert's project, and shapes the trajectory of this study.

In both Church and society Hebert was remarkably prescient. *Liturgy and
Society* as well as *The Parish Communion*, which he edited, helped shape an
understanding of the Church in the post-war period which only came to
be challenged towards the end of the twentieth century.[49] In society he saw
clearly the twin, and apparently mutually exclusive, threats of individualism
and fascism. His theology resists the autonomy of individualism and also
the corporatist nature of fascism.[50] Corporatism and fascism are parodies
of the corporate life of the Church in Christ. The individual is significant
and finds identity within the Body, but is not subsumed by it. The antidote
to individualism, simply put, is to be found in the eucharistic worship of
the Church. Such worship is corporate. In this he is indebted to Maurice,
especially *The Kingdom of Christ*.[51] It is the extent to which that profoundly
corporate worship *shapes* the Body and to what extent it *reflects* the unity of
the Body that is Hebert's distinctive contribution. As Morris comments, 'The
full implications of [Maurice's] emphasis, at least in practical worship, were
to await development in the twentieth century, in the liturgical movement
associated with the parish communion and the name of Gabriel Hebert.'[52]

This raises the issue of romanticism as 'a reaction against the optimism,
utilitarianism, and individualism of the eighteenth century'.[53] Yet, Hebert
claims, 'we are not reactionaries, taking refuge from the dangers of the future
in a romantic return to the past'.[54] Hebert uses the word 'romantic' in a different way from that of Forbes, who sees the Liberal Anglican school as sharing
traits of Romanticism. This has a Maurician dimension in its attitude to history which Hebert does not explore. Hebert is convinced throughout *Liturgy
and Society* that what he advocates, which he argues is recovered from the deep
riches of the Christian tradition, is all the more pertinent and necessary when
addressing the modern world, in its post-Enlightenment, post-Darwinian and
inter-war realities. This becomes all the more pressing in the light of the rise
of the individual, which elsewhere he also attributes to the rise of National
Socialism in Germany as he excoriates totalitarianism. *Liturgy and Society*
engages deeply in the concrete realities of the world.

Hebert valued liturgy and understood it to be the articulation of faith and
its summation. This is nowhere better understood for Hebert than in the
Eucharist. The test of his theology and its application is how it sits alongside

the function of the Church in the modern world. The place in which it is contextualised is the eucharistic parish, which has to be a demonstrably plausible vehicle for witness, mission and Church growth today.

The Theology of *Liturgy and Society*

It is legitimate to ask if *Liturgy and Society* is ecclesiology, sociology or liturgical; systematic, practical or moral theology. In one sense it is a combination of all of the above. It is not only the area of theology that is significant but also that manner in which it is spoken. Rowan Williams' 'typology of theological activity' can be deployed as a means of asking what 'voice' or 'mode' Hebert is using in his writing.[55] This enables a move beyond easy categorisation but also to hold the shape of Hebert's theology. Exploring Hebert in this way is foundational since it draws out his preferences in his theological, ecclesiological and liturgical quest. In his typology Williams outlines three ways, styles or 'voices' of approaching theology: celebratory, communicative and critical.[56] Theology, he proposes, begins as a *celebratory* phenomenon: 'an attempt to draw out and display connections of thought and image so as to exhibit the fullest possible range of significance in the language used'.[57] This is typically the language of hymnody and preaching, and therefore it might be suggested is the style most familiar to the majority of Christians. This is not, as it becomes more sophisticated, without rigour; but Williams' caution is the danger of it 'being sealed in on itself'.[58] This is an allegation that could be levelled at *Liturgy and Society* on first reading – that his eucharistic source of ecclesial life constantly references itself. To rebut that, Hebert's constant reference back to society means his theology has a wider frame of reference than the dogmatic tradition of the Church. It is this conceptual move that echoes Williams' second theological 'voice', namely the *communicative* style. Williams identifies this when the process is undertaken of ensuring that theology does not become turned in on itself: that is to say, 'a theology experimenting with the rhetoric of its uncommitted environment'.[59] In some senses this shows theology being deployed in the culture in which it finds itself, a doctrine finding a language that is not of its essence from the ecclesiastical, if that can ever fully be the case. Thirdly, the category that nags away at fundamental meaning is the *critical* voice which can find itself engaged in thorough re-evaluation of given doctrinal understandings, or in a rejection of them. Williams acknowledges that all three categories should not be regarded as sealed in themselves; and indeed he acknowledges something of a cyclical movement within them, and each should properly shape and inform the insights of the other.

Liturgy and Society, as a work, is thoroughgoing in its delight in the Church and her tradition. It is written in a primarily celebratory voice.[60] This does not mask its insightful nature. Furthermore it does not in any way imply that Hebert cannot speak in a critical or analytical manner about the Church. It is hard to see in *Liturgy and Society* a sense of critical theology in the way Williams uses it. This is in part because Hebert's method does not seek to repair Christian language. Hebert assumes that Christian language, if not the language spoken by Christians, is fundamentally sound but that it is not heard properly and is disregarded as being irrelevant, which is the fault of the Church. The only sense in which it might be critical in the sense described by Williams is in the way in which Hebert seeks to return to the sources to regenerate theology. Hebert is not a speculative theologian. He is overwhelmingly celebratory in his method. The interesting area is the one that in a sense comes in between; this is the *communicative* voice. In this voice he demonstrates a nascent missiology. The nature of the relationship Hebert envisages between the Church and society is never neatly resolved. There is a generous approach to people in wider society, and yet he also writes: 'it is to Christians after all that this book is really in the first place addressed, and especially to those of the Church to which I belong'.[61] *Liturgy and Society* contributes a celebratory flavoured theology to the Church of England.

The full title of the book, *Liturgy and Society: The Function of the Church in the Modern World*, suggests the interface of two different, potentially hostile worlds. This is not to suggest that Hebert is a dualist, but that his project is one of addressing the Church's liturgy to the world and the world to the Church's liturgy. This is not what happens in *Liturgy and Society*. There is a sense that the purpose of *Liturgy and Society* is at best muddled or at worst flawed from the outset. Hebert claims that what could have been 'a treatise on the principles of Christian worship, inspired by a large extent by the Liturgical Movement' became a book not 'limited to a purely religious and ecclesiastical treatment'.[62] And yet in the opening pages of the preface it becomes clear that this is not the communicative work it might be; it is not a two-way conversation. Granted, Hebert says, 'it is necessary to envisage the condition of modern Europe'; but then he asserts that the book must start with the question: 'What has the Church to give to the modern world?'[63] Understood generously, this is the language of gifting, less generously of imposition; either way it is not reciprocity. Hebert starts, not unreasonably, from the presumption that what the Church is, and what it offers, is of benefit to the world and that the relationship between Church and world somehow has a hierarchy, with society subservient to the Church and the arena of the Church's mission.

Williams describes the celebratory approach as drawing out the fullest range of significance in the language used. This describes Hebert's language and aesthetics. He is comfortable with using essentially doxological language and expression.[64] He is also unashamed to quote and use the poetry of T.S.

Eliot, especially *The Rock*.[65] And, as noted above, this extends to using photography and art. In this way Hebert builds a case that is imaginative and generous in a way that is generated by the liturgy he has received. If *Liturgy and Society* was simply a work of liturgical theology, or even an attempt at systematic theology, Hebert may have been more bashful in using 'unacademic' modes of writing. In this way he is more celebratory in *Liturgy and Society* than ever the influential Maurice would have been: Maurice's works were both dense in style and, unlike *Liturgy and Society*, lack illustrations.

Hebert's approach to dogma reveals his unease with the notion that it is reducible to ideas or opinion.[66] Pointing to the example of Christian martyrs, he comments that martyrs do not give their lives for 'mere opinions'.[67] This moves Hebert to point to that which may motivate such witness. His answer is inevitably celebratory: such faith (of the martyr), he suggests, is 'an apprehension of something divine, something not of man nor from man, something which is to him a well-spring of life'.[68] There is a strong element of Hebert treating wider society as he wishes it to be and not as it really is. As already noted, *Liturgy and Society* is 'essentially an appeal to the authority of the Church'.[69] This is not a contemporary approach to missiology. This is principally a matter of tone, born of historical setting, and not of substance. Hebert is primarily a celebratory theologian, but not to the exclusion of a genuine communicative instinct. The impulse to write *Liturgy and Society* in the first place, as stated in his aims and priorities, does not come from a world-hating point of view but from a deep sense of the gift of the Church to the world. Hebert's deep appreciation of the gifted nature of the Church and her liturgy is evident throughout the text. It is most explicitly revealed in the poem-cum-prayer-cum-confession, 'What I learnt in the House of God'.[70]

Liturgy and Society: Innovative Conservative

The transforming impact of *Liturgy and Society*, along with the wider intellectual and pastoral developments in the life of the Church of England that shaped the Parish Communion Movement, makes the question of *Liturgy and Society* as a conservative work an apparently odd one: how can such a radical book and movement possibly be described as conservative? Like one of Hebert's key influences, Maurice, he is open to the charge of being simultaneously conservative and innovative.[71] Also, like Maurice, Hebert's theology is both of its time and ahead of its time.[72] Maurice is summarised by Morris as best considered 'as a Christian apologist and as a polythematic theologian'.[73] Hebert inherits from Maurice the sense that the catholicity of the Church is not to be found in doctrinal postures, be they Catholic or Protestant. His account of dogma represents a retrieval of Chalcedonian and Nicean orthodoxy, with a good measure of Tractarian interpretation. Like Maurice, he continues to detect the catholicity of the Church even in a splintered history of Christendom. This is the basis of Hebert's passion for Church unity. It also enables him to take the Eucharist and forms of its celebration away from defining a 'party Catholic' and to allow the Church to express her Catholicity. Hebert's concern is for Catholicity in its widest, most generous sense – not rooted in nostalgia or party. This is a key contribution for the contemporary Church.

The parallels between Hebert and Maurice should not be overworked, not least because Hebert evades simple categorisation. Irvine 'confidently describe[s]' *Liturgy and Society* as a work of liturgical theology, but goes on to qualify this assertion.[74] It is liturgical theology he suggests, 'not in the sense of seeking to explicate the theological significance of given liturgical themes and motifs, but in seeing the gathered worshipping Church as being the first arena of theological apprehension and response'.[75] Such activity of the Church demands an ecclesiology.[76] Equally, Hebert works from an ecclesiology that demands a liturgiology. Either way *Liturgy and Society* makes clear that ecclesiology and liturgy are both generative and expressive of the other.[77] Hebert touches on these questions but does not address them directly. Rather, he somewhat nostalgically speaks of 'the great days of the liturgy the ceremonial of the rite expressed its corporate character as the common act of the Body of Christ'.[78] In that statement Hebert sees the Eucharist as something to be done by the Church, an exterior action that has the consequence of *expressing* its corporate character; but he does not suggest that it *forms* that character. Hebert explores the nature of the Church as the Body of Christ further:

> The offering of the gifts must always have been the speaking symbol of the people's will to offer up themselves to God; and here the self-oblation of the Church, the *Corpus Christi*, is set forth as the matter of the sacramental *Corpus Christi*. Here, as in St Paul, the two senses of 'the Body of Christ' are allowed to run together: the offering up of the Body of Jesus Christ in the Sacrament is one with the offering-up of His Body which is the Church.[79]

Hebert's approach should not be surprising given Maurice's approach to the Eucharist. As Morris notes, '[Maurice] could speak of the Eucharist as a means through which believers 'really receive . . . all the spiritual blessings', including 'that strength and renewal by which [the individual spirit is] enabled to do its appointed work'.[80] In similar vein Hebert approvingly quotes Abbot Herwegen of Maria Laach: 'the celebration of the Christian Mysteries is a social act, by which the worshippers are brought out of their isolation into fellowship with one another in the Church, which is Christ's mystical Body'.[81] Hebert is properly *radical* in his writing in the sense that he is rooted in Church tradition. He has a deep sense of that which is handed on. Thus he writes in the preface, 'this way of approach starts from the consideration of the Church as an existing fact, and as the inheritor of a long tradition'.[82] Hebert has a vibrant sense of the radical character of the Church, resisting any portrayal of him as a stuffy traditionalist.

Hebert is less concerned about a hierarchy of Church and Eucharist and setting the priority of one over the other, but is concerned with how the Church 'uses' the Eucharist and what it says of the nature of society.[83] This is not social engineering, but a social liberation. Hebert's 'eucharistic ecclesiology', as it might be called, regards the Eucharist as contingent upon the Church and the social life of the Church contingent upon the Eucharist. Hebert sees the effects of the Eucharist as being part of his project to counter individualism: 'Thereby [at the Eucharist] not only their religious life but all their individual and social life is re-orientated towards God as its centre, and is transformed, sanctified, and glorified.'[84] This is an uncompromising statement on the Eucharist. Seen in the context of Hebert's self-disclosure in *Liturgy and Society* it has another character. Hebert demonstrates very clearly the celebratory character of his theology in doxological and theophanic terms.

What I Learnt in the House of God: Personal Disclosure

Liturgy and Society is, as we have been exploring, a conventional work in many ways; and yet in its use of illustrations, poetry (T.S. Eliot) and novelists (D.H. Lawrence) it refuses to be categorised easily. Another idiosyncratic, yet formative passage is Hebert's 'statement of faith': 'What I Learnt in the House of God'. As we shall see, this is a pivotal section in understanding Hebert and *Liturgy and Society*. Hebert's deployment of personal experience and theological influences roots him as a person of Christian faith. The title Hebert gives is of interest: 'What I *learnt* in the House of God'. Given his liturgical principles it would not have been surprising if he had entitled the statement of faith 'What I *apprehended* or *sensed* in the house of God'; it perhaps reflects the more didactic approach of his time. In it we see forming influences, principles and self-disclosure that are rarely uncovered in theological writers.

The poem is in three parts. The first part is explicitly a search for the meaning of the individual within the corporate context of family, common life and nation. It gives an account of settings in which the individual is located and given meaning. Curiously, given the nature of his emphasis on the corporate life of the Church in *Liturgy and Society*, Hebert does not refer explicitly to the doctrine of the Communion of Saints. We might find this a surprising omission given his background and theology. Hebert's rich sense of the fellowship of the Church and her character as the Mystical Body of Christ lacks the articulation of, for example, the Swiss theologian Hans Urs von Balthasar. Whilst both come from very different ecclesial backgrounds and there is no formal link between them, the resonances are remarkably similar. So, for instance, von Balthasar, writing about the Communion of Saints, remarks that nothing in the communion of saints is private, although everything is personal. But 'persons', in the Christian sense, are just such as, in imitation of the divine-human person Jesus, 'no longer live for themselves' and also 'no longer die for themselves'.[85] This articulates the same point that Hebert makes in his imperative of the anthropology of persons in relationship to others.

The social theme continues in the second part of the poem, which names the Church as existing 'to bear witness/that there is an universal King and Father of all mankind'.[86] It is in the social setting of the 'universal spiritual Family and Kingdom' that individual and personal sinfulness is redeemed. The second part closes with a declaration that 'the root of all evil is godlessness', which Hebert explicitly links again to 'the exaltation of the self, / the claim of the self to live as it pleases without God'.[87]

Hebert's approach is captured in Von Balthasar's statement, 'holiness is something essentially social and thus saved from the caprice of the individual'.[88] The final section is a doxology which is again described in terms of the 'common life'. This poem is at the heart of *Liturgy and Society* but could not be described as classical liturgical theology, but very much as evidence of mystagogy, 'that cyclic and cumulative engagement in catechesis' which is also liturgical in character.[89] It reads far more as a piece of confessional writing that is shaped and formed by liturgy and liturgical action and rooted in a distinctive and highly social ecclesiology; it is, in Clarahan's phrase, how 'ritualised bodies give rise to understanding and growth in faith'.[90]

A close textual and theological analysis of the text of 'What I Learnt in the House of God' will now follow, opening up these new dimensions in understanding Hebert.[91]

1   'What is your name?'

The opening line of the 'statement of faith' comes from the Catechism of the Church of England as set out in the Book of Common Prayer (1662). The Catechism is subtitled 'An Instruction to be Learned of Every Person before he be Brought to be Confirmed by the Bishop'. This reveals Hebert's sense that faith is to be taught as well as apprehended, so faith is not *solely* generated or shaped by liturgy. It also shows an innate sense of the teaching authority of the Church. So 'What I learnt' begins in a profoundly relational way:

2 'Who gave you this name?'

This second question, which is the second interrogation of the Catechism, places his name firmly in a baptismal context as in the Catechism the question elicits the answer: 'My Godfathers and Godmothers [gave me this name] in my Baptism; wherein I was made a member of Christ, the child of God, and an inheritor of the kingdom of heaven.' This question then prompts Hebert into situating his personal faith in a wider context, which is entirely typical of Hebert's ecclesiology.

3 I was born into a family, and into a nation;
4 The head of the family was my father,
5 The head of the nation is the king.
6 But where could I find the eternal Father, the universal King,
7 Claiming the allegiance of my spirit?
8 Where were the signs of His Family and His Kingdom?

This paragraph gives the sense of a pervading paternalism and Erastianism, yet Hebert can be read more generously than that. It is the case that Hebert uses familial imagery, mentioning the family three times in those lines. He appears to draw from the second chapter of the First Letter of Peter. The reference to a 'holy nation' (1 Peter 2.9) is picked up, as is the sense of national paternity in the King (cf. 1 Peter 2.13–14). The questions that seek after the 'eternal Father' and the signs of his kingdom move him beyond an uncritical state or inherited religion, much as Keble's Assize Sermon did in inaugurating the Tractarian movement, to whom Hebert is indebted.

9   At my baptism I received my Christian name.
10 There I was born anew,
11 a child of an unseen Father,
12 a member of a spiritual Family,
13 the Church, the Body of Christ,
14 an inheritor of an eternal Kingdom.
15 God had a meaning for my life.

Hebert's naming in baptism is clearly significant, as it is referred to in the paragraph above and also in the first two questions of the poem. There are rich biblical sources for this interest in the name, such as the renaming of Abram (Genesis 17.5), the call of Samuel by name (1 Samuel 3.10ff), the call of Israel and Jacob by name (Isaiah 43.1b) and the renaming of Saul to Paul.

The use of the image of the spiritual family is of interest ecclesiologically since the concept of family as an image of the Church is not widespread in the New Testament, whilst not being absent (Romans 8.29, 1 Corinthians 8.12, Galatians 1.2, 6.10, 1 Peter 2.17). Indeed, the image of the Church as Body of Christ is far more dominant. However to answer Hebert's question, in line 8, about the location of the signs of God's family and Kingdom, his emphatic answer is that they are found in the Church into which through baptism the individual becomes a member. The reference to being born anew speaks of his understanding of baptismal regeneration. Here too we see the first assertion of and interest in *meaning* in life. The origin of that meaning is God. So from the mystery of God, and we might add the *social* reality of God, the believer finds meaning for his individual life. This individual meaning is tempered by Hebert's hostility to individualism which is illuminated further by the way in which he sets his own baptism within the corporate setting of the Church, and it is within that setting that he is able to claim 'God had a meaning for my life'.

16   My father and my mother
17   had become man and wife before God's altar:
18   A new family had come into being;
19   God had a meaning for that family.

The search for meaning, or perhaps more properly the *gift* of meaning for his life is set in the wider context of the family. Again, perhaps typical of his age, Hebert has no scruples about referring to the biological, nuclear family in an unabashed way. The verse evokes the first 'cause for which Matrimony was ordained' in the Book of Common Prayer 1662: 'First, it was ordained for the procreation of children, to be brought up in the fear and nurture of the Lord, and to the praise of his holy Name.'[92] Hebert was a man of his time in terms of how he understood and articulated marriage and his place as the fruit of a marriage. His individual meaning starts within the family context and the family is by definition a social entity. Hebert uses the word family (with both lower and upper case 'F') on 11 occasions in the poem. Five of those references are to the human family, including a reference to Abraham's family. The Church as family is mentioned a further five times, and there is one reference to God's family. The implication of this is that Hebert is shaped and defined by sociality from his earliest days, which is something he retains throughout his life as a priest in community and in his writing on the nature of the Church.

In the whole of *Liturgy and Society* Hebert refers only once to the Established nature of the Church of England. When he does it is not addressing the ecclesiological complexity of what establishment might mean. It is not clear if this is through any embarrassment or if it simply was not deemed to suit his central purpose. Except for the reference in 'What I learnt' there is no reference to the Sovereign and there is critical distance set between the Kingdom of God and the Kingdom of Man.[93] This does not prevent a connection being made with earthly and sacral authority and the pursuit of a common life.

20 The king of England was crowned before God's altar,
21 by the Archbishop, the Primate of the Church:
22 The kingship is a sacred office;
23 God has a meaning for common life and labour.

Hebert appears content to pursue his ecclesiological vision aside from establishment. He does however allude to the position of the Church of England following the Civil War, which he sees as the time when 'a change set in'.[94] The change is that the 'classical period of Anglican theology' passed and moved from 'the old basis, as the Church of God in England, and the faith to which these great writers appeal is a common faith'.[95] The principal rupture of the Civil War for Hebert is not on the grounds of Royal Supremacy and Establishment; more problematic is the loss of a 'common faith'.[96] Given the language of the 'statement of faith', Hebert's remarks about the aftermath of the Civil War are consonant with his approach: 'Englishmen now could no longer fully take the Church for granted, as the mother of whom they had been born: it was open to them to choose to belong to the Church or to the Independents.'[97] The historiography of Hebert's assertion about the impact of the Civil War may be unconvincing, but his statement is telling in terms of the romantic cultural memory it carries. It highlights Hebert's discomfort with the sense of *choice* of religious preference; but secondly, and more significantly in the context of his 'statement of faith', it sees the Church in maternal terms and therefore reinforces Hebert's familial imagery.

24 The Church exists to bear witness
25 that there is an universal King and Father of all mankind.

These lines (24 and 25) constitute the only missiological reference in the 'statement of faith' and are not wholly explicit. Hebert's missiology will be explored further below, but here he conceives mission as *missio Dei*, bearing witness to God's mission in the world. These lines form a prelude to the portion of the statement that reads in a credal manner and echoes both the

Letter to the Hebrews (Hebrews 11.4–end) and Stephen's speech in the Acts of the Apostles (Acts 7.1–53). Hebert begins with Abraham 'the father of a family' and points to Jesus as son of David reconciling the 'nations and families into one':

26   Her Bible tells
27   of Abraham the father of a family,
28   of David the king of a nation,
29   both confessing the universal Father and King.
30   It tells also of other kings, as Nebuchadnezzar,
31   making men their slaves,
32   claiming the title of the Man-god.
33   It tells of the GOD-MAN, Jesus Christ,
34   of the seed of Abraham,
35   of the line of David,
36   who came to proclaim the Kingdom of God,
37   to reconcile all nations and families into one,
38   having slain the enmity
39   by the suffering of the Cross,
40   by the Resurrection-victory.
41   Into this faith the Church baptizes us,
42   faith in the eternal Father and King,
43   in Jesus Christ the Reconciler,
44   in the Holy Spirit, the Life of her life.
45   The Church is a Family and a Kingdom;
46   The head of the Family, in each place,
47   is the Bishop, consecrated before God's altar
48   as the successor of the Apostles of Jesus Christ,
49   to be Father-in-God to God's people,
50   Shepherd of Christ's flock,
51   Priest, in Christ's Name.

The prominence of family thus far is clear. Two other social entities are important to note: Church and nation. Lines 26–51 reflect all three. This recalls Maurice: Morris notes that 'he [Maurice] spoke constantly of a "divine order", and found that order represented particularly in three levels of social identity – family, Church and nation'.[98] In this passage the themes emerge and develop. In words that could describe Hebert in lines 26–51, and indeed the whole poem, Morris comments, 'at times it seems almost as if he [Maurice] reduces human history to the interaction of these absolute but abstract concepts'.[99]

Hebert applies those 'absolute but abstract concepts' to salvation-history as revealed in the Bible. In relation to Maurice, Morris goes on to argue:

> The Platonism, such as it is, is there in this very tendency to discern an underlying pattern in the varied matter of human history. And yet it would be quite wrong to think that what he does is to absolutize and justify existing social relations. The 'divine order' for him, like the concept of Christ's Kingdom, was a dynamic notion, but represented as much as anything an ideal which Christians were called to discover and embody in their lives . . . for Maurice, Christian discipleship is at once deeply personal and yet also socially responsible, we can see that the 'divine order' is actually a call for social transformation.[100]

The notion of divine order as a call to social transformation is intriguing because social order is often sacralised and deemed 'divine order' and precludes social transformation. Hebert, like Maurice, is able to retain the sense of 'divine order' and hierarchy alongside the call for social transformation.

The recurring pattern in 'What I Learnt' is threefold: family, Church and nation – precisely that of Maurice's 'divine order'. Hebert clearly alludes to an *ordered social hierarchy* of family, Church and nation. The repeated references to meaning (lines 15, 19 and 23) may be more appropriately viewed in this context. The meaning to which he alludes may not be in a personal therapeutic sense but as being in accord with a 'divine order'. This would suggest a social conservatism on Hebert's part, and it is indeed hard to see any call for social transformation in 'What I Learnt'. However, social transformation is not absent from *Liturgy and Society* as a whole, and the impact of liturgy upon society and the ecclesiology and anthropology that accompany it is transformative.

52 The Church meets on the Lord's Day to offer the Holy Sacrifice,
53 using universal symbols, bread and wine,
54 proclaiming therewith God's redeeming love in Christ:
55 'This is My Body which is given for you; take, eat'.
56 'This is My Blood of the Covenant; drink ye all of this'.
57 In eating and drinking at the Table of the Lord
58 the brethren of the family, my neighbour and I,
59 are shown as reconciled with Him
60 and in Him with one another:
61 God has a meaning for our lives, singly and all together:
62 'What I do thou knowest not now, but thou shalt know
63 hereafter'.

Lines 52 and 57 contain a clear reference to one of the slogans of the Parish Communion Movement that referred to the character of the Eucharist as Sunday worship: 'the Lord's People, gathered around the Lord's Table, on the Lord's Day'. In practical terms that motto has come to be regarded in the twenty-first century as a millstone around the Church's neck. Mission and pastoral planning, including the deployment of clergy, becomes problematic when there is an expectation of a Sunday Eucharist even if that is not practicable in every community of faith because of a decline in clergy numbers. Nevertheless the purpose and potential of the slogan articulates Hebert's aspiration of a community shaped by and around the Eucharist on the normative day of Christian worship.

Lines 52–63 appear to relate to the sermon of St Augustine which Hebert includes earlier in the book in an abbreviated form.[101] It is a sermon to the newly baptised at Easter. The explicit connection is Augustine's exploration of the nature of the Body of Christ and the themes of unity (cf. line 59) and peace.

Hebert deploys the word *meaning* (lines 15, 19 and 23) referring to self, family and common life and labour. His understanding of meaning is reliant on Maurice's notion of 'divine order'. However the references to meaning may also be understood as being part of Hebert's anthropology, and more specifically what might be called the 'liturgical self'. In this understanding, to be explored further below, Hebert is not focusing on the autonomous individual but on the individual *in relation to* the common life of the Church and liturgy. The 'liturgical self' is a profoundly social vision for Hebert. This can be developed further since this anthropology is not only about the individual but also about the Body of the Church. Therefore meaning is to be found in the fullest expression of individual flourishing and authenticity. For Hebert this is when worship happens both for the individual and the Church: 'God has a meaning for our lives, singly and all together' (line 61). Irvine notes, 'Hebert repeatedly argued that the Church was most clearly seen to be the Church when the people of God gathered for worship.'[102]

This search for meaning has a limited eschatological dimension in *Liturgy and Society*. Line 57 echoes St Paul's words that, 'For as often as you eat this bread and drink the cup, you proclaim the Lord's death until he comes' (1 Corinthians 11.25) Hebert judges Liberal Protestantism to be seeking 'to discard as completely as possible the eschatological forms in which [the essence of Jesus' message] is clothed'.[103] *Liturgy and Society* does not fully explore the eschatological possibilities or implications of his own work. He later states that '[f]ulfilment means transformation',[104] but this sense of transformation is very much social, to be realised in the present, rather than eschatological. Hebert's reticence with regard to eschatology may stem from his debt to Maurice and awareness of Maurice's treatment following his publication of *Theological Essays* (1834) and reinforced by his lectures, *The Religions of the World* (1847). Maurice lost his job, and his reputation was tarnished in some quarters. It is intriguing too that Hebert entitles one of his chapters 'Christ the Fulfiller' and a section 'the problem of world-religions'. Similarly intriguing in that regard is the quoting of John 13.7: 'What I do thou knowest not now, but thou shalt know hereafter' (lines 62 and 63). It is a verse which speaks of a social/servant role of washing feet and serving. Located as it is in the Farewell discourses of St John's Gospel, it is assumed to be in the equivalent setting of the Synoptic Gospels' Last Supper. For Hebert the quotation has eucharistic and ethical imperatives.

As he continues, Hebert makes explicit and intensifies his assessment that it is individualism, and the related phenomenon of self-exaltation, that is hamartological and not simply sociological, for example weakening of the social nature of the Church. Godlessness is the root of all evil and is unambiguously linked to the exaltation of self.

64 Here we see that the root of all evil is godlessness,
65 practical godlessness,
66 the exaltation of the self,
67 the claim of the self to live as it pleases without God.
68 Here we see the root of all evil in ourselves,
69 and confess and are absolved:
70 'Thou hast broken my bonds in sunder'.

'Here we see' (line 64) appears to relate back to 'the House of God' rather than the preceding lines; that is to say it is the worship and being in the House of God, the Church, that illuminates humanity's sinfulness. In lines 64–7 we see the leitmotif that underlies the whole of *Liturgy and Society*.

Line 70 is a direct quotation from Psalm 116.14. His use of it reinforces what he believes and states in lines 68 and 69, that to see the root of evil, confess it and be absolved looses the bonds of evil. It is important not to give more meaning to this choice of verse than might be sustainable; nevertheless it is noteworthy that it is not the whole of the verse that is quoted. Hebert's partial quotation of the verse suits his purpose in the context of the preceding lines (68 and 69), but the full verse is, 'Behold, O Lord, how that I am thy servant: I am thy servant, and the son of thine handmaid; thou hast broken my bonds in sunder' (Psalm 116.14). However the whole verse elucidates other themes in the poem and is in the context of the familial relationship. Living the monastic life, Hebert would no doubt be readily familiar with the context of the verse. It is a verse that in the context of his poem and statement of faith is significant; it is also a verse quoted, in its entirety, by Augustine.[105] First, it identifies him as God's servant, and therefore not godless. Secondly, it places him in a relational framework as being the 'son of thine handmaid'. Thirdly, it is the relationship with God and biological parent that breaks his 'bonds in sunder'.

Hebert's understanding of freedom and liberty, meaning and fulfilment, is in God's service, 'whose service is perfect freedom'.[106] The wider context of Psalm 116 is one of relationship with God, and has a eucharistic and sacerdotal reference: 'I will receive the cup of salvation: and call upon the Name of the Lord' (Psalm 116.12). Indeed Brilioth quotes a medieval Swedish rhymed prayer for the elevation in the mass: 'Which now I see in the priest's hands / Loose me from all my sins' hard bands / O glorious King, O living Bread, / Be thou my help in utmost need'.[107]

With bonds 'broken in sunder' Hebert moves to the doxological climax of the statement of faith. He restates his conviction that redemption is enacted in the movement from godlessness and self into the 'common life which is in Him / into the universal spiritual Family and Kingdom' (lines 74 and 75).

71 Thanks be to Him who has redeemed us and continues to
72 save us
73 out of this godlessness,
74 into the common life which is in Him,
75 into the universal spiritual Family and Kingdom,
76 And has promised the perfecting of this salvation and
77 fellowship in the life everlasting.
78 Glory be to God for all things. Amen.

Hebert is clear: the Church is indispensable in the work of redemption and the Cross. This is at the heart of Ramsey's *The Gospel and the Catholic Church* as he explores the relationship between 'the Church and the Passion'.[108] Its relevance is that Ramsey refers to Hebert approvingly and bears some of his influence. Writing in the foreword to *The Gospel and the Catholic Church*, Geoffrey Rowell states: 'Ramsey was appreciative of Gabriel Hebert's *Liturgy and Society*, and shared with Hebert an indebtedness to Maurice on the one hand and an awareness of the nascent Liturgical Movement on the Continent'.[109] Rowell further comments that Ramsey's 'concern [was] to overcome the endemic individualism of much Western Christianity in both Protestant and Catholic forms, and to recover the sense of the organic life of the Church as the Body of Christ'.[110] Hebert also reviewed Ramsey's book in *Theology*. In that review, cited by Rowell, Hebert affirms Ramsey's assertion of the link between the Passion of Christ and the believer through baptism, and goes on to comment that '[the baptised] had died to the old self-centred life, they had received a share in a new life of *koinonia*. These are the two poles around which the New Testament conception of the Church revolves – the death and the *koinonia*.'[111] The corollary of this is that the Church is not incidental to the proclamation of the gospel, but is integral to it.

Finally Hebert quotes Isaiah (Isaiah 42.19) in a self-deprecating and humble way:

79 'But who is blind, but My servant?
80 'Or deaf, as My messenger that I send?
81 'Who is blind as he that is at peace with Me,
82 'And blind as the LORD'S servant?'

With this a distinctive and somewhat idiosyncratic, yet defining, passage closes. 'What I Learnt in the House of God' gives real insight into the character of *Liturgy and Society*. It represents the 'celebratory' character of his theology. Whilst it is deeply personal, it is also relational and not individualistic.

Conclusion

This chapter has traced a number of key strands that form the basis of understanding Hebert's thinking in *Liturgy and Society*. Each of the areas covered has yielded fruitful possibilities to engage with it in ways hitherto little explored. Hebert was a man of his time who could draw from Christian tradition, in a distinctive and imaginative way, as well as being aware of the imperative to engage with wider society. Hebert roots his theology robustly in the Church and generously in the flourishing of persons. He is able to do this employing a theological voice that is primarily *celebratory* in tone. The integral place of the Church in Hebert's theology is developed in the next chapter. It is through the Church and her worship that he accounts for the individual's relationship with God, fellow human beings and society.

Notes

1 Christopher Irvine, *The Art of God: The Making of Christians and the Meaning of Worship* (London: SPCK, 2005), xv. Michael Marshall, *Free to Worship: Creating Transcendent Worship Today* (London: Marshall Pickering, 1996), 1–4.
2 Eric L. Mascall, *Saraband: The Memoirs of E.L. Mascall* (Leominster: Gracewing, 1992).
3 Mascall, *Saraband*, 166–9.
4 Mascall, *Saraband*, 166–7.
5 Mascall, *Saraband*, 167.
6 Mascall, *Saraband*, 167.
7 Mascall, *Saraband*, 167.

8 Mascall, *Saraband*, 167.

9 Hebert, *Liturgy and Society*, 234–6.

10 Irvine, *Worship, Church and Society*.

11 Yngve Brilioth, *Eucharistic Faith and Practice*, x.

12 Hebert, *Liturgy and Society*, 210 and 34.

13 Irvine, *Worship, Church and Society*, 62.

14 Irvine, *Worship, Church and Society*, 78.

15 Irvine, *Worship, Church and Society*, 78.

16 Mascall, *Saraband*, 167.

17 Mascall, *Saraband*, 167.

18 Hebert, *Liturgy and Society*, 11.

19 Hebert, *Liturgy and Society*, 10.

20 Hebert, *Liturgy and Society*, 12.

21 Book of Common Prayer, 244.

22 This is the starting point for further thinking I will undertake in engaging with the work of Samuel Wells drawn from a parish context in Norfolk; furthermore it takes on an ethical edge in Wells' work with Stanley Hauerwas in Stanley Hauerwas and Samuel Wells, eds, *The Blackwell Companion to Christian Ethics* (Oxford: Blackwell, 2004).

23 Hebert, *Liturgy and Society*, 13.

24 Hebert, *Liturgy and Society*. 13.

25 Hebert, *Liturgy and Society*. 14.

26 Hebert, *Liturgy and Society*. 14.

27 Hebert, *Liturgy and Society*, 3.

28 See Spinks, *The Worship Mall*.

29 Ronald, C.D. Jasper, *The Development of the Anglican Liturgy 1662–1980* (London: SPCK, 1989), 162–86.

30 Jasper, *The Development of the Anglican Liturgy*, 162.

31 Jasper, *The Development of the Anglican Liturgy*, 162.

32 Michael Ramsey, *The Gospel and the Catholic Church* (London: SPCK, 1990). Lionel Thornton, *The Common Life in the Body of Christ* (London: Dacre, 1941).

33 Jasper, *The Development of the Anglican Liturgy*, 166, 194.

34 Jasper, *The Development of the Anglican Liturgy*, 167–72.

35 The Archbishops' Council, *Common Worship: Christian Initiation* (London: Church House, 2006).

36 Article XXV, *Of Sacraments*, Book of Common Prayer, 621.

37 Jasper, *The Development of the Anglican Liturgy*, 178.

38 Jasper, *The Development of the Anglican Liturgy*, 178.

39 Jasper, *The Development of the Anglican Liturgy*, 178–9.

40 Evelyn Underhill, *Worship* (London: Nisbet, 1936), 164.

41 Dix, *The Shape of the Liturgy*.

42 Jasper, *The Development of the Anglican Liturgy*, 179.

43 Hebert, *Liturgy and Society*, 7.

44 Romano Guardini, *The Spirit of the Liturgy* (New York: Herder, 1930).

45 This is arguably the tone of Joseph Ratzinger's retrospective of the same title, Joseph Ratzinger, *The Spirit of the Liturgy*, trans. John Saward (San Francisco: Ignatius Press, 2000).

46 Hebert, *Liturgy and Society*, 7.

47 Irvine, *Worship, Church and Society*, 3.

48 Hebert, *Liturgy and Society*, 8.

49 Arthur Gabriel Hebert, ed., *The Parish Communion* (London: SPCK, 1937).

50 The world in which Hebert lived had experienced the ravages of the First World War which had traumatised Church and society, as had the subsequent economic

and financial turmoil. See Hylson-Smith, *The Churches in England from Elizabeth I to Elizabeth II*, 154 and Alan Wilkinson, *The Church of England and the First World War* (London: SCM Press, 1978, 1996), 8–12.

51 Jeremy Morris, ed., *To Build Christ's Kingdom: F.D. Maurice and His Writings* (Norwich: Canterbury Press, 2007), 98–9.

52 Jeremy Morris, 'Building Community: Anglo-Catholicism and Social Action', in *Generous Ecclesiology: Church, World and the Kingdom of God*, ed. Julie Gittoes et al. (London: SCM Press, 2013), 50.

53 Jeremy Morris, *F.D. Maurice and the Crisis of Christian Authority* (Oxford: Oxford University Press, 2005), 66.

54 Hebert, *Liturgy and Society*, 13.

55 Rowan D. Williams, *On Christian Theology* (Oxford: Blackwell, 2000), xiii.

56 See also Mike Higton, *Difficult Gospel: The Theology of Rowan Williams* (London: SCM Press, 2004), 10–12.

57 Williams, *On Christian Theology*, xiii.

58 Williams, *On Christian Theology*, xiv.

59 Williams, *On Christian Theology*, xiv.

60 We will explore this 'voice' further through the particular lens of Hebert's 'What Learnt in the House of God'. Hebert, *Liturgy and Society*, 234–6.

61 Hebert, *Liturgy and Society*, 12.

62 Hebert, *Liturgy and Society*. 7, 8.

63 Hebert, *Liturgy and Society*. 8.

64 Hebert, *Liturgy and Society*. 234–6.

65 T.S. Eliot, *The Complete Poems and Plays of T.S. Eliot* (London: Faber, 1969), 147–67.

66 Hebert, *Liturgy and Society*. 87–111.

67 Hebert, *Liturgy and Society*. 88.

68 Hebert, *Liturgy and Society*. 88.

69 Hebert, *Liturgy and Society*. 12.

70 Hebert, *Liturgy and Society*. 234–6.

71 Morris, *F.D. Maurice and the Crisis of Christian Authority*, 195–6.

72 Morris, *F.D. Maurice and the Crisis of Christian Authority*, 207.

73 Morris, *F.D. Maurice and the Crisis of Christian Authority*, 196.

74 Irvine, *Worship, Church and Society*, 109.

75 Irvine, *Worship, Church and Society*, 109.

76 Irvine, *Worship, Church and Society*, 109.

77 Paul McPartlan explores this relationship in a dialogue between Henri de Lubac and John Zizioulas. Paul McPartlan, *The Eucharist Makes the Church: Henri de Lubac and John Zizioulas in Dialogue* (Edinburgh: T&T Clark, 1993).

78 Hebert, *Liturgy and Society*. 75.

79 Hebert, *Liturgy and Society*, 77, his italics.

80 Morris, *F.D. Maurice and the Crisis of Christian Authority*, 81.

81 Hebert, *Liturgy and Society*, 65.

82 Hebert, *Liturgy and Society*. 8.

83 I will explore further the theology of the mystical Body of Christ in Chapter 7 in relation to the work of William Cavanaugh in Chile and some of the practical consequences of it for the life, worship and witness of the Church in Chile.

84 Hebert, *Liturgy and Society*. 65.

85 Hans Urs von Balthasar, *Credo: Meditations on the Apostles' Creed*, trans. David Kipp (Edinburgh: T&T Clark, 1990), 85–6.

86 Hebert, *Liturgy and Society*, 235.

87 Hebert, *Liturgy and Society*, 236.

88 Hans Urs von Balthasar, *The von Balthasar Reader*, eds Medard Kelh and Werner Löser (Edinburgh: T&T Clark, 1982), 377.

89 Mary A. Clarahan, 'Mystagogy and Mystery', *Worship* 83/6 (2009): 508.

90 Clarahan, 'Mystagogy and Mystery', 512.

91 Hebert, *Liturgy and Society*, 234–6.

92 Book of Common Prayer, 302.

93 Hebert, *Liturgy and Society*, 187–9. He also draws from Maurice's, *The Kingdom of Christ*.

94 Hebert, *Liturgy and Society*. 175.

95 Hebert, *Liturgy and Society*. 175.

96 Hebert, *Liturgy and Society*, 175.

97 Hebert, *Liturgy and Society*, 175–6.

98 Morris, *To Build Christ's Kingdom*, 14.

99 Morris, *To Build Christ's Kingdom*, 14.

100 Morris, *To Build Christ's Kingdom*, 14.

101 St Augustine, An Easter Sermon to the Newly Baptised, No. 227 abbreviated by Hebert, *Liturgy and Society*, 85–6.

102 Christopher Irvine, ed., *They Shaped Our Worship: Essays on Anglican Liturgists* (London: SPCK, 1998), 66.

103 Hebert, *Liturgy and Society*, 60.

104 Hebert, *Liturgy and Society*, 63.

105 Henry Chadwick, trans., *St Augustine: Confessions* (Oxford: Oxford University Press, 1991), *Confessions IX i[1]*.

106 Book of Common Prayer, 13.

107 Brilioth, *Eucharistic Faith and Practice*, 229.

108 Geoffrey Rowell, foreword to *The Gospel and the Catholic Church*, by Michael Ramsey (London: SPCK, 1990), iii.

109 Rowell, foreword, ii–iii.

110 Rowell, foreword, ii.

111 Rowell, foreword, iii.

3   Let these Dry Bones Live

Ecclesiology

Hebert very clearly sets out his purpose in writing *Liturgy and Society* in the preface, saying:

> This book is an essay on the Church and her message, particularly as embodied in the actual order of the Church and her liturgy, in relation to the problem of belief and of a true social life in the confused world of today.[1]

Hebert's reflection on the Church is fundamental to *Liturgy and Society*; it coexists with, and is bound into, the two other key themes of the book, liturgiology and missiology. Whilst he makes the case that ecclesiology and liturgy both inform each other, it is ecclesiology that is primary because liturgy is principally an embodied and performative ecclesiology. This shapes how the Church learns to be the Body of Christ *acting* in society and not simply *being* in it. Therein lies a challenge for 'gathered' Churches of any tradition – either those with a preference for 'fine liturgy', esoteric or contemporary forms and expressions of Church. The test of the Church is both its imperative to worship God and to function plausibly in the world. This is Hebert's intention. Hebert's credibility in contemporary ecclesiology necessitates an interrogation of the cultural memory under which he operates. In *Liturgy and Society* Hebert goes beyond nostalgia and his conventional upbringing to develop a nimble, reflective and radically traditional approach to the Church and her mission.

Hebert's ecclesiology and method are valuable today. One of the ways in which this is the case is that he insistently establishes a doctrinal basis for what he writes. So, for example, Hebert's understanding of, and case for, the Church are intimately related to the doctrine of the Incarnation. This also relates to his emphasis on the necessity of understanding dogma in relation to truth, and as a critical part of that which guarantees the Church's identity and faithfulness to the gospel. Such reflection is primarily about the Church's identity, a self-understanding which is at risk if mission is too associated with an attractional model of the Church in which church attendance becomes an end in itself. The Church is integral to the *missio Dei*.

Hebert ecclesiology will be examined as connections are made with the work of Daniel Hardy (1930–2007). Hardy's work constitutes a recent example of the exploration of the social meaning of the Church.[2] Hebert's unfolding of *The Function of the Church in the Modern World* considers not only the Church's inner meaning but her social meaning too. In *Liturgy and Society* Hebert is staking a claim in the search for the Church, and what the Church of England might be. Hardy is a recent writer who was exploring similar questions in a generous and generative way.[3] To that extent there is a theological connection that can be made between Hebert and Hardy (aware that Hardy does not at any point quote or cite Hebert). Significantly, both demonstrate participation in the life and purposes of God, and show how they are made known through history and in the practicalities of particular situations.

The Case for the Church

The relationship between continuity and development in ecclesiology is one that Hebert negotiates successfully. His negotiation necessitates an appraisal of the language used about the Church. The framing of language, usage of words such as 'authentic', 'pure' or 'sound', in relation to the Church, can never be neutral. Hebert has a vision of the Church that rises above ecclesiology seen as *either* retrieval *or* innovation. In *Liturgy and Society* Hebert is doing ecclesiology as he reflects on the nature of the Church, and brings that to bear on how it functions in the modern world. The Church is what can be named when those baptised gather to worship corporately in the name of the Trinity in their task of engagement with the world, and in worship, primarily the Eucharist. Ecclesiology is the way in which Christians shape and inform their understanding of the nature of the Church. Nostalgia does not serve the Church well. Avoiding it, Hebert accounts for the Church's varied character, saying, 'The Church on earth belongs to time and eternity: it is at once human, imperfect, militant here on earth, and divine, the heir now of the eternal kingdom of God: "our citizenship is in heaven".'[4]

Ecclesiology, like liturgiology, is sometimes perceived – somewhat derogatively – to be an archaeological exercise: however, both ecclesiologists and liturgists reject this.[5] Nevertheless their appeal is, of necessity, to that which gives a basis for their current work, and that is very often historical. The nature of that appeal and its outworking is something that rarely goes uncontested: put simply each ecclesiological model will necessarily implicitly draw from a chosen model of the Church from the past. The temptation in a report such as *Mission-shaped Church* is to assume that 'inherited Church' can be set aside and a new conception of what the Church is be developed. That in itself is a task of ecclesiology.[6]

Hebert approaches ecclesiology from his concern for the function of the Church in the modern world and what it means to 'proclaim [the faith] afresh in each generation'.[7] Hebert's ecclesiology is embodied and cannot therefore be a neat and tidy system. Dependent on people, as individuals and corporately, ecclesiology and pneumatology are intimately related as in the Apostles' and Nicene Creeds:

> I believe in the Holy Spirit
> the holy catholic Church
> the communion of saints . . .[8]

The life of the Church in the Creeds is linked explicitly to the operation of the Holy Spirit. Hebert's pneumatology in *Liturgy and Society* is underdeveloped. It is in the later *The Form of the Church* (1946) that Hebert develops his pneumatology; echoing Ezekiel 37 and speaking of the Church, he writes that:

> These four things, Bible, Creed, Sacraments, Apostolate, form the structure of the building of the Church, the bones of the body of the Church; but also the building has a Tenant, the body is animated by a spirit of life, the Holy Spirit of God . . .[9]

This picks up Hebert's point in *Liturgy and Society* that the Church is social and not individualistic. To put it another way, the dry bones of individualism are given sinews and flesh and are bound into a vibrant and living social body by the breath of the Lord. Ezekiel addresses a corporate entity, Israel, just as Hebert addresses the corporate entity of the Church. The Holy Spirit cannot be used as a panacea or gap-filling explanation for how Church, worship and mission exist and operate, but it is fundamental to the Anglican impulse of Church order, liturgy and mission. Hebert has an implicitly charismatic ecclesiology not just a liturgical one.

Method and Motivation in Ecclesiology

One starting point for ecclesiology is the early Church. The early Church can be approached nostalgically or as source that is generative and keeps fidelity to that which has gone before. Either way it is a *cultural memory*.[10]

The concept of cultural memory can reveal the motivation of any particular approach to ecclesiology, and this is true of *Liturgy and Society* too. This is significant in positioning Hebert and therefore his contribution to ecclesiology today. A cultural memory drawing on the early Church justifies itself by providing a more pure and less sullied version of Christianity than subsequent developments of later ages. This is typically summed up in the dictum of the Anglican Bishop John Cosin (1594–1672), who in *The Catholic Religion of the Realm of England, Primitive, Pure, Purged (Volume V)* wrote:

> To us in the Church of England the perpetual standard of our Religion and our Faith is this:
>
> One Canon of Scripture delivered by God in two Testaments. For in those truths which manifestly rest on Holy Scripture are contained all things that regard faith and morals. After them our authentic Instruments are these:
>
> The Three Creeds
>
> The Four Councils
>
> The First Five Centuries, and throughout them the succession and consent of the Catholic Fathers.
>
> For in them is discovered and set forth that early Faith once for all delivered to the Saints, – primitive, pure, and purged from all defilement, apart from the human corruptions and later accretions.[11]

The context of Cosin's writing is the theological antagonism between Puritanism and Catholicism, but its tone and timbre are deeply resonant for a significant body of Anglicans. In the life of the English Church even from before the Reformation, for instance the Lollards, the supposed purity of the early Church is invoked, and is significant both to those like Cosin and also the other Anglican Divines of the seventeenth century. Later in the eighteenth century John Wesley's Holy Club in Oxford, nicknamed the Methodists, is notable for its appeal to the Patristic Era, as was the Tractarian movement in the nineteenth century. The 1662 Book of Common Prayer roots its liturgy in a nostalgic ecclesiological understanding, '[b]ut these many years passed, this godly and decent order of the ancient Fathers hath been so altered, broken, and neglected'.[12] In that account Anglican ecclesiology and liturgy is an attempt at re-pristinisation of the Church.

Cosin's approach has been challenged. The 1938 Church of England report *Doctrine in the Church of England*, of which Hebert would have been aware, highlights the impossibility of deriving one form of Church order from either the New Testament or early Church, and 'we no longer regard precedents, as such, as decisive for all time'.[13] The report traces this line of thought to Richard Hooker in *Laws of Ecclesiastical Polity*, who concludes:

> [Matters of ecclesiastical polity] are not so strictly nor everlastingly com-manded in Scripture, but that unto the complete form of Church polity much may be requisite which the Scripture teacheth not, and much which it hath taught become unrequisite, some time because we need not use it, some time because we cannot.[14]

This is true of *Liturgy and Society* too, as Hebert relates 'the actual order of the Church' to 'the confused world of today'.[15]

The shaping of ecclesiology is about cultural memory and is therefore contested. Problems come when different Churches, inter or intra Church, hold competing definitive and formative memories. Jan Assmann explores the notion of cultural memory by describing 'semantic memory' as a pre-eminently social way of remembering that refers to 'everything we have learned and memorized'.[16] 'It is called "semantic"', he continues, 'because it is connected to meaning and reference'.[17] This way of remembering he distinguishes from 'episodic memory', which refers to our experiences. He suggests such memories can be unsocial; they also 'possess a meaning-ful structure much of the time'.[18] So, in Assmann's terms, the relationship between 'individual' and 'social' memory is where the contested cultural memory is forged: 'remembering means pushing other things into the background, making distinctions, obliterating many things in order to shed light on others'.[19] This is something that Hebert begins to tease out about the Church in order to establish her function and identity in the modern world.

Josef Lössl reflects on the tensions between history and memory.[20] He makes the distinction between critical scholarship and cultural memory, and emphasises the need for scholarship to engage with cultural memory, in a critical, self-reflective process. For instance, he identifies emerging ways of studying the early Church in the fifteenth and sixteenth centuries exempli-fied in the entrenchment of conservatism and growth of reform.[21] Another example is the way in which the contemporary Eastern Church perceives its ecclesiological identity in continuity with the early Church.[22] Reflection on the motivations of early Church historiography is significant for us because it reveals the need to acknowledge the lack of objectivity that anyone can have in accounting for the Church. This is especially the case when it comes to applying 'historical' insights to contemporary practice, which is decisive in *Liturgy and Society*. Lössl rightly identifies that study of the early Church must first begin with what it is, but that the *motivation* to study it is as much about 'memory' as it is about 'history'.[23]

To suggest that the motivation of the study of the Church is as much about memory as it is about history immediately opens up the possibility that historical objectivity, whilst possible, is not what is often most sought after when it comes to study of the early Church. This is partly because the detail is hazy; references to different patristic sources can be used to justify different standpoints. Elements of early writing such as the *Apostolic Tradition* of Hippolytus can be used to reconstruct what it is supposed is early liturgy, and therefore dislodge liturgical texts that have continuity and identity within a tradition. Appeal to the early Church as an ecclesiological source is also about cultural memory. Hebert is doing more than drawing nostalgically from the early Church because of his desire to account for the agency of the Church in society of his own times. His vision of the Church is shaped by, but not dependent upon, cultural memory, but a cultural memory that is generative of mission.

The distinction between cultural memory and critical scholarship is further important in ecclesiology because it exposes theological and personal *motivation*. In this regard *Liturgy and Society* is a case study which unfolds how a cultural memory informs ecclesiology and is an exercise in determining the 'agendas', influences and theologies that dictate them. When cultural memory and critical scholarship become fused, or confused, then the danger is that an ecclesiastical ideology rather than ecclesiology is created. The peril of this in the current Anglican ecclesiological debate is the ideologising of ecclesiology. *Mission-shaped Church* and *For the Parish* can be appropriated, and thereby represent contested cultural memory (rather than critical scholarship) and the move to ecclesiastical ideology. It may be expected that these will be entirely divergent, and some have sought to demonstrate such divergence very sharply.[24]

Liturgy and Society engages in dialogue between cultural memory and critical scholarship and does not meld the two. This is its value in contemporary ecclesiology because it reveals the false dichotomy between seeing ecclesiology as either innovation or retrieval. *Liturgy and Society* reflects on Church in relation to society by narrating its story embodied in liturgy, the proper place of anamnesis.[25] Our consideration of Hebert thus contends that the nature of historic Christendom was little more than enculturation by the Church, examples of which include feudalism, the Act of Uniformity and Establishment. *Liturgy and Society* represents the beginning of the need to reflect ecclesiologically in a predominantly, but not exclusively, post-Christendom society in which an intimate relationship between

Church, society and politics cannot be assumed, and where dominant cultural memories are unpicked.[26]

Roots of Hebert's Ecclesiology: Liturgical and Doctrinal

The defining, but by no means the only, ecclesiological influence on Hebert was the continental Liturgical Movement. Hebert states this explicitly at the beginning of his preface, although there is a restlessness about his engagement with the Liturgical Movement: a centrifugal force impels him to go beyond 'a purely religious and ecclesiastical treatment' issuing in his question 'What has the Church to give to the modern world?'[27]

It is important not to regard the influence of the Liturgical Movement as a Romanising one on account of its continental background. The Roman Catholic author J.D. Critchton celebrates Hebert, along with Dix, as Anglican liturgists who were 'forerunners of the Liturgical Movement'; and in that regard the flow of the Liturgical Movement was not all one way.[28] For our purposes it is important to be aware of the developments of the late nineteenth and early twentieth century since they form the hinterland of the influences upon Hebert. Any overlap between Hebert's thought and the continental Liturgical Movement derives from the shared cultural memory and fascination with the early Church.[29]

Hebert also drew from other sources, notably the work of the Lutherans Yngve Brilioth and Gustaf Aulén.[30] Hebert translated Brilioth's *Eucharistic Faith and Practice*, and in his translator's preface he writes that he is indebted to Brilioth's exposition of his subject.[31] In that preface Hebert acknowledges Brilioth's insights that enable those of a catholic mind, like him, to see beyond the caricature of Lutheranism. This takes him beyond stating (Roman) Catholic 'abuses' because he seeks to uncover those truths 'that mediaevalism had lost sight of, and of which even our revived Catholicism has need to be reminded'.[32] This is very similar to Hebert's appreciation of Aulén's account of the atonement. Both Brilioth and Aulén account for doctrine in ways that enable it to become a gift to the whole Church and prevent it being the possession of a particular Confession. In the same way *Liturgy and Society* is a voice that reframes the received understanding of Church parties and traditions, thus becoming available to the whole Church and resisting deployment *against* contemporary ecclesiological expressions for the sake of it.

Hebert's engagement with the Swedish Lutherans dispels any sense that his later writing is introspective or narrowly bound to England. That is important to bear in mind. It is through work such as the translation of Brilioth that Hebert's wider hinterland allows him to explore the nature of the Church of England and her engagement with society. Despite his openness to Lutheran insights and Brilioth's work he still highly values the association of the Church of England with place and not theological system: 'we stand before the nation as the Church of England: that, and not some theological system, is our title'.[33] This is echoed in *Doctrine in the Church of England*, which refers to the Thirty-Nine Articles of Religion which, 'have not, at any rate from the early seventeenth century onwards, taken in our system the place occupied in the Lutheran system by the Augsburg Confession'.[34] Hebert makes the point that the title Church of England is a geographical term, and that it is not a confessional Church named after a doctrine or person. He sees the Church of England as the means by which the hope of unity may be achieved.[35] He is happy to refer to the *Faith and Order* meeting at Lausanne in 1927 that saw Anglicanism as a 'Bridge-Church'.[36]

What is clear from Hebert's preface to Brilioth's work is that unity is a priority, but not something to be naïve about. Brilioth describes the Eucharist as the sacrament of unity; yet, as Hebert notes, it is also the point where disunity is most intensified and obvious. This anticipates Healy's warning of the danger of idealising doctrine against the lived out forms of the Church.[37] The impact of this is that the sacrament of unity judges the Church, revealing that the sacrament is not a possession of the Church but is instituted by Christ: indeed at the same time the sacrament of the Eucharist defines the Church and holds it to account. Hebert locates that searing judgement at the heart of the mystery of Christ; his death and resurrection. This is like Ramsey, who saw the inextricable relationship of the Church to the passion and resurrection of Christ.[38] Therefore Hebert dismisses the familiar lament of those who would love to be able to share in Holy Communion with people of other Churches before visible unity as 'a superficial remark'.[39] This is not out of pastoral hardheartedness but an act of deduction. Hebert asserts that Christianity is 'the answer to the problems of life', and so the sacrament at the centre of its life is at the centre of controversy because it simultaneously acknowledges disunity whilst calling the Church to unity.[40] He states this in the context of the passion and resurrection of Christ:

> All the issues of life meet there, all the problems of faith in God and His Kingdom, all life's contradictions and difficulties, and all man's sin; *therefore* all our controversies are found there too, for all our differences from one another are there reflected. But there is also found the reconciliation of the differences; their reconciliation, not through some happy formula of concord devised by men, but through the Divine act of redemption which triumphs over our separateness . . .[41]

Such a statement is in the spirit of Brilioth, Ramsey and Aulén. So for Hebert, 'the Sacrament of Unity stands as a perpetual witness against our divisions'.[42]

And in this he is particularly indebted to Brilioth. This helps to give Hebert a realistic sense of ecclesiology, and the space between doctrine and practice.

The *Doctrine in the Church of England* report, and its handling of ecclesiology, prefigures some of Hebert's themes. In its section on the Church and sacraments the report notes that many people at that stage 'find difficulty in seeing any necessity for a Church at all'.[43] *Liturgy and Society* is very much more a work of apologetics than the Doctrine Commission report. The report gives biblical foundation for the Church, the fourfold structure given by the Nicene Creed to describe it – one, holy, catholic and apostolic – and a substantial account of the sacraments including Church order and ministry. *Doctrine in the Church of England* works from the same premise as Hebert writing about 'many people to-day':

> They regard religion as a purely personal and individual activity, and recognise the utility of associations of like-minded people in order that they may effectively announce their convictions for whoso will to heed and perhaps accept. But they see no need for a Christian community which is bound up with the Gospel entrusted to it in such sense that to accept the Gospel in its fullness must involve membership in that community, so that the Church is part of its own creed.[44]

Hebert shares the concern that when Christian community is seen as expendable in the living of a life that claims to be a Christian one it is problematic.[45] However he makes a different conceptual move because he adds the theological imperative of claims about Truth. The report continues, 'the nature of man is inherently social, and the way of progress has always been found to lie in and through the development of some form of community life'.[46] That is dangerously like the reification and sacralising of community and human sociality, something Hebert constantly resists by locating the Church principally in dogma. Nevertheless both *Liturgy and Society* and *Doctrine in the Church of England* reflect a concern about individualisation and the atomisation of the social character of human being, and thereby locate Hebert in the mainstream of Anglican thinking and theology of the time.

Social Meaning and the Gift of Dogma

Hebert poses the question, 'What has the Church to give to the modern world?'[47] In asking that, his purpose is to demonstrate that the Church has a coherent internal social meaning, whilst acknowledging, and describing in some detail, that in many instances sociality in Church, and wider society, is impaired. This is done, most obviously in *Liturgy and Society* and, following

closely on from it, *The Parish Communion*, in which he, and the other contributors, articulates that impairment in terms of the tension between individualism and the social vision of the Church. *Liturgy and Society*, on one level,
recalls the Church to the sociality of the gospel and early ecclesiology that
sees its sociality expressed in a vigorous theology of baptism and Eucharist:
in this subsists the mission of the Church.[48] Embodied in the Church and
expressed in liturgy, the gospel enriches society and gives a framework for
living. It is not an 'add-on extra' or set against society. This is a key area that
Fresh Expressions and *For the Parish* have to consider.

In Hardy's terms Hebert is engaged in seeking the 'social meaning' of the
Church. This is his awareness of the danger of the Church becoming preoccupied with her 'inner meaning' such that she fails to attend to the coming
kingdom or to the way in which she functions in the modern world. Hardy's
word for this is 'sociopoiesis', which is more than looking for social meaning
but how the Church look beyond even herself to the kingdom. Hardy has a
number of key concepts within his theology – extensity, intensity, attraction
and abduction – which relate 'to the way in which our human lives are lived
out in the world, our creaturely condition; our focus on God and his presence
with us that reorders our desires; the way in which we are drawn to God,
generating and reshaping our relationships'.[49] Julie Gittoes sees sociopoiesis as
'the energetics of attraction – that is, the generation and shaping of relationships in relation to the divine'.[50] It works on personal, societal, national and
global levels. This means Church and society are neither independent nor
mutually exclusive. This is an intricate economy where the Church moves
society towards the Kingdom of God, in which 'the former speaks into and
within civilisation to call it to something better; the latter stands within
civilisation, relating it to that by which it is perfected'.[51] The worship of the
Church has a pivotal place in this; facing God and performing that worship
in human social life. Thus for Hardy God's self-giving holiness forms the
Church and shapes both freedom and ethical responses.[52]

Hebert does this by exploring the interaction of liturgy and society. For
Hebert liturgy is embodied ecclesiology not rubrics, or even Dix's pursuit of
'ritual patterns'.[53] When Hebert speaks of society he refers both to the society
of the Church and wider human society: 'One must ask whether the Church
does not show the way, the only way, to the recovery of a common faith and a
true social life.'[54] Hardy's notion of social meaning as applied to the Church is
predicated on the presumption that 'a Church is a society', and he continues: 'In
the most general terms, a *society* is meaning – potentially wisdom – structured in
social terms.'[55] As a parallel he uses the image of architecture in which buildings
are 'an important way of folding space around us to allow us to be and do what
we need': architecture is this process done 'intentionally and systematically'.[56]

Hardy's generous and nuanced description of the fragility of social net-works is different in tone but not in essence from Hebert's. Both in their own way acknowledge, to use Hebert's expression, 'the manifold divisions, confusions, and distractions' of 'the present age'.[57] For Hardy wisdom needs structures that work towards the common good of society. Prior to that, 'lived wisdom is the dynamic of human knowledge, understanding and practice on the one hand, and God and the fulfilment of God's purposes on the other'.[58] For both Hardy and Hebert the Eucharist is the place of enactment of this social meaning.[59] Hardy has themes in common that enable a reassessment of Hebert and which position him in contemporary ecclesiological debate.

Like Hardy, Hebert does not seek to propose a complete 'theological syn-thesis'. Rather, quoting T.S. Eliot, he states: 'There are many questions which *we* are not capable of answering satisfactorily. It is rather for us to "take no thought of the harvest, but only of the proper sowing".'[60] As has been shown, Hebert gives particular prominence to Eliot, and especially the quotation which is repeated at the end of *Liturgy and Society*.[61] In this context Hebert's is an approach of humility, grace and trust, in that for all his assertions about the merits of his thesis he recognises that one sows and another reaps. It echoes Ecclesiasticus: 'Come to [wisdom] like one who ploughs and sows, and wait for her good harvest' (Sirach 6.19). Hebert, like Sirach and Hardy, has a patient teleology. This patience is able to hold together the unresolved nature and provisionality of the Church with a vision of the Kingdom of God. Hardy gives a useful balance in that he holds patience and impatience together.[62] Hebert's patience, however, does not cause him to foreclose his reflection on who the Church is and the nature of its function in the world.

Hebert identifies political consequences of ecclesiology. Some of these are negative – for instance, he warns of the dangers of totalitarianism; and some are positive, such as the way in which a vibrant social conception of Church can influence society for the good. This raises two significant issues: first, the relationship between the individual and the social, and the place of autonomy within that; secondly, the way in which the social nature of the Church and its dogma can be regarded as a *gift*. Hebert identifies the suppres-sion of individuality in totalitarian regimes, in which the social is paramount and stifles individual expression.[63] Hardy likewise notes that a government, if it is 'to be permitted to deal with the issues of a society, must submit itself to re-election'.[64] For Hebert the social nature of the Church as a gift is really at the heart of the interaction of liturgy and society. Deep within this lies freedom, about which he says:

> the discussion, as will be seen, leads up to the conclusion that the confession of the common Christian faith, so far from involving any

renunciation of intellectual freedom, is in reality its indispensable condition: 'the Truth shall make you free'.[65]

Hardy likewise highlights freedom and meaning in the sociality of faith:

> The distinctive character of a *Church* is that it finds the meaning of society in God, and seeks to bring society into closer and closer approximation to the truth that also frees people to be fully themselves, that is to the truth of God.[66]

The handling of truth within the life of the Church is a contested area. Church polity often finds the truth uncomfortable rather than liberating. The overlap between Hebert and Hardy shows the affinity of Hebert with contemporary theology and the contribution that he can make as a partner in ecclesiological thinking, and that therein lies his great value today.

The Church and Truth

Hebert's approach to truth is twofold. First, he locates truth within God.[67] This springs from his consistent wariness about personal opinion and its relation to truth, more specifically 'the blurring of the fundamental distinction between dogma and human opinion'.[68] In this regard Hebert wants to maintain the Church's insistence on the divine and 'a genuine faith in the supernatural'.[69] Hebert analyses the relationship between dogma and truth so that 'knowing the truth' is not confused with 'holding true beliefs'.[70] In this regard Hardy's quoting of an aphorism of Samuel Coleridge Taylor is salient: 'He, who begins by loving Christianity better than Truth, will proceed by loving his own Sect or Church better than Christianity, and end in loving himself better than all.'[71]

Hebert's second approach is in what he calls 'the fundamental distinction between the thing-in-itself and our concept of it'.[72] In speaking of the atonement, Hebert notes that 'there is no official theory of the Atonement, authoritatively sanctioned and guaranteed', so we may ask how we should regard this. He continues, 'The Church believes in and lives by the fact of the Atonement, as a reality which can never be exhaustively defined.'[73] He says this too of the Christian sacraments, and the nature of God, as a reality which can never be exhaustively defined, and yet in which Christians believe and by which they live. Truth claims, not ambivalence to the truth, are, to many modern minds, part of the problem of Christianity and formal religion, hence the designation many are prepared to make about being 'spiritual but not religious'.[74] Hebert does not have an exclusivist view of truth. In Williams' terms of theological voices he is being *communicative*, experimenting with the language of the uncommitted environment. Nevertheless he addresses the issue of God's truth by quoting Isaiah (55.9): 'As the heavens are higher than the earth, so are My ways higher than your ways, and My thoughts than your thoughts.' These approaches to truth mean that Hebert rejects *systems* of truth, both religious and non-religious.

The question of truth also has a bearing on reason and humanity's ability to grasp wisdom beyond themselves. Hebert's anthropology is firmly rooted in humanity made in the image of God.[75] Being made in the image of God gives human beings reason, reason in which they can trust; but that does not render them capable of constructing 'the scheme of the whole universal order'.[76] To make reason the final arbiter of truth exalts the human mind to that of God, which it cannot possibly be; the making of meaning and sense in 'the midst of a changing universe' in which human beings are also subject to change can only be resolved by positing the existence of something outside itself.[77] Hardy describes this in similar terms: it is truth that is the foundation of Christianity, not the other way round, 'a truth in which Churches find their meaning, and in which – as truthful Christian Churches – individuals find their meaning. So truth – God – is what/who confers the meaning of Christian Churches and individuals.'[78] Hardy's appeal is for ways of thinking in these terms, which is something Hebert does as he thinks 'both about the Church and the source and goal of its social meaning in the truth of God'.[79] This further highlights Hebert's contemporary value when seen alongside Hardy.

Hebert engages precisely in these ways of thinking, by asking the question, what is the function of the Church in the modern world, and his continuing contribution to the liturgical and missional life of the Church is to encourage that thinking. The antithesis of Hebert's thinking is that a particular 'model' of the Church is superior to another, although he is ready and willing to critique different approaches – such as Medieval Catholicism, Liberalism, Protestantism, Anglo-Catholicism – acknowledging what is worthy in them.[80] An example of this is his approach to Liberalism, which was an ideology that Hebert shared in his earlier life. Indeed it is important to note that Liberalism to Hebert was not the derogatory term it has become for some, and a badge of honour for others – a party label – but rather a way of thinking which he came to find over-expanded from the given tradition, for example, in seeing the person of Jesus as reduced to his moral and spiritual teaching and discarding 'the eschatological forms in which it is clothed'.[81] Hebert appreciates the optimism of Liberalism but demonstrates its limits.[82] Similarly, Hebert applauds Modernism because of 'its desire to face facts honestly and courageously, accepting new methods and results of modern historical investigation'.[83] His critique of Modernism comes from another angle – 'It is to be criticized, not for being critical, but for not being critical enough, and uncritically accepting the dogmas of the professors: not for being too modern, but for not being modern enough.'[84]

This is partly a rhetorical flourish; but Hebert's underlying point is that it is 'an attempt to adapt Christianity to the belief in Progress – to belief not in God but in man'.[85] If this is so then Modernism, as accounted for by Hebert, does not engage with the 'architecture' of the social meaning of the Church but in the construction of a similar but different building. The corollary is the fear of modern insight which is equally corrosive: '[The] evasion of the appeal to history in panic at the seeming results of Biblical criticism, has given rise to the Fundamentalist movement.'[86] Hebert negotiates the two strands of the social meaning of the Church, orthodoxy and orthopraxis, '[h]ere is the central principle of Christianity: the manifestation of the Divine Goodness in the flesh, in Jesus as the Son of God first, and then through the Holy Spirit in the members of His mystical Body'.[87] This matters because Hebert's concern is not 'obtuse traditionalism or stuffy ecclesiasticism' but vibrant orthodoxy that is rooted in the dogma of the Church.[88] Ben Quash illustrates that this view of orthodoxy and heresy prevails and is not entirely without value because, '[heresies] have forced us to think our belief out more deeply and thoroughly'.[89] Hebert accounts for, and dismisses, some early heresies on the grounds of their inadequate outworking of social meaning. In the same vein Stephen Pickard identifies 'natural ecclesial heresies', amongst them Docetism and Pelagianism.[90] From inherent Docetism the Church 'lurches from one extreme to another', having lost its 'transcendent reference', thus behaving like any other historical community; from Pelagianism the Church becomes toxically anxious and, 'suffering the loss of its of its own inner transcendence is for the most part a Church left to its own devices'.

Hebert's emphasis is less on the loss of transcendence *per se* but truth. Thus he ranges from Gnosticism to Pelagianism, drawing out the insufficiency of their lack of materiality and corporality. For example, of Gnosticism he writes:

> [It] believed in a salvation by Gnosis, by lofty contemplation and wonderful mystical experience and speculations about the unseen world . . . could not believe that marriage was holy or that there was any possibility of glorify-ing God in the common actions of daily life. For them salvation meant an escape from the body, not redemption of the body.[91]

A leitmotif of *Liturgy and Society* is that of truth-telling. This reflects Hebert's attraction to St John's Gospel, '[s]o for St John, "truth" is reality: "to know the truth" is to recognise God as real. And Christ is the truth.'[92] This leads to an examination of the nature of dogma in Hebert and how the truth is told and honoured dogmatically. It places dogmatic considerations as something to be engaged with and negotiated with in the contemporary Church.

Conclusion

This chapter has set out Hebert's case for the Church and its significance. In relation to Hardy this illustrates that Hebert has a credible voice in current debate and that, whilst from another generation, his is not an isolated voice. Hardy represents a modern theologian with a clear and generous engagement with society, and is concerned about the social meaning of the Church and its relationship to the Kingdom of God. Pickard, who is theologically influenced by Hardy, sees a 'renewed sociality' as the antidote to the ecclesial heresies that threaten the sociality of the Church.[93] Hebert's contribution in contemporary ecclesiology is in recalling the Church to the significance of dogma, rooted in God's truth, and the liturgical expression of the social character and benefit of the Church. Renewed sociality will have a eucharistic shape. This will be developed further in the next chapter by considering dogma through the Incarnation and its social consequences which help shape how mission is approached and understood, which is the subject of Chapter 5.

Notes

1 Hebert, *Liturgy and Society*, 7.
2 Daniel Hardy, *Finding the Church* (London: SCM Press, 2001).
3 Hardy, *Finding the Church*, 238–59.
4 Hebert, *Liturgy and Society*, 152.
5 Famously, Dean Inge, when asked about his interest in liturgy, said he had no interest in it, just as he had no interest in collecting stamps.
6 Rowan Williams negotiates the tension in 'Theological Resources for Re-examining Church', in *The Future of the Parish System: Shaping the Church of England for the Twenty-First Century*, ed. Steven Croft (London: Church House, 2006), 49–60.
7 '[The Church of England] professes the faith uniquely revealed in the Holy Scriptures and set forth in the catholic creeds, which faith the Church is called upon to proclaim afresh in each generation. Led by the Holy Spirit it has borne witness to Christian truth in its historic formularies, the Thirty-nine Articles of Religion, *The Book of Common Prayer*, and the Ordering of Bishops, Priests and Deacons.' The Declaration of Assent in the Archbishops' Council, *Common Worship: Services and Prayers for the Church of England* (London: Church House, 2000), xi.
8 Archbishop's Council, *Common Worship*, 35.
9 Arthur Gabriel Hebert, *The Form of the Church* (London: Faber, 1944), 136.
10 Jan Assmann, *Religion and Cultural Memory*, trans. Rodney Livingstone (Stanford CA: Stanford University Press, 2006).
11 Arthur Middleton, *Fathers and Anglicans: The Limits of Orthodoxy* (Leominster: Gracewing, 2001), 183.
12 Book of Common Prayer, viii.

13 William Temple, ed., *Doctrine in the Church of England: The Report of the Commission on Christian Doctrine Appointed by the Archbishops of Canterbury and York in 1922* (London: SPCK, 1938), 117.

14 Temple, *Doctrine in the Church of England*, 118.

15 Hebert, *Liturgy and Society*, 7; quoted more extensively at the beginning of this chapter.

16 Assmann, *Religion and Cultural Memory*, 2.

17 Assmann, *Religion and Cultural Memory*, 2.

18 Assmann, *Religion and Cultural Memory*, 2.

19 Assmann, *Religion and Cultural Memory*, 3.

20 Josef Lössl, *The Early Church: History and Memory* (London: T&T Clark, 2010).

21 Lössl, *The Early Church*, 34.

22 Kallistos Ware, *The Inner Kingdom: Volume 1 of the Collected Works* (New York: St Vladimir's Seminary Press, 2000), 10–11.

23 Lössl, *The Early Church*, vii.

24 Davison and Milbank, *For the Parish*.

25 Julie Gittoes, *Anamnesis and the Eucharist: Contemporary Anglican Approaches* (Aldershot: Ashgate, 2008).

26 Calls for a post-Christendom ecclesiology fail to note that Christendom as a paradigm still exists as a continuing feature of modernity. This relates to Healy's 'ecclesial bricolage' and engagement with pluralism.

27 Hebert, *Liturgy and Society*, 8.

28 Critchton, *Lights in the Darkness*, 87–102.

29 Critchton, *Lights in the Darkness*.

30 Gustav Aulén, *Christus Victor: An Historical Study of Three Main Types of the Idea of the Atonement*, trans. Arthur Gabriel Hebert (London: SPCK, 2010). Originally published in 1931.

31 Brilioth, *Eucharistic Faith and Practice*, ix–xiii.

32 Brilioth, *Eucharistic Faith and Practice*, xi.

33 Hebert, *Liturgy and Society*, 174.

34 Temple, *Doctrine in the Church of England*, 9.

35 Hebert, *Liturgy and Society*, 169.

36 Hebert, *Liturgy and Society*, 169.

37 Healy, *Church, World and the Christian Life.* 25.

38 Ramsey, *The Gospel and the Catholic Church*.

39 Hebert, *Liturgy and Society*, ix.

40 Hebert, *Liturgy and Society*, ix.

41 Hebert, *Liturgy and Society*. ix.

42 Hebert, *Liturgy and Society*. ix.

43 Temple, *Doctrine in the Church of England*, 99.

44 Temple, *Doctrine in the Church of England*, 99.

45 Hebert attributes this phenomenon, and relates it to mysticism, to the Way of Eros and contrasts it with the Way of Agape. Hebert, *Liturgy and Society*, 139–42.

46 Temple, *Doctrine in the Church of England*, 99–100.

47 Hebert, *Liturgy and Society*, 8.

48 Gray, *Earth and Altar*, 201–2.

49 Julie Gittoes, 'Where is the Kingdom?' in *Generous Ecclesiology: Church, World and the Kingdom of God*, eds Julie Gittoes et al. (London: SCM Press, 2013), 103.

50 Gittoes, 'Where is the Kingdom?', 104.

51 Gittoes, 'Where is the Kingdom?', 105.

52 Gittoes, 'Where is the Kingdom?', 107.

53 Simon Jones, introduction to *The Shape of the Liturgy*, by Gregory Dix (London: Continuum, 1945, 2005), xviii.

54 Hebert, *Liturgy and Society*, 9.

55 Hardy, *Finding the Church*, 238.
56 Hardy, *Finding the Church*, 238–9.
57 Hebert, *Liturgy and Society*, 12.
58 Hardy, *Finding the Church*, 41.
59 Hardy, *Finding the Church*, 241.
60 Hebert, *Liturgy and Society*, 12, his italics.
61 Eliot *The Complete Poems and Plays*, 148.
62 Thomas Greggs, 'The Eschatological Tension of Theological Method: Some Reflections after Reading Daniel W. Hardy's "Creation and Eschatology"', *Theology*, 113/875 (2010): 339–47.
63 Hebert, *Liturgy and Society*, 30–31.
64 Hardy, *Finding the Church*, 240.
65 Hebert, *Liturgy and Society*, 12.
66 Hardy, *Finding the Church*, 240. There are also parallels in Daniel Hardy, *Wording a Radiance: Parting Conversations on God and the Church* (London: SCM Press, 2010).
67 Hardy does this too.
68 Hebert, *Liturgy and Society*, 100.
69 Hebert, *Liturgy and Society*, 100.
70 Hebert, *Liturgy and Society*, 109.
71 Hardy, *Finding the Church*, 240.
72 Hebert, *Liturgy and Society*, 102.
73 Hebert, *Liturgy and Society*, 103.
74 Linda Woodhead, 'Introduction', in *Religion and Change in Modern Britain*, eds Linda Woodhead and Rebecca Catto (London: Routledge, 2012), 6–7.
75 Hebert, *Liturgy and Society*, 101.
76 Hebert, *Liturgy and Society*, 101.
77 Hebert, *Liturgy and Society*, 101.
78 Hardy, *Finding the Church*, 240.
79 Hebert, *Liturgy and Society*, 240.
80 The proliferation of Anglican subgroups continues in Evangelical, Liberal and Anglo-Catholic circles, all of which make claims about ideal models of Church and where truth resides.
81 Hebert, *Liturgy and Society*, 60.
82 Hebert, *Liturgy and Society*, 251.
83 Hebert, *Liturgy and Society*, 34.
84 Hebert, *Liturgy and Society*, 34–5.
85 Hebert, *Liturgy and Society*, 35.
86 Hebert, *Liturgy and Society*, 105.
87 Hebert, *Liturgy and Society*, 95.
88 Hebert, *Liturgy and Society*, 34.
89 Ben Quash and Michael Ward, eds, *Heresies and How to Avoid Them: Why it Matters What Christians Believe* (London: SPCK, 2007), 7–8.
90 Stephen Pickard, *Seeking the Church: An Introduction to Ecclesiology* (London: SCM Press, 2012), 75–7.
91 Hebert, *Liturgy and Society*, 95.
92 Hebert, *Liturgy and Society*, 110.
93 Pickard, *Seeking the Church*, 81–99.

4   Ecclesiology, Incarnation and Dogma

This chapter will develop Hebert's ecclesiology further by examining his use and treatment of the Incarnation and dogma and how they are located in the concrete actualisation of the Church. Hardy continues to inform this examination. In this Hebert seeks to 'find' the Church in response to the societal changes of his day. This serves as a way of contributing to contemporary Anglican theology in the wake of the *Mission-shaped Church* report. Likewise, Hardy did so in the wake of the 1998 Lambeth Conference of Anglican bishops, revealing deeper issues at stake than the presenting ones. Thus Hardy's task echoes Hebert's as he writes, 'Anglicanism ideally follows a distinctive pattern in which the gift of God in Jesus Christ is embodied in worship, wisdom and service in an historical continuity of contextually sensitive mission.'[1] Thus the worship, order and practice of the Church in the breadth of mission in each place means that 'the Church is *necessary* – if always *incomplete*'.[2] The Church therefore does not grow numerically by attraction, but through *living out its own narrative and social meaning, maintained by its dogma as a guarantee of its faithfulness to the gospel.* This is far more than a sectarian battening down of the hatches and retreat into liturgy. Indeed it is at the heart of Hebert's project since it propels the Church outwards from herself into the social and political realities of the world which she then embraces and offers in intercession.

In other words, the Church is the interconnectedness of Christian people for the sake of the Kingdom and for the world. Without being nostalgic, Hebert's ecclesiology allows for a vibrant and current self-understanding of the Church that can be subjected to analysis, reflection and development. This lies at the heart of the enduring contribution of Hebert in critiquing the contemporary Church's self-understanding.

Dogma and Freedom

Hebert is keenly alert to the challenge made to the notion of dogma in the life of the Church. There is potential for dogma to suppress the human will and subsume the individual into a corporatist and totalitarian Church. *Liturgy and Society* is in part a negotiation between the Liberal approach that rejects dogma and the overbearing dogmatic approach. That is his approach as he explores the consequence of Incarnation upon the Church and Christian life. In keeping with the Catholic Anglican theologians of the late nineteenth century onwards, the doctrine of the Incarnation is of critical importance to Hebert.[3] Its importance is related both to social doctrine and to the existence of the Church. This is classically expressed in Mascall's *Christ, the Christian and the Church: A Study of the Incarnation and its Consequences,* in which the connection between the Incarnation and the Church is made explicit, saying: 'I have attempted in this book to exhibit the Incarnation of the Son of God as the foundation and the unifying principle of the life and thought of both the individual Christian and the Church of which he is a member.'[4] Consideration of interplay between Incarnation, Church, social life and meaning also necessitates exploration of the place of the sacraments of Baptism and Eucharist. The sacraments are themselves consequences of the Incarnation: for Hebert they also have a further consequence flowing from them in the particularity of human society and interaction. The sacraments are the principal forms of the Church's life, and intimately related to them is the 'order' of the Church.

Hebert speaks very freely about dogma and the Incarnation, and relates the two very closely. This chapter will first explore Hebert's understanding of dogma, before relating that to his understanding of its relationship to the Incarnation *qua* dogma. Hebert's understanding of dogma is derived from his understanding of the Church and its corporate rather than individualistic character. For Hebert dogma is about the holding of opinions; not opinions constructed on 'reasonable grounds', but on the guarantee of Church authority.[5] He rejects a definition, which he sets up as an Aunt Sally, that dogma 'consists of a set of opinions about religious matters imposed by ecclesiastical authority'. He rejects this by demonstrating that dogma does not restrict the freedom of the individual, whilst conceding that theology has often given a contrary impression. Individualism has a 'fragmenting influence'.[6] He is not however terribly interested in individual views unless they are consonant with the teaching of the Church.[7] Thus he asserts, 'we can argue about beliefs and opinions: but there is something in faith which is of a different order from the mere assent of the intellect to propositions'.[8]

Hebert quotes Father Herbert Kelly of the Society of the Sacred Mission in giving a down-to-earth explanation of the difference that *faith* brings to opinions, and what makes them dogma.[9] Kelly's example is to demonstrate how people can agree with the thrust of dogmas, for instance the very existence of God, but that that does not guarantee faith: 'The man who can only see opinions to agree with has plainly no least idea of what I was talking about.'[10]

This demonstrates Hebert's rich sense of Christian tradition, which contrasts with his belief that Liberalism strips out faith and mystery.

It is not Liberalism's concern for freedom and lack of imposition that sits uneasily with Hebert, since he shared that sensibility by instinct and temperament as someone who rejects repression and coercion. Essentially, Hebert cannot accept that obedience is necessarily restrictive. So he suggests that Liberal Theology asks, 'How can a man be intellectually free, if the Church by imposing on him one set of opinions, deprives him of freedom to adopt a different set of opinions?'[11] Hebert also dismisses scholastic tendencies, with their identification of faith with *correct* belief. The point is the corrosiveness of the pietistic and individualistic forces that, in Hebert's view, have dogged the Church since the Middle Ages, whose scope includes Protestantism, Liberalism and Roman Catholicism, such as in the work of Thomas à Kempis.[12]

Reference to God is of critical importance to Hebert, because reference to God is reference to truth: he presages Hardy's notion of 'layers of social meaning referred to God'.[13] Hebert appropriates Maurice to himself in this regard. He sees Maurice as a 'seer and prophet of the future' whose importance 'has not yet been recognised'.[14] What is fundamental to him is Maurice's rejection of Liberalism, as he sees it; indeed to Hebert, 'there never was a theologian more radically opposed to the spirit of Liberal Theology, or a more thorough dogmatist'.[15] Hebert drives home the importance of not simply using human reason but also reference to the Divine in this consideration of Maurice: 'The whole centre of [Maurice's] teaching was his faith in the reality of God and the reality of God's saving work through Christ, and his constant endeavour to distinguish between the Divine and human.'[16] Hebert contrasts that view with a Liberal theology that treats dogma as opinion and 'always has misgivings about subscription to the creeds'.[17] The Church does not, in Hebert's view, demand a rigid adherence; but it does demand fidelity. The profession of the Creed, for instance, is not a shackle on truth but a source of freedom, because 'it is an act of personal allegiance; a man is speaking, confessing his faith in God, in Jesus Christ the Revelation of God, in the Holy Ghost the Lord and Life-giver'.[18] Such a view of the emancipatory character of dogma is not evident in the Church today. The re-imagination of the place of dogma is potentially one of Hebert's contributions to contemporary ecclesiology.

The nature of the freedom to believe is a delicate one for Hebert. He has to negotiate between fundamental freedom of belief and conscience that everyone has and the dogma held by the Church. His answer is to see, in the spirit of Maurice and his own statement 'What I Learnt in the House of God', a familial loyalty to Church teaching: his acceptance of Church teaching and dogma is as a loyal child, albeit a child who can think and apprehend God, because, for Hebert, 'faith is an effort to apprehend something which exceeds the grasp of the apprehending mind'.[19] This is freedom. It is also a profoundly important point for ecclesiology since it draws people into a relationship in which belief is forged.

In wrestling with the Johannine notion of the truth, Hebert devotes a sub-section of *Liturgy and Society*, the title of which – 'The Truth Shall Make You Free' – alludes to John 8.32.[20] Hebert is clearly attracted to St John's Gospel, and he asserts that 'to identify "knowing the truth" with "holding true beliefs" would betray a complete misunderstanding of the thought of St John's Gospel'.[21] Hebert had a reputation as a biblical scholar.[22] Despite that, *Liturgy and Society* does not represent a thoroughgoing engagement with John's Gospel. In his assertion of the necessity of dogma to bind the family of the Church he does not equate coming to know the truth with holding true beliefs. Assent to the Church's teaching must be on the basis of truth and not a sense of the totalitarian Church arbitrarily insisting on its own formulae. Rather, he wrestles with freedom and truth, personal conscience and ecclesial discipline: it is a fine balance and it is never fully resolved in *Liturgy and Society*, or indeed in his other writing. They are a crucial set of tensions to hold:

> In being thus under authority, man is freed from the domination of other men's opinions and of his own; he is free to obey his own conscience, in so far as he has learnt to obey the truth. And thus the creed, which is man's act of allegiance to God and his acknowledgement of the authority of God's revelation in Christ is our charter of freedom.[23]

This emphatic statement situates Hebert's understanding of dogma as, in anachronistic terms, an acceptance of the genetic coding of the Church's faith as patterned on Christ. The centrality of the dogma of the Incarnation holds the Church faithful to that. It also reflects part of Hebert's particularly *Anglican* heritage in that it echoes the second collect at Morning Prayer in the Book of Common Prayer: 'There is no freedom except in allegiance to the truth – to God, *whose service is perfect freedom*. This is the paradox of Christianity.'[24]

Hebert does not use R.W. Moberly's phrase in *Lux Mundi* (1889), 'The Incarnation as the Basis of Dogma', despite showing an affinity with that claim. Like Hebert, Moberly believed that dogma begins in the apprehension of, and judgements about, the life of Jesus of Nazareth. Williams, writing on Moberly, sums him up as saying that, 'The settling of questions to do with this history is where dogma begins; and it is necessary if faith is not to be irrational.'[25] Williams notes that Moberly's interest is not (as with Hebert) in the *how* of the Incarnation; what concerns Moberly is the 'conviction that the

Church, must be able to give a response it holds to be true to the question, "Who is it that is the object of your faith?"'[26]

In his critique of Moberly, Williams is very alert to the pitfalls of an overly dogmatic approach to Christianity. Hebert uses the word dogma in a nuanced way, and even invokes Origen in suggesting that the Church cannot be dogmatic about dogma: 'It is always possible, therefore, in the case of any given doctrine, that the truth which is seeking to find adequate expression may not have found for itself an adequate vehicle.'[27] Williams sees the theologian's task as being to 'urge that we stand aside from some of the words we think we know, so that we may see better what our language is *for* – keeping the door open to the promises of God'.[28] The simple asking of the question 'Do you believe in "the Incarnation"?' is, says Williams, a 'futile question' unless it has something to do with the 'serious question', which is 'How do you proclaim, and how do you hear proclaimed, the judgement of Christ?'[29] Hebert's emphatic answer would be that liturgy is the place where that proclamation is most properly made, and where the *how* of the proclamation is uttered and heard.

Williams offers two points which pick up the tension of identifying ecclesiology with ecclesiasticism, and the danger of its appropriation of the Incarnation. First, he describes the 'long-standing enthusiasm' of Anglican theology for the incarnational principle, which has often risked blurring that question of *how* to proclaim, 'because the *image* of incarnation, the fusion of heaven and earth, the spiritualizing of matter, has proved so wonderfully resourceful a tool for making sense of a sacramental community with a social conscience and a cultural homeland'.[30] Williams' thinking raises a question of Hebert in relation to the 'sacramental community with a social conscience and a cultural homeland'. This is Hebert's theological hinterland and historical context. As Morris says of Maurice, and which is also true of Hebert:

> The theological inspiration of this tradition unquestionably lay in the heavy accent that High Church Anglicans came to place on the doctrine of the incarnation, but they pursued an integrated vision of faith in which community action, liturgy, personal devotion, education and theology cohered in a sacramental and incarnational way of viewing the world, and not least in the Eucharist.[31]

His disillusionment with Liberalism stems from the trenches of the First World War, something Moberly and Maurice did not live to see. The incarnational principle has a different sense for Hebert because the 'spiritualising of matter', to which Williams refers, becomes profoundly difficult when matter was so degraded in the trenches.

The second question Williams raises for the theologian is the relationship between dogma and worship; a relationship which when divorced opens up the 'inevitable temptation to treat dogma as a solution, a closure'.[32] This drives to the heart of what *Liturgy and Society* is about. Williams notes, 'the theologian will share the concern of those who want the Church's liturgy properly to open up a congregation to wonder and newness of life, and will understand the reticence of the contemplative'.[33] Hebert associates dogma with the worship of the Church, 'the change with regard to dogma is closely parallel with liturgical change'.[34] He is aware that dogma has been responsive and responded to in the history of the Church. *Pace* Hebert, Williams does not seek to defend the dogma of the Incarnation: 'It is not a theologian's business first and foremost to defend this or that dogmatic formula, but to keep alive the impulse that animates such formulae – the need to keep the Church attentive to the judgement it faces, and the mission committed to it.'[35] Hebert inhabits the incarnational principle; and, far from ideologically driving an agenda, uses the Incarnation as a source and point of reference in which the social nature of the Church and her embodied worship 'keeps alive the impulse that animates' the dogma.

As has been shown, Hebert never claims the Incarnation as the *basis* of dogma. Williams' critique of Moberly, to whom Hebert was indebted, also highlights their dissimilarity. This means that it is necessary to demonstrate *how* Hebert can be said to describe the relationship between dogma and liturgy by not being 'piously uncritical', to use Williams' phrase, in defence of dogmatic formulae 'on the grounds of liturgical use or adherence by holy people' but in 'helping to articulate the critical dimension of worship itself'.[36] Hebert notes that it is common to assign the primacy of liturgy, dogma and personal religion to religious experience, but this is something he seeks to counter. This means that Hebert can be expansive about all three without being defensive because his argument is that experience is not the basis or validation of any of them.[37]

Dogma is not sufficient in itself for a faith that engages with the gospel and society because, as Hebert suggests, 'without piety and personal devotion, liturgy becomes external and formalistic, and dogma becomes arid and intellectualist'.[38] Hebert's conviction is that the basis of keeping the impulse of piety and personal devotion is what animates dogma. The personal conviction is not generated by feeling but by the initiative that God takes – 'Christianity is the proclamation that God has made a way to man, in the Incarnation: "Herein is love, not that we loved God, but that he loved us."'[39] The dogmatic-liturgical interplay runs through *Liturgy and Society*. Hebert's gripe with the Counter-Reformation is that it did not address the weakness of the Church pre-Reformation, which was its doctrine of the Church. He sees the pre-Reformation Church as an earthly Church which sustained 'the vast fabric of theology and of canon law'.[40] The Counter-Reformation did not address the Church, but rather it 'set in hand a devotional reformation'.[41] So piety and personal devotion has to be set in the context of the Church as Christ's mystical body with a 'strong realisation in worship of this common life'.[42] This is salutary in relation to Fresh Expressions of Church. Analysing them in relation to Hebert raises the question of ecclesiological identity and impact today: are *Fresh Expressions* essentially devotional and/or liturgical reforms or a renewed ecclesiology?

Society and the Function of the Church in the Modern World

The appeal of Hebert and others to the Incarnation addresses Hardy's urging that thought be given to Church and the source and goal of its social meaning in the truth of God.[43] So what about the Church and society? 'It is wrong to assume', writes Hebert, 'that the concern of Christianity is only with the religious life of the individual and the endeavour of a select circle of devout people to live a sanctified life and attain an individual perfection: it is the denial of the Incarnation'.[44] What follows from that statement is that to affirm the Incarnation is to see that Christianity embraces the whole of an individual's life and places the individual within a society that is wider than religious affiliation. Sectarianism is not plausible or sustainable. Hebert broadens this further in his argument that the Incarnation, the manifestation of God's goodness in the flesh, involves the redemption of the body, 'and therefore also of the social relations of the life lived in the body, and of the whole social, economic and political structure'.[45] This sense of the Incarnation compelling the Church to exist outside the narrow confines of ecclesiasticism and 'very much *in* the world'[46] is far-reaching in its consequences.

The impact of this is that it makes Hebert a politically astute and aware writer, with sensitivity to societal issues. Hebert does not comment directly on the politics of his time, other than his critique of totalitarianism. Nevertheless there is a communitarian tenor to his reflections on the impact of the Incarnation which echoes the thinking of one of the key figures in the creation of the Welfare State, Archbishop William Temple:

> The common view is that the Church is concerned with spiritual issues and eternal destiny, the State with temporal issues and economic prosperity. But you cannot cut the two apart in this way; for the two consist of the same people, and they cannot act on divergent principles without an inconsistency which amounts to hypocrisy.[47]

Hebert picks up leads left by Temple, who writes: 'We have to work out again the social principles of the Gospel; we must hope to be able to offer to the distracted world a Christian sociology which all Christians agree to propagate.'[48] Temple says the Church *should* engage with the social, political and economic structure of society: in *Liturgy and Society* Hebert acknowledges that call and suggests *how* the Church might do that.[49] It is not a programme, but more of a manifesto outlining the Church's existing self-reflective capacity to offer a Christian sociology to 'a distracted world'. This marks a departure from the Temple of 1926, in that part of the capacity the Church already has, which is an incarnational gift, is not only a social conscience shaped by the gospel but also the embodiment of that gift in the embodied life of the Church, principally in the Eucharist – 'Here is part of the ideal: that all those who live in one place should eat and drink together before God.'[50] This is distinctly about gathering as a Church as an expression of society not a flight from it.

This is an account of the hallowing of everyday life, hence why 'the Eucharist is the Lord's Supper [which] makes the family dinner also a holy meal'.[51] It would be easy now, even more than in Hebert's day, to regard this as somewhat nostalgic or utopian: however he is insistent that this is what the Church can exist to offer society in her politics and economics, and that harder for the Church is 'to lay down a rule of ethics and draw up a programme of social action'; and 'The first and chief thing is that we should so learn to believe in the Incarnation that we learn to see more and more clearly the contrast between the actual and the ideal which is the truly real.'[52] A somewhat wistful side of Hebert comes out in his description of rural and urban life – it echoes William Cowper's lament that 'God made the country, and man made the town' – how towns are 'for the most part aggregations of unrelated families and individuals', whereas 'dwellers in villages' are happier because 'every one knows every one else'.[53]

Nevertheless he is alert to just how far all this is from the practice of Christians. Yet Hebert remains insistent about the generative capacity of the Church from within herself through her fidelity to the gospel and doctrine of the Incarnation: 'The task of the Church in the future will be to re-create a social life.'[54] The diagnosis is clear; the prescription that follows is for the Church to recover the sacramental ideal that 'includes all'.[55] That ideal shall not be recovered, he writes, 'till in each parish the chief Sunday service is the offering of the Eucharist with the communion of the people'.[56] This is the clear and direct influence of the Liturgical Movement, and also Hebert's conviction that the Eucharist shapes the Body of Christ and as a consequence of the Incarnation is a gift to the world.

The trajectory of Hebert's argument gives it contemporary significance in its inclusive sociality. Hardy notes the need to 'begin from where we are', in that social meaning within the Church is already structured and inhabited.[57] He further suggests that 'we need first to focus on how the indefinitely rich meaning of society provided by God is already present in the Church'.[58] This is a rich vision of the meaning of society that is already present in the Church. The source and outworking of that vision is the Eucharist; more specifically, a Parish Eucharist which is 'not one service among many, but the centre of all'.[59] This vein of thought is one articulated by Hardy as he says, 'Eucharistic worship is the major way by which the social meaning of the Church is consistently referred to God's decisive formation of its meaning in Jesus Christ as continued through the Holy Spirit.'[60] This 'social meaning' is described by Hebert in *Apostle and Bishop* as 'Frontier Studies'.[61] In this Hebert draws on the work of Lesslie Newbigin in acknowledging the interface between the gospel and the world 'which runs across every place where men live and work'.[62] The significance of this is that: 'The answers which are to be found are not only the answers of a few experts within the Church, but also of the Church itself in the persons of its members dispersed throughout the world, functioning through regular meetings for serious discussion.'[63] This is not to say that either Hebert or Hardy see the Church as simply a pragmatic societal way of organising a group of like-minded individuals who derive authority from each other; but rather there is something of the gift of being that demands eucharistic living. Neither does it preclude the pneumatological or grace-filled presence in non-eucharistic communities, but suggests a diminished social meaning in them. It does have consequences when it comes to decision making within the Church. The etymology of the word 'synod', *together on the way*, is suggestive of companionship which is better reflected in the practices of the 2008 Lambeth Conference, with its *indaba* reflection and intentional conversations, than the quasi-parliamentary governance of the Church of England.[64]

Form and Order: Church Shaping

In Hebert's day the ecclesiological alternatives were a retrenched conservatism represented in anti-Modernist Roman Catholicism, a radical reworking of ecclesiology of a Calvinist nature or a liberalism that fostered a fractured relationship between Church history and theology that superseded both in benign notions of progress. As Hebert speaks of the 'authority of the Church' he envisages this as a shared enterprise and not that of a magisterium. He writes:

> If [*Liturgy and Society*] were an apologetic or personal statement of views, it would rightly be required to answer a thousand and one questions in

order to vindicate itself. The questions are there to be asked; to many of them I have tried to give an answer. But the pith of the matter is, not that *I* am able to answer them, but that members of the Church, you and I, have the duty of tackling them in common, and that it is only on the basis of the common Christian faith and within the unity of the common Christian fellowship that they can fruitfully be answered at all.[65]

Hebert initially accepted the Liberal approach, but came to reject it in the aftermath of the First World War, when such optimism around progress was shattered along with other factors in science, societal change, psychology and other disciplines. The previous chapter showed that Hebert was inspired by a cultural memory of the early Church but was not bound by it. Indeed, his interest is in the formation of an authentic post-Constantinian ecclesiology and a foundation for a post-Christendom ecclesiology. In such a way he avoids what Lössl suggests:

> The most intensive and most informed interest in the early Church, however, can still be found in the mainstream Western Churches. It is true that as these Churches have in the past been threatened by the revisions and deconstructions of academic study of early Christianity, so they have increasingly lost interest in the early Church as a normative entity for their own conduct. Like all modern institutions, the great modern Churches tend to be orientated towards the future and to conduct their business in tune with the social and political systems around them.[66]

In the interplay between the contested claims for the Church under consideration, ecclesiology is the vibrant and current self-understanding of the Church that can be subjected to analysis and reflection. It is not destined always to be retrospective, engaging in retrieval, or nostalgia, in the pursuit of a Church that is in tune with theological fashion rather than the authentic Church of Jesus Christ. Hebert's direct answer is to be found in his later work, *Apostle and Bishop*, in which he states categorically:

> The new Reformation [flowing from the Liturgical Movement] both of the Reformation and Counter-Reformation, which is now taking place, cannot be a return to the primitive Church, or to the middle ages, or any other period which we may be tempted to idealize; it is never possible to put the clock back in that way. The return always has to be to the Gospel itself, to the Lord who once lived on earth and died and rose again, and who lives and reigns, and who, remaining the same, says, 'Behold, I make all things new.'[67]

This is the conclusion of a section on 'static' and 'dynamic' views of the Church, which Hebert discusses in relation to the issue of Church order, and particularly the place of episcopacy within it. Hebert had already contributed to *The Apostolic Ministry* in 1946. Of that book he says that he reaffirms its 'positive thesis and upholding of the Catholic view of valid orders, but rejecting the inference that all non-episcopal sacraments and ministries are invalid'.[68] This is a more irenic and less dogmatic position than might at first be supposed and inferred from *Liturgy and Society*. Hebert's irenicism on this point is illustrated by his statement on dialogue and the refutation of arguments because '[i]t is a mistake in controversy to try to refute one's opponents. In that case, if one wins the argument, one has really lost it; for those whose views have (perhaps) been successfully refuted will only be hardened in their opposition.'[69] He sees a 'better way' in which principles are set out and that in disagreement is the opportunity to learn.

Church Governance

Reference to Hebert's *Apostle and Bishop* is significant here because he develops a wider account of Church governance that is illuminating. In it, and in *Liturgy and Society*, Hebert does not present a view of an ossified Church, or a Church seeking nostalgically to recover past positions, or even to sacralise the present. In considering episcopacy he sketches out the styles of episcopal ministry, pointing out the great differences between 'the pre-Nicene bishop and the missionary monk of the Dark Ages, and the mediaeval prelate, and the Hanoverian grandee' and so on. Yet there is, he writes, 'a continuity and unity in these various episcopacies, which depends on the nature of the office itself'.[70] He restates his position that, in the case of episcopacy, it is a many-sided office and that it cannot be justified because it is 'a venerable form of Church government' or 'the Historic Episcopate'; but rather it has to appeal to gospel roots.[71] Hebert's appeal is not simply to offices and rites as they have been received, or even to recovery, but to a dynamic sense of how the Church expresses herself in concrete form today. This is evident in his analysis of the approach to episcopacy taken in the Church of England:

> [It has been] a common fault among us Anglicans to present the Episcopal Office as if it were primarily a matter of Law and Constitution of the Church, and to fail *to trace any special connection of it with the Gospel which our Lord proclaimed and entrusted to his Apostles.*[72]

This illustrates two significant points in any critique of Hebert more generally. First is his acknowledgement that forms of the Church and its order are not rigid but can be responsive. Secondly, they cannot be any more innovative than fidelity to the gospel and Christ allows; how such fidelity is judged is another matter. He is a radical conservative. He states clearly in *Fundamentalism and the Church of God* that '*The Visible Church is part of the Gospel*'[73] and that '[n]othing could be plainer than this in Holy Scripture'.[74] The shape and form of the 'visible' Church' is what is at issue, since how it is formed and how it expresses itself are integral to its engagement with society.

Hebert is alert to the ruptures that socio–political and historical forces brought to the Church: whether the rise of Islam and its impact on the Eastern Church; or the demise of Greek and then Latin as common languages; or the assimilation of tribes along with their chieftains in northern Europe; or the vestiges of Arianism.[75] All these forces he sees as implicated in fostering 'individualistic piety, a personal religiousness'. This is broad brush stroke history – and, as is the case with Dix, reflects flawed liturgical archaeology too – and he uses it to position his assault on those liturgical expressions that do not conform to his principles:

> In the Church of England today [it] still leads people to desire the 'nice quiet service' at eight o'clock on Sunday, and to take their place in Church by preference away from their fellow-worshippers, at a service which is the successor of the private masses of the middle ages in being a clerical monologue.[76]

This teases out the way Hebert in *Liturgy and Society* relates individualism and the associated loss of the sense of the *plebs sancta Dei* to the clericalisation of the Church.[77] In *Apostle and Bishop* 27 years later, this is undiminished. Here Hebert assails both, 'then the priest said mass for the people; now he celebrates Holy Communion for them', and goes on, 'yet our Prayer Book is called the Book of *Common* Prayer'.[78] All this represents a *deprivation* of the part of the whole people of God in the liturgy which properly belongs to them.

In *Apostle and Bishop* Hebert also explores the meaning and place of the Communion of Saints; surprisingly this is lacking both in reference and in substance in *Liturgy and Society*. Hebert's unease with 'the individualistic piety and personal religiousness' is not simply its ecclesiological impropriety, but the origin of the vacuum which it filled. He traces it to Arian tendencies that, combined with sixteenth-century manifestations of Apollinarianism and Monophysitism, denied the 'true manhood' of Christ, and that, 'whenever this happens, we get a wrong idea about the Church and the Ministry also, so that the priest is thought of as an exalted personage who is above the level of ordinary men'.[79] However the humanity of Christ returns in the realism of the crucifix and pieta scene. What is missing, in Hebert's analysis, is 'the 'Mystery of Christ', the glory of the risen Lord.[80] Such an analysis is pertinent to a critique of contemporary functional or bureaucratic notions of the Church.

Eberhard Bethge notes that Dietrich Bonhoeffer traces a similar move in 'the old extreme Calvinism' which is in error when 'it ends by preventing the complete entry into this world of the majesty of God', something which Bethge suggests Bonhoeffer sees in Karl Barth.[81] Put simply, Bethge suggests that 'the early Barth, desiring to proclaim God's majesty, begins by removing him to a remote distance, Bonhoeffer, inspired by the same desire to proclaim his majesty, begins by bringing him into close proximity'. This relates closely, Bethge suggests, to Bonhoeffer's *Act and Being* so that one of the principal themes of *Sanctorum Communio* is that:

> The Church is the basic givenness of theology. It is the reality of the Church, again conceived of as 'Christ existing as community' that makes fruitful the tension between the respective legitimate interests; of the existentialist theology of Act on the one hand, as developed theocentrically in Barth and anthropocentrically in Bultmann, and on the other of the neo-orthodox theology of Being of the 'pure doctrine'.[82]

In some ways Hebert's work is an attempt to engage with what Bonhoeffer had pursued in his early work; and, like Bethge's description of Bonhoeffer's approach to the Church, 'it was both a riddle and an aspiration'. Bethge asks if Bonhoeffer (and the later commentator Althus) fall between stools when they try 'to reconcile such powerful tendencies as historicism and sociology on the one hand and the theology of revelation on the other'[83] This is a significant question to Hebert as well, and one that *Liturgy and Society* addresses not by solving the riddle but by being faithful in living within it the aspiration of what the Church is.

Hebert does not record any debt to Bonhoeffer, but there are interesting parallels and echoes. Bonhoeffer has the aim of 'establishing the word of God in a sociological community'.[84] Hebert's response to any suggestion that theological tenets become more 'fluid' when he revealed their 'thoroughly social character' is through the restatement of the significance of dogma in relation to the sociological community of the Church. That said, Hebert is open to the charge levelled at Bonhoeffer also that his identification of Christ with the community violates something of the eschatological nature of the Church; and arguably, in Hebert's case, his denigration of the Church shaped by historical forces underemphasises the historicity of the Church. To be part of the *plebs sancta* and *Communio Sanctorum* also involves inheriting mistakes as well as glory. Hebert likewise is harder on the liturgical lapses of the Church than those of ministry, for instance, episcopacy.

Into this discussion Hebert adds the notion of what he calls 'a false doctrine of the holy'. This can be traced to the 'Double Standard' described more fully by Kenneth Kirk in *The Vision of God* (1931), to whom Hebert attributes the analysis.[85] Simply put, Kirk describes the idea that clergy and religious are held to have different standards of holiness from laypeople:

> A high standard of those who lived in monasteries and the 'clerical' class generally who were educated and knew Latin – though there was much transgression among them also – and a lower standard for the layman in the world, who was indeed reckoned to be doing well if he kept clear of grave offences against the moral law.[86]

Hebert's ecclesiology cannot accept the possibility that some people have a higher way to pursue than others. Such a concept is itself related to individualism since it exalts certain individuals over others and denigrates the whole Body. It is a form of individualistic Gnosticism and tends to exalt clerics above the whole People of God.[87]

Conclusion

Hebert sets out a robust, generous, yet dogmatic case for the Church. This is decisive and fundamental to our understanding of Hebert and what he offers distinctively today. The Church is the articulation of sociality because it is the place in which the individual flourishes as a person, a person-in-relationship within the Church and wider society. Hebert's case stands or falls on its validity theologically and ecclesiologically. This is all a consequence of the Incarnation and continues to be the guarantee of the fact of it. The actuality of the Church in society is the key to the 'function of the Church in the modern world'. This situates Hebert's place in the continuum of Anglican ecclesiology and, in his affinity with Hardy, as capable of having a contemporary ecclesiological voice.

The next chapter will turn to scrutinise *Liturgy and Society* through the lens of mission and vice versa. In considering mission, the indispensability of the Church as part of gospel and consequence of the Incarnation remains. The Church is how the Kingdom of God is anticipated and made known, whilst never usurping the Kingdom. Without the Church Christ is not made visible in society. The missional dilemma of the Church, and Hebert's ecclesiology and missiology, is how fidelity to the gospel, dogma and the reality of God relate to the empirical reality of the Church. This continues and sustains the proposition that Hebert's understanding of the Church is not as a nostalgic cultural memory, but as the vessel of the narrative of God's presence in the world in the Incarnate Christ, which in the power of the Spirit defines mission. *Liturgy and Society* is grounded in the idea that Christian faith is transmitted in a familial generational way, as expressed in the personal testimony 'What I Learnt in the House of God'. However through his restatement of the significance of the Church, dogma and liturgy Hebert begins to sketch out the possibility of developing a missiology that sees faith as being narrated through the concrete forms of Christian life and practice. This forms the background of the treatment of mission in the next chapter.

Notes

1 Hardy, *Finding the Church*, 3. I am not suggesting a definitive link between the two, simply that there are similar theological and ecclesiological themes that are common to both.
2 Hardy, *Finding the Church*, 3.
3 For instance, Charles Gore, Maurice and the *Lux Mundi* school; and more in the early and mid-twentieth century, such as William Temple, Mascall and Ramsey.
4 Eric L. Mascall, *Christ, the Christian and the Church: A Study of the Incarnation and its Consequences* (London: Longmans, Green, 1946), v.
5 Hebert, *Liturgy and Society*, 87.
6 Pickard, *Finding the Church*, 76.
7 Hebert, *Liturgy and Society*, 87.
8 Hebert, *Liturgy and Society*, 88.
9 Hebert, *Liturgy and Society*, 88–9.
10 Hebert, *Liturgy and Society*, 89.
11 Hebert, *Liturgy and Society*, 109.
12 Hebert, *Liturgy and Society*, 113. Pickard also notes that individualism is not a new phenomenon in the Church: Pickard, *Finding the Church*, 76.
13 Hardy, *Finding the Church*, 241. I am not suggesting a causal link between the two.
14 Hebert, *Liturgy and Society*, 108.
15 Hebert, *Liturgy and Society*, 108.
16 Hebert, *Liturgy and Society*, 108.
17 Hebert, *Liturgy and Society*, 108.
18 Hebert, *Liturgy and Society*, 109.
19 Hebert, *Liturgy and Society*, 89.
20 'And you will know the truth and the truth will make you free.'
21 Hebert, *Liturgy and Society*, 110.
22 Critchton, *Lights in the Darkness*, 88.
23 Hebert, *Liturgy and Society*, 111.
24 Hebert, *Liturgy and Society*, 110.
25 Williams, *On Christian Theology*, 79.
26 Williams, *On Christian Theology*, 80.
27 Hebert, *Liturgy and Society*, 90.
28 Williams, *On Christian Theology*, 85.
29 Williams, *On Christian Theology*, 85.
30 Williams, *On Christian Theology*, 85.
31 Morris, 'Building Community', 35.
32 Williams, *On Christian Theology*, 86.
33 Williams, *On Christian Theology*, 86.
34 Hebert, *Liturgy and Society*, 98.

35 Williams, *On Christian Theology*, 86.
36 Williams, *On Christian Theology*, 86.
37 Hebert's chapter on 'Liturgy, Dogma and Personal Religion' allows that exploration through Hebert's own words and images. *Liturgy and Society*, 112–15.
38 Hebert, *Liturgy and Society*, 112.
39 Hebert, *Liturgy and Society*, 114.
40 Hebert, *Liturgy and Society*, 117.
41 Hebert, *Liturgy and Society*, 117.
42 Hebert, *Liturgy and Society*, 122.
43 Hardy, *Finding the Church*, 240.
44 Hebert, *Liturgy and Society*, 191.
45 Hebert, *Liturgy and Society*, 191.
46 Hebert, *Liturgy and Society*, 191, his italics.
47 William Temple, *Personal Religion and the Life of Fellowship* (London: Longmans, Green, 1926), 54.
48 Temple, *Personal Religion and the Life of Fellowship*, 75.
49 There is a fertile area for research in relation to John Milbank, *Theology and Social Theory: Beyond Secular Reason* (Oxford: Blackwell, 1996, 2000).
50 Hebert, *Liturgy and Society*, 193.
51 Hebert, *Liturgy and Society*, 193.
52 Hebert, *Liturgy and Society*, 193.
53 Hebert, *Liturgy and Society*, 193.
54 Hebert, *Liturgy and Society*, 193.
55 Hebert, *Liturgy and Society*, 194.
56 Hebert, *Liturgy and Society*, 194.
57 Hardy, *Finding the Church*, 241.
58 Hardy, *Finding the Church*, 242.
59 Hebert, *Liturgy and* Society, 207.
60 Hardy, *Finding the Church*, 242.
61 Arthur Gabriel Hebert, *Apostle and Bishop: A Study of the Gospel, Ministry and the Church Community* (London: Faber, 1963), 140.
62 Hebert, *Apostle and Bishop*, 142.
63 Hebert, *Apostle and Bishop*, 142.
64 Anglican Communion News, 'Indigenous and Culture found in Lambeth Indaba Reflections', http://www.anglicannews.org/news/2008/08/indigenous-and-culture-found-in-lambeth-indaba-reflections.aspx [accessed 22 January 2013].
65 Hebert, *Liturgy and Society*, 12.
66 Lössl, *The Early Church*, 41–2.
67 Hebert, *Apostle and Bishop*, 20–21.
68 Hebert, *Apostle and Bishop*, 9.
69 Hebert, *Apostle and Bishop*, 10.
70 Hebert, *Apostle and Bishop*, 15.
71 Hebert, *Apostle and Bishop*, 16.
72 Hebert, *Apostle and Bishop*, 15, my italics.
73 Arthur Gabriel Hebert, *Fundamentalism and the Church of God* (London: SCM Press, 1957), 121, his italics.
74 Hebert, *Fundamentalism and the Church of God*, 121.
75 Hebert, *Apostle and Bishop*, 78–81.
76 Hebert, *Apostle and Bishop*, 81–2.
77 Hebert, *Apostle and Bishop*, 82.
78 Hebert, *Apostle and Bishop*, 82, his italics.
79 Hebert, *Apostle and Bishop*, 81.
80 Hebert, *Apostle and Bishop*, 81.

81 Eberhard Bethge, *Dietrich Bonhoeffer: A Biography* (London: Collins, 1970), 98.

82 Bethge, *Dietrich Bonhoeffer*, 98.

83 Bethge, *Dietrich* Bonhoeffer, 58.

84 Bethge, *Dietrich* Bonhoeffer, 59

85 Kenneth E. Kirk, *The Vision of God* (Cambridge: James Clarke, 1931).

86 Hebert, *Apostle and Bishop*, 82.

87 This is has an interesting consequence in relation to the House of Bishop statement *Issues in Human Sexuality: A Statement by the House of Bishops of the General Synod of the Church of England, December 1991* (London: Church House, 1991).

5 Liturgy and Mission

A Case of Jacob and Esau or Mary and Martha?

In the previous two chapters the necessity of the Church as posited in *Liturgy and Society* was established. This chapter will attend to mission to draw out the proposition that *Liturgy and Society*, when placed in dialogue with contemporary voices, has a significant contribution to make. Mission is the contemporary way of framing Hebert's consideration of the function of the Church in the modern world. This will be done in relation to the work of Andrew Walker and Paul Roberts because both, from different perspectives, help to position him in contemporary missiological discourse.[1]

Roberts offers Jacob and Esau as a biblical metaphor for the relationship between liturgy and mission.[2] Roberts refers directly to the Parish Communion Movement and Hebert himself. He uses the biblical motif of the estranged twins Jacob and Esau to suggest that liturgy and mission have become separated if not alienated. Roberts refers to Hebert directly as he explores the relationship between liturgy and mission.[3] *Liturgy and Society* is missional in the sense that the function of the Church in the modern world is clearly located in public space. In this it is not as explicit in the language of mission, unlike Hebert's *God's Kingdom and Ours*.[4] *Liturgy and Society* is a profoundly missionary work, and that frames its own missiology.[5]

Having considered Roberts, Walker's work is a means of positioning Hebert alongside a contemporary theologian who analyses the relationship between gospel, mission and culture. Walker takes on the same challenge as Hebert: 'the function of the Church in the modern world'. There are direct, but not causal, links between Hebert and Walker, including the indispensability of the Church in mission as both the bearer and teller of the story.

Having established Hebert's relevance in contemporary missiology and stated the generative capacity of his work, an alternative relational biblical metaphor for the relationship between liturgy and mission arises, that of Mary and Martha. Some writers have seen Mary and Martha psychologically as two sides of human personality; they can also be seen as representing styles of mission, one active and one contemplative.[6] This reappraisal of Hebert generates two key points: first, to inform the way in which the contemporary Church approaches mission in a non-anxious way; and, secondly, that liturgy is intimately related to mission.

Mission, Hebert and the Liturgical Movement

That Hebert features in the current debate about the relationship between mission and liturgy is both interesting and encouraging.[7] Interesting because, as this study contends, Hebert has something to say today and that this is a hitherto unrecognised element of his corpus, especially *Liturgy and Society*. It is encouraging because Hebert's ecclesiology and liturgical anthropology are not totally neglected but offer a starting point for the relationship between liturgy, society and mission. And so it is that Roberts asks if mission and liturgy are akin to the estranged twins Jacob and Esau, 'whose struggle for a hearing in both church and academy has tended to blind each to the important role the other can play in their self-understanding'.[8] In what can be called Hebert's 'missiology' this divergence is not apparent because it is not systematic.

In his discussion of liturgy and mission Roberts sees the origins of the Liturgical Movement as missiological.[9] This is contested. Roberts argues that this was generated by the observation of the impact of faith in the life of industrialised communities. Roberts offers a brief critique of *Liturgy and Society* and suggests that it was not simply motivated by social concern, but by 'a call to a new attention to mission'.[10] The assertion is open to question. Colin Buchanan, for example, attributes Hebert's work to a pastoral impulse, but not noting a missiological dimension.[11] Louis Luzbetak sees it the other way round by suggesting that the Liturgical Movement took on new life after the First World War, which was a development that 'later affected mission models'.[12] Fenwick and Spinks identify what they call 'forerunners and false trails' of the Liturgical Movement in England, stretching back to the time after the Reformation and encompassing the eighteenth-century High Churchmen and John Wesley; the Tractarians and the Camden Society; and, following Gray, Christian Socialism with its particular and characteristic incarnational emphasis.[13] Immediately prior to Hebert they identify the work of Walter Frere, the experience of chaplains in the First World War and the 1928 Prayer Book controversy. Fenwick and Spinks' conclusion is that the Liturgical Movement, in England the Parish Communion Movement, was essentially driven by pastoral concern that was primarily about 'education and pastoral action'.[14] Thus, based on the indispensability of the Church, Hebert makes his ecclesiological concern also generative of mission because liturgy articulates ecclesiology.

Liturgy and Society is identified by Roberts as the best articulated statement of a 'wide agenda' for the renewal of the Church's life, beginning with worship. Roberts rightly identifies Hebert's sense that the Church's life renewed has an impact on liturgy and would allow the Church 'to perform its function in demonstrating the gospel and the vocation of the church'.[15] Roberts states: 'This is important: the initial impetus for liturgical renewal was in order for the liturgy to function missiologically.'[16] What Roberts fails to account for is Hebert's sharp critique of modern culture. For Hebert renewal of liturgy is not to make it more relevant or understandable but to counter the forces that see worship only as a generator of mission or as an activity done by the Church rather than being integral to its life; something which equally applies to mission. Furthermore it is about being and becoming the Body of Christ, offering 'acceptable worship' and acting in the world.

Roberts' account of *Liturgy and Society* is insufficient. The thesis already advanced is that Hebert's starting point is ecclesiological, which means that worship is not primarily something to be renewed in order that lives may be changed; rather it is something offered by the Church in order that the Church is most true and authentic to herself through which lives are changed. The worship of the Church embodies what the Church is, and in what she does her function in the modern world is defined, expounded and (literally) articulated.

Roberts also suggests that the Liturgical Movement understood that renewed liturgy made for a renewed and transforming Church for the world.[17] He dismisses that supposition: 'The snag was that liturgical renewal was itself such a large task that it dominated ecclesial agendas for decades.'[18] And so the transformation did not materialise. This appears to suggest a causal link between the renewal of liturgy and the failure of the transformation of society, and implies that the Church when reflecting on worship and liturgy is necessarily introspective: a case of *post hoc ergo propter hoc*. However society was itself in flux and transformation, primary global examples of which include the Great Depression, the Second World War, the impact of the Holocaust and the subsequent Cold War.[19] The underlying implication is that there is a fissure between ecclesiology, Hebert's principal concern, and missiology: for Hebert the ecclesiology is prior to the liturgiology. To this end Hebert's insight lends contemporary weight to those who argue that the current emphasis on mission is at the cost of ecclesiology.[20]

Liturgical Renewal and Mission

The heart of this argument is that Hebert helps reframe contemporary discourse because of his understanding of the meaning of liturgical renewal and its relationship to mission. This is exemplified in the production by the

Church of England of *Common Worship*.[21] A time of considerable missional reflection was accompanied by significant liturgical revision. The report *Mission-shaped Church*, following the Decade of Evangelism, saw the terms 'Pioneer Minister', 'Fresh Expressions' and 'Bishops' Mission Orders' becoming part of the lexicon of Anglicanism as much as 'Parish Communion', 'Offertory procession' and 'the gathering on the Lord's Day' had become some 70 or so years before. This illustrates that whilst a substantial amount of ecclesial effort has been expended on official liturgy, there has been a transformation of the liturgical and missiological sense of the Church. Furthermore the Parish Communion Movement in general, and certainly Hebert, in the case of *Liturgy and Society*, has perhaps surprisingly little explicit to say about liturgical revision of texts.[22] He identifies that:

> [T]he main effort of the Liturgical Movement is to recall the faithful to the treasures which they possess in the liturgy, and to realize anew the ancient ideal of Christian worship as the common prayer of the Church, the act of the whole Body, in which all the members have a part.[23]

That statement is about liturgical renewal rather than revising texts, thereby being similar to Roberts' statement that, 'Unrenewed worship is still worship, but it fails to realise its potential in shaping the church's role in the world.'[24]

For Hebert liturgical renewal and liturgical revision are not the same things. It is not that one is good and one is bad. The starting point for liturgical renewal is ecclesiology; the starting point for liturgical revision is a more technical, and not always misplaced, concern for liturgical correctness. It is the difference between Hebert (renewal) and Dix (revision). Roberts is right however to note that there was an assumption – although wrong to suggest it was totally unspoken – that renewed liturgy would help people somehow to *get it*.[25] This *getting it* is what might be called *liturgical catechesis by osmosis* or *lex orandi, lex credendi*. Hebert works on the assumption often, for which he may be challenged, that people will *get it* as he *got it*.[26] This is a clear area in which Hebert is vulnerable to the suggestion that his liturgical/missional connection is aesthetic. 'What I Learnt in the House of God', Hebert's personal and confessional account, is seminal in his understanding of the formative nature of liturgy. Nevertheless it also serves as an example of a lack of accounting for religious subjectivity.[27] Hebert himself recognises this as he poses the question:

> Will it then be right to regard personal religion as really the most fundamental of the three elements, and to say that liturgical worship is of value primarily in order that the individual soul may be trained up in the way

of holiness, and that dogma is the intellectual formulation of religious experience, so that the *lex orandi* of the individual is his true *lex credendi*?[28]

It is important to note that Hebert's account of what formed and shaped him 'in the House of God' was not renewed worship. The Church faithfully engaging in her worship formed and trained him in a liturgical, missional sensibility. Hebert was in Morris' terms part of an 'innovative and creative tradition'.[29]

Roberts goes on to propose that some of the social and missiological insights of Hebert and others, such as Beauduin, were 'flawed from the start'.[30] He suggests that they mistakenly assume that society operated as a series of parishes, even in urban situations, noting that even if this were ever correct, other social changes, 'such as the emancipation of women, the invention of the television and the emergence of multiple generation gaps in a single family unit', quickly eclipsed them.[31] Hebert's social and religious background could lead to the assumption that he was not entirely in tune with the range of patterns of living in his day. Missiologically this would be a tremendous problem. As Vincent Donovan convincingly demonstrates, ignorance of the cultural terrain of the mission landscape hinders both effective mission and liturgy.[32] Hebert is perhaps more alert to the way in which communities were working by the 1930s than it might at first seem. He was acutely aware of the social devastation of the Great War, one of the reasons that his modernist optimism in progress evaporated.[33] He also writes frankly about what he sees in modern society:

> In the midst of the levelling, disintegrating, and de-humanizing influences of the modern social system, the Church even now creates a true social life: the modern man, isolated among a multitude of strangers in the modern suburb, is drawn out of his loneliness into the fellowship of a spiritual family.[34]

Furthermore, in asking what the Church has to give to the modern world, he notes:

> But the trouble is that all this theology is failing at present to reach the mind of the modern man. It is not that it is rejected as untrue. It is set aside as irrelevant. It fails to make contact with his life. It seems to belong to another world than the world in which he lives.[35]

Roberts asserts that 'confusion of liturgical renewal with renewal of mission became one of a series of flawed assumptions accepted by local churches, which have led to a growing suspicion when regarding liturgy as an agency for mission'.[36] Roberts misattributes this confusion to Hebert. Yet Hebert's sense of liturgical renewal is precisely to enable the Church to be the embodied presence of Christ in the world, a profoundly missional intention. Roberts also posits that the 'worship wars' and the 'seeker services' that emerged in North America in the mid-1990s exemplified the expendability of formal liturgy, itself an inverted form of liturgical renewal, in attempting to engage with cultures for whom the notion of liturgy was remote.[37] Hebert helps redress that confusion by insisting on the integrity of liturgy in relation to ecclesiology, and therefore to mission.

Three Approaches to Liturgy and Mission

Hebert's missiology assumes an intimate relationship between liturgy and mission. The nature of that relationship is critical in evaluating the merit of *Liturgy and Society*. Thomas Schattauer helpfully explores issues around 'worship in an age of mission' which help explore just this relationship.[38] Schattauer claims that mission takes place *in* the eucharistic assembly, and that the liturgy of the eucharistic assembly is the 'locus of mission'.[39] This is a rarely articulated proposition. His three categories of liturgical missiology – 'conventional', 'contemporary' and, his preferred, 'radically traditional' – give a starting point in considering Hebert's missiology and its contribution in contemporary discourse.[40]

Schattauer first characterises the conventional approach as 'inside and out'. In this approach the assembly understands worship to be an activity for those inside the church, and mission what happens when worship ends. Typical of this is the phrase of unclear origin, 'when the worship ends the service begins'. This is developed in the notion that at the end of the Eucharist 'we are sent out to participate in God's mission of love'.[41] Schattauer accounts for this saying that, 'Mission is what takes place on the outside when the gospel is proclaimed to those who have not heard or received it or, to broaden the notion of mission, when neighbor [sic] is served in acts of love and justice.'[42] Liturgy in this model is the engine room and inspiration for mission which happens outside the Church. In this approach mission and liturgy are related in a functional way because, as Schattauer notes, the Church's liturgical life is independent of mission in this approach.[43] This approach also locates worship to that which happens within a church or 'worship space', and thereby forecloses what worship is about. Sarah Coakley describes *leitourgia*, 'in the best theological sense, as service to the world in humility and hope'.[44] That is another expression of the sense that liturgy, properly conceived as public service in which worship happens, does not end with the formal worship in church.

Secondly, in the 'contemporary' approach which Schattauer calls 'outside in' the separation of the conventional model collapses in which 'the sacred precinct' of the liturgy becomes 'either a stage from which to present the gospel and reach out to the unchurched and irreligious, or a platform from which to issue the call to serve the neighbor [sic] and rally religious commitment for social and political action'.[45] In this model the *tasks* of mission, conceived as activism and numerical growth, become the principal purpose of the Church's worship. This recalls Pickard's warning above about the heresies inherent in ecclesial life. The danger of the discussion of the relationship between liturgy and mission is that it becomes self-defeating and short-circuiting: in more clichéd terms it is a chicken and egg argument. Does liturgy generate mission, or is liturgy to receive the fruits of mission? Both approaches assume that liturgy and mission somehow diverge and are discrete areas. So, to add to Roberts' bifurcation of liturgy and mission separating in the academy, it is also true of pastoral practice.

Schattauer's third approach is 'radically traditional'. In it he recasts the question of which generates the other. His claim is that the 'radically traditional' approach sees the liturgical assembly as *locus of mission*. This could be seen as too ecclesiastically based; however both other approaches are bound up in the Church, albeit in impaired or inadequate ways. Schattauer is emphatic: 'This approach locates the liturgical assembly itself within the arena of the missio Dei.'[46] That is his 'radically traditional' approach to the relationship between liturgy and mission: this is an 'inside out' approach to liturgy and mission. The key distinction in this approach is that liturgy and mission are inseparable: 'The visible act of assembly (in Christ by the power of the Spirit) and the forms of this assembly – what we call liturgy – enact and signify this mission.'[47] Worship, which seems to be so internal to the Church, is directed outwards towards the world: 'The liturgical assembly is the visible locus of God's reconciling mission toward the world.'[48] In pragmatic terms Stephen Platten notes that all church members 'encounter God in the liturgy', in a way not true of those who 'attend home groups, house groups or adult Sunday schools, let alone lectures and specialist courses'.[49]

The 'inside out' notion is problematic for liturgists. For example, Gordon Lathrop uses the language of 'inside out' to describe the relationship between liturgy and mission, whilst employing an 'inside and out' model, not least in his treatment of 'Organizing the Assembly for Mission'.[50] By contrast, Platten notes that 'mission and liturgy stand and fall together', and that Christian people are 'shaped and strengthened so that their own lives may be instruments of mission within the wider world'.[51] He acknowledges that this is not solely utilitarian because it conveys and has a direct impact upon, knowledge of, confidence in and living of the faith.[52] Michael Perham states that 'the truth is that the deep purpose of worship is not to evangelise, nor to teach, nor to engender fellowship, but to be in touch with the living God'.[53] All of this represents a reclamation of the sense that liturgy, *leitourgia*, is in itself a sacrificial act of service of the whole people of God which is another way of framing mission and the function of the Church in the modern world.[54] This means that the mystery celebrated in the liturgy remains ever present in the mission and practical life of the Church.[55]

Gabriel Hebert and Andrew Walker: Telling the Same Story?

The above discussion of Schattauer's models enables us to consider *Liturgy and Society* in relation to Walker because both Walker and Hebert uncover the way in which liturgy relates to the handing on of the Christian story as a narrative. Schattauer's contribution is to give a missional framework for the context of the telling of the story. Walker describes the cultural realities that affect the handing on of the gospel story in contemporary society, and Hebert undertakes a similar task, albeit in a different cultural and historical setting.[56]

One account of *Liturgy and Society* is that it is a reflection on how the Christian 'story' has been lost. Hebert speculates on reasons why that might be, and he does so at a time when many might still assume a Christian supremacy in England in particular, and Western Europe more generally.[57] This quest for a missiology after hegemony is pressing. Hebert sees the 'story' as retained in dogma and the enacted ecclesiology of liturgy. Walker's point is that the story of the gospel is a story that has become one among many in a culture that, after Lyotard, is no longer driven by narratives, and that Christian faith has been driven from public life into a privatised world of personal choice and leisure pursuits, an environment in which the gospel is difficult to maintain.[58] Hebert's account of the competing choices and claims is prescient and he states that: 'It is clear that when religious belief is regarded as the exclusive concern of the individual, social life can no longer be based on faith in God. Private theological beliefs cannot be allowed to influence industrial, commercial and political affairs.'[59] In similar vein he sees the exhilarating riding of a motorcycle at high speed which 'is a lonely pastime that isolates him from his fellows'.[60] Hebert sees in society 'the fear of a breakdown of civilization through spiritual exhaustion; we live in fear of another war which might be the end'.[61] He sees clearly the end of common values: 'The modern world has moved away from Christian morals, and has no fixed standard of right and wrong, and no common faith that there is a right and a wrong.'[62]

Morris describes an Anglican tradition of social criticism which is an attempt 'to look at contemporary society through a vision of what the church might be'.[63] The antidote to this for Hebert is an ecclesiologically plausible liturgical approach because:

> [T]he way of approach which I have called 'liturgical' is essentially an appeal *away from* personal beliefs and opinions, my own included, to the common faith of the Church, to the authority of the Church, to the dogma by which the Church lives.[64]

In the face of gospel amnesia, described by Walker, Christians face the challenge of passing the story on.[65] It may just be that Hebert had spotted the very earliest symptoms of this malaise, and is articulating much the same thing. He addresses it not simply as amnesia but also as a certain distaste for the Christian story. This is also identified by Linda Woodhead in her survey of religion and change in modern Britain, something that has taken on the language of toxicity so far as the Church in particular and religious faith expression in general is concerned.[66]

Walker accounts for the pivotal role of liturgy in the early life of the Church that ensured that the gospel was not simply about the hearing of the word but had visual impact too: 'If Judaism was essentially a religion of the ear, as Islam and Protestantism would later be, early Christianity developed a healthy balance of the eye and ear.'[67] In this way early Christian liturgies were a 'retelling of the divine drama of salvation'.[68] Walker's account is, by his own admission, 'a highly selected, compressed and idealized ethnography of early gospel culture'.[69] Nevertheless, the normative status of Christian liturgy, albeit with abuses, enabled the communication, presentation and re-presentation of the Gospel story.

Hebert's account of the loss of the Christian story in society presages that of Walker's. The Enlightenment is seen as the beginning of Christian amnesia: the forgetting of the Christian story saps energy for witness and mission. Walker sees in theological modernism the concern to find new or adequate grounds for believing. He praises its 'undoubted insights', but believes that it 'has eclipsed the gospel as narrative'.[70] Walker suggests that this is at the cost of telling the gospel story, the break between academic theology and ecclesiastical authority, and that all the central tenets appear to be negotiable products in a free market of ideas. Into this account Walker adds the way in which metanarratives displace the Christian story. In short he characterises these metanarratives as optimism in strands of philosophy and sociology.[71] Theology is not immune from the prevalence of such metanarratives. Hebert found the relentless optimism of Liberal theology to be unsustainable. Walker includes the American ideal and scientism in those unsustainable metanarratives, which see themselves as superior to all other methodologies and philosophies.[72] Hebert identifies totalitarianism as a parody of society. It inverts society not by personal individualism but by the corporate individualism which subsumes the ecology of society. An example of Hebert's day is Nazism:

> These [National] movements are messianic in character: but plainly they have in view the welfare of one nation at the expense of the rest, and in spite of the Nordic myth of the Chosen Race, it must be hard for any one who asks questions really to believe that God is a German.[73]

Walker describes the Age of Reason as also the age of religious revival; both phenomena sharing a prevailing individualism. He concludes that, 'Evangelicals share in common with modern westerners both an emphasis on the pre-eminence of the individual, and the desirability of being with the like-minded crowd.'[74] There is a common cause in Walker and Hebert identifying the pre-eminence of the individual because both identify it as a way in which the common, corporately held narrative of the Christian faith is lost. Hebert repeatedly notes it throughout *Liturgy and Society* as not just limited to evangelicalism but to pietism and secular individualism. Hebert identifies what Walker asserts, that 'theological liberals are humane, but gospel amnesiacs'.[75] Hebert is a little more generous, as he states: 'Nor do we fail to appreciate the virtues of the Liberal theologians, their desire to be honest and open-minded and to love the truth.'[76]

Hebert wants to re-liturgise congregations for mission by participating actively in liturgy. Walker, having in mind the world of televangelism in the United States, notes that 'an audience is not a congregation'.[77] And yet congregations become audiences if they are treated as consumers. Hebert describes the consumerism of his time. From a similar context Walker, through his critique of the North American experience, states that the evangelist's role is not to tell tales but to initiate people into the Kingdom of God. Liturgy effects that initiation. Hebert does not see the congregation as an audience, and goes further in suggesting even that where the congregation has a voice, there is a concern that '[we are i]n an age when Christian worship is commonly degraded into the familiar duet between minister and people'.[78] That bears the hallmark of individual consumerism. The task of mission, as Hebert notes with his concern about dogma, is not the selling of a product, but a story that they need to indwell by getting up from sofas and joining with fellow Christians in the churches. Hebert's concern is the structure that dogma and liturgy give to the story.[79] *How* this is done is Walker's concern. Walker has subsequently been influential in 'Fresh Expressions' thinking, but Hebert does not feature in it. This is where Hebert can make a contemporary contribution and can help negotiate the tension between the priorities of mission and liturgical observance. Hebert makes clear that liturgical churches can be mission minded and active as they engage in the modern world.

The diagnoses and prognoses that Walker and Hebert offer converge in their treatment of liturgy. Hebert displays, in Schattauer's terms, an approach to liturgy and mission which shows 'conventional' and 'radically traditional' tendencies. Roberts casts Hebert as a liturgical elitist who sees liturgy as always prior to mission, and that this is somehow unique to the movement of which Hebert was a part. Yet Walker, with his missiological urgency, gives liturgy a significant place: what he terms the 'indwelling of the story'.[80] Hebert sees the gathering for worship as the antidote to 'gospel amnesia'; a prerequisite for mission:

> We who assemble there are to think of ourselves as keeping the hearth-fires burning and the door of their home open for the multitudes who have strayed away: we are worshipping the Father of men on behalf of those who have forgotten Him: we are keeping a tradition alive in trust for those who have lost it.[81]

The notion of 'recovering collective memory in the context of postmodern-ism' is not restricted to Walker, but explored by the contemporary writer Wendelin Köster, who states:

> The issue is not that memory is a collective of knowledge and capable of memorizing things. More significant is that deeper memory capable of knowing and understanding who I am, where I come from and where I'm going. Liturgy *is* that collective memory of the Church, I think, and that memory's centre is the Eucharist.[82]

Hebert presages Köster's thought in this regard, enabling us further to situate Hebert in contemporary thought and show that he has a vibrant contribu-tion to make.

Indwelling the Story: Conventional, Contemporary or Radically Traditional?

Walker's treatment of the cultural currents that have given rise to 'gospel amnesia' does not lead him to a 'contemporary' approach to liturgy and mis-sion as described by Schattauer. Walker sees Christians being involved increas-ingly in political, moral and social activities and environmental improvement, and seeing them as good in themselves. He suggests Christians need to recapture a sense of civic responsibility because it is where the story can be narrated and given context. The way he proposes this should be done is 'by being church again, and not attempting to become model citizens of a secular age'; and this is because, he suggests, there is no such thing as a morally neutral state.[83] This is in accord with Walker's rejection of narratives, such as the American Dream, which should not be brought into the Church's lifeblood but should be viewed in light of the gospel.[84] This is, like Hebert, a rejection of a 'contemporary' account of the relationship between liturgy and mission. This is not a rejection of the secular world but the reassertion of the place of the sacred in the secular sphere.

Schattauer's threefold division is not as neat as he describes. So, for example, in 'conventional' terms Walker sees liturgy and its renewal as critical for mission because, 'Liturgical renewal is not archaeological and antiquarian, not the restraining of the Spirit in a formal straitjacket of tradition. It is nothing less than *a preparation* for mission in a world where literary culture is moribund.'[85] That is (renewed) liturgy as preparation for mission. Yet Walker's 'radically traditional' approach is evident too as he describes the renewal of liturgy as a recapturing of the gospel that has been handed down in different mediums and cultures. And he continues, '[t]he down-handedness of things reminds us that they have a history, an embeddedness in past cultures: they are a treasury of blessings to be appropriated by every new generation'.[86] The handing down of things is mediated by liturgy.[87] Walker's analogy of missionary work is the long-term plan for creating a vineyard, 'digging in, establishing roots, and nurturing the young vines in order that others, in time, may harvest the grapes and make the good wine'.[88] Arguably the Church is already tending a vineyard, and it is the renewal and regeneration of the vineyard that is the pressing missionary task.

Walker proposes three 'missionary imperatives' for the future: building new plausibility structures, renewing the liturgy and becoming a holy people. Those three imperatives drive to the heart of the discussion of *Mission-shaped Church* and *For the Parish*. This is one of the ways in which Hebert enables us to negotiate the impasse between the two. Renewing liturgy is not a 'party' line approach. Hebert would be quick to point out that renewing the liturgy is precisely about 'becoming a holy people'. This is how he helps us to see what a 'new plausibility structure' might look like. It is one based not on tactical positioning within an agenda within the Church. Plausibility comes from wholehearted Christian faith, dogma and practice. This plays out in how Walker and Hebert see the significance of the parish. Hebert cannot envisage anything such as the *structures* that Walker wants to see. Hebert is deeply conventional in assuming that the mission of the Church is primarily associated with the parochial system, which is something that Walker can see beyond, commenting that parishes are 'no longer plausible viability structures'.[89] This has consequences for the missional value and impact of a movement today that was known as the *Parish* Communion Movement.[90]

Liturgical renewal for both Walker and Hebert is not about liturgical tinkering but rather engaging in liturgical theology and ecclesiology. In his account of the necessity of liturgical renewal Walker demonstrates precisely Schattauer's 'radically traditional' ('inside out') understanding of the relationship between liturgy and mission, even going as far as identifying liturgy with mission.[91] Liturgy itself is a plausibility structure, or what Walker calls 'both the institutional and charismatic expression of "God with us"'.[92] Following Derrida, Walker proposes that, as there is no reality outside the text, the coming age will be an age of signs with no meaning, in that 'we will be so immersed in images that have no iconic value'.[93] Liturgy gives the capacity to reach beyond pictures and sounds to their source and creator. Walker sees this authenticity and transparency as missional and evangelistic, since 'it is the way to the heart of our story [in the] second orality that will dominate postmodernity'.[94] And in a passage that touches on Hebert's interests in liturgical renewal, anthropology and architecture Walker writes that: 'It is not a question of importing light and colour from the outside, but re-establishing a holy liturgy where architecture and dramaturgy – with its icons, words and music – tell again, and again, the old, old story.'[95] This is, again, a rejection of the 'contemporary' or 'outside in' approach to liturgy and mission. In justifying his appeal to a renewed liturgy Walker states, 'liturgy in postmodern culture *is* mission', which is the articulation of the 'radically traditional' approach so evident Hebert.[96]

Ecclesiology and Mission

Both Walker and Schattauer demonstrate a 'high' missional ecclesiology; that is to say, they do not see the Church as incidental to mission, or as an accident that followed Jesus' preaching of the Kingdom of God, but rather as integral to the preaching of the Kingdom and of mission today. Hebert shares that approach. In question is the ecclesiological understanding of mission as much as its liturgical generation. There is also a case being made for a missional anthropology, because people need to be formed for mission. Consideration also has to be given to the nature of human transformation that mission effects. For Hebert this is an ecclesiological issue that directly relates to liturgy because it is generative of mission. This is significant in understanding *Liturgy and Society*, since its project is wider than liturgy. Hebert's writing challenges Roberts' statement that, 'you can no more renew a local church's mission solely by renewing its worship than can you plant a church by constructing a

building'.[97] Hebert's understanding of worship, ecclesiologically and anthro-
pologically rooted as it is, would concede that it is not *solely* the renewing of
worship that renews a local church's mission, but it is integral to it. So, the
renewal of worship, and its proper understanding, will, in Hebert's thinking,
renew a church's mission. This is because liturgy must reflect ecclesiology,
'thereby not only their religious life but all their individual and social life is
re-orientated towards God as its centre, and is transformed, sanctified, and
glorified'.[98]

The key task as Hebert sees it is not one of synodical liturgical revision,
although some of that would be inevitable, but the task is more one of catechesis and reaching the mind of 'modern man'.[99] A Church is dependent on
the real presence of a community of faith, not by constructing or inhabiting
an ecclesiastical building. That congregation has principally to be the Church
as it worships: the community of faith has to be involved and engaged in its
worship. For Hebert this being the Church is not confined to worship in a
church; it is more engaging and wide-ranging. As Roberts notes, '[m]ission
must involve activity which is non-liturgical and extra-mural'.[100] Hebert
makes this extra-mural connection through reference to art.[101] This is most
often ecclesiastical art and public architecture, but he engages other cultural
references in literature and poetry, most notably that of D.H. Lawrence and,
as we have already seen, Eliot.[102]

Art and literature is a case study of Hebert's attitude to liturgy because
they lie parallel to each other. A narrative reality, the Church, shapes the
lived reality, in liturgy and life. Hebert takes this critique of art further in
that not only is any one piece of art never solely the work of one person
as if they are entirely isolated, but that even if one pair of hands created the
art it always comes from a wider 'story', a tradition. This is true also of contemporary scientific endeavour: extensive teams work behind lead scientists
who are then attributed with discovery. The tyranny of individualism and
suspicion of tradition in art has both stripped the social out of the narrative
of the creative process and has dislocated the art from the story, and therefore
Hebert suggests, from its beauty: the 'tragedy of modern art is the divorce
between art and the people' and 'there is no popular art, because there is no
common mind'.[103] Hebert sees the solution – which links work, creativity
and offertory – as beginning to come when 'the artist is a Christian living
the Church's life; for the Church still has something of a tradition and a
common mind'.[104] So abstract, modernist or challenging art that is born out
of tradition can still speak and be engaged with attentively. This is interesting in relation to the work and phenomenon of the artist Banksy in the way
that a city's social space is claimed as a space for art, albeit illicit, and protest.
Furthermore popular, or vulgar, art is increasingly becoming of interest to

art collectors, thereby robbing it of its popular and particular connection. It must be conceded that *Liturgy and Society*'s illustrations have been described as 'unexceptional'.[105] They do look somewhat conservative in their themes if not in their design. Hebert's understanding of liturgy may be seen in a similar aesthetic.

In this sense of the danger of individualism in art there is a connection with George Guiver, who links art to the drama of liturgy.[106] He identifies the German word *Gesamtkunstwerk*, in connection with a Wagnerian sense of a total work of art in which music, literature, theatre and art come together.[107] Guiver rightly distinguishes the performance of Wagner and the performance of liturgy in which applause from spectators is appropriate to the former and inappropriate in the latter: the all-embracing intensity of worship is captured in *Gesamtkunstwerk*, performed in 'attentive cooperation with God'.[108] Guiver quotes Ildefons Herwegen, one of Hebert's direct influences, as he uses *Gesamtkunstwerk* as a description of the liturgy of the fifth and sixth centuries as a 'complete art-synthesis'.[109] It is this *Gesamtkunstwerk* that shapes Hebert's approach to art, liturgy and life.

Hebert is certainly open to the accusation of being most interested in 'churchy' art and architecture, but he takes this further – 'the Bible and the Liturgy do not merely provide symbols of which art can make use: they themselves partake of the nature of art.'[110] Hebert sees the need for churches to be of their time whilst honouring their past and the Christian tradition as reflective of the common life of the Church; and so in commenting on the appearance of churches he adds:

> And if churches, why not also railway stations, post offices and banks? It is not that these should be made to look like churches, it is that they should become themselves, and be seen to be products of the common life of the people of the town. When this begins to happen, art has begun to come into its own.[111]

Hebert appeals to the concrete form of the reality as an authentic one that faithfully reflects the inner reality and purpose of the building. Hebert's problem with modern art is not simply a question of aesthetics, but '[i]n general the tragedy of modern art is the divorce between art and the people'.[112] He attributes this again to individualism, which is the greatest problem for mission because, 'there is no common mind'.[113] Hebert's appeal to art rooted in tradition takes on a distinctly (post)modern flavour given current interest in Eastern iconography in all Christian traditions. However Hebert's approach to icons is again not on aesthetic or taste grounds, but rather that they are rooted in an ecclesiological social and liturgical understanding of their purpose. Icons, and any religious art, are not for the gallery, but rather to serve the Church:

> [The] classical tradition of Christian art illustrates the liturgical use of the Scriptures, according to which a Gospel story, such as that of the healing the blind man, is read both as an historical story and a symbol of the continuing activity of the living Saviour.[114]

Echoing Eliot, Hebert associates art with the iconic quality of liturgy: 'If anyone is present merely as an onlooker, he misses all the meaning that matters.'[115] We have seen that Hebert's missionary aesthetic is thoroughly ecclesiological and cannot be separated from his missiological understanding, because it projects the Church into public space. This is what his cultural and artistic references achieve.

Mary, Martha and Proper Sowing

Schattauer usefully relocates 'the assembly as the locus of mission'. Evading neat categorisation, Hebert's approach to mission is first an appeal to liturgy, not because liturgy will replace mission, or even that liturgy equips mission, but because liturgy, in essence, is missional. Liturgy places the assembly within the *missio Dei* rather than it being another *missione ecclesiam*. Roberts suggests that mission and liturgy are like estranged twins, somehow competing for the birthright and proximity to the Father.[116] Hebert does not conceive of liturgy and mission in the same way; if anything, a more appropriate image may be that of the sisters Martha and Mary. This is not to stereotype the sisters in an idealised femininity; and the suggestion that patience and a sense of gestation is essential to this missiology is not intended to succumb to that. Rather, Martha and Mary engage a biblical image in the way in which liturgy and mission can come together. This further reinforces our exploration of the relatedness of the two.

A liturgical framing of this relationship between liturgy and mission coheres in the treatment of Harvest Festival and Rogationtide by churches in their corporate and liturgical life.[117] Rogation has a practical origin and an ecclesiological application. The practical element of rogation is of sowing the seed on the land and asking and trusting God for its growth; so the missional application is one of careful, patient and attentive expectation. Likewise, harvest is about thanksgiving for something that the land has yielded; missionally it can be seen to be about numerical growth and yield.[118] Tom Greggs, in reflections on Hardy's 'creation and eschatology', proposes that theology properly has a 'patient impatience'.[119] This introduces the possibility of an eschatological dimension to a critique of *Liturgy and Society* because of the concept of results-based mission. It warns against the Church losing her patience with the world, with herself and God. Related to this, Martyn Percy suggests, 'the church might not be about holding our own in the world, but rather recognising that we are to become a radical form of counter-culture'.[120] A harvest church is interested primarily in the yield.[121] It does have an eschatological resonance, but harvest-centric mission is distorting because it focuses on results and is also used as a very 'outside in' mission approach to boost numbers.[122] For Hebert harvest, yield and numbers are for God; rogation – proper sowing, cultivation of habits and virtues, of right decisions and of truthful living – is the task of the Church.[123]

In 2014 the Church of England published a document conducted by the Church Growth Research Programme, *From Anecdote to Evidence*.[124] The report reveals the anxieties around Church growth in the contemporary Church of England. This is perhaps most evident in the commissioning body, the 'Spending Plans Task Group'. The evidence-based decision making it appeals to is in terms of deployment of ministry.[125] The anxiety reveals itself in the way that mission is consistently equated to Church growth. The approaches of Hebert, Walker and Schattauer, let alone Bosch, are not discernible. Rather it lists key ingredients for the different recipes for growth, whilst repeatedly quoting 1 Corinthians 3.6 ('I planted the seed, Apollos watered, but God made it grow'). It would be wrong to dismiss the report out of hand, but our purpose is to note the anxiety that Church growth – as opposed to a missional understanding of the life and worship of the Church – can generate.

The story of Mary and Martha has had a considerable variety of readings throughout Christian history.[126] A classic reading takes Mary and Martha to be emblems of contemplation over and against activism.[127] To use the paradigm of Mary and Martha is not to suggest that one is better than the other (cf. Luke 10.42), but it reframes the competitive model. Classically Mary would be the worshipful sister and Martha the more activist, which would seem to fit neatly with a characterisation of Mary representing liturgy and Martha as mission. Mary then can be portrayed, along with worship, as devoted, reverent and steady; Martha is a doer, an activist in mission. But Martha is also anxious.[128] Martha's anxiety reflects *anxiety-driven mission*, in which anxiety grows in direct proportion to numerical achievement, as some would suggest about *From Anecdote to Evidence*. Mission can be driven, when dislocated from liturgy, by such a sense of anxiety, of fear of failure or disapproval, or trying to shout over voices in a contested space.

What would Hebert make of that distinction? He notes in the closing paragraphs of *Liturgy and Society* that:

> In these days of anxiety and fear and impending tribulation, Christians have their witness to bear, of the reality of God as the owner of His world and the Master in His own house . . . so that the bodily life of even the lowest has an eternal meaning; and of the vocation of the Church to express in her worship and the common life of her members the pattern of the Foundations of the City of God.[129]

Hebert's approach to mission is the antithesis of anxiety, but is rather a steady and confident sense of witness, worship and the common life that Mary represents, placing the mission of the Church in the adoring service of Christ. It also is dependent upon an understanding of the nature of patience in the way that Greggs describes.

Hebert's sense of missiological patience is borne out in 'proper sowing'. The final words of *Liturgy and Society* are a quotation from Eliot:

> I say unto you: Make perfect your will.
> I say: take no thought of the harvest.
> But only of proper sowing.[130]

This encapsulates Hebert's missiology. Taking no thought of the harvest implies a confidence in grace and a rejection of activism. It rest on God giving the growth, and being totally implicated in the sowing and watering (cf. 1 Corinthians 3.6). So often churches exuberantly celebrate Harvest Festival, taking *every* 'thought of the harvest' when little consideration has been given to the sowing – perhaps thereby subconsciously echoing the anxiety approach to mission.[131]

Conclusion

This chapter has explored the relationship between liturgy and mission, and demonstrated that neither is sustainable if estranged like Jacob and Esau. *Liturgy and Society* holds worship and mission together creatively and shows that both are integral to the life of the Church. Any caricature of Hebert or the Parish Communion Movement as being ecclesiastically introspective and not interested in mission is fallacious. What Hebert does is demonstrate that liturgy is significant because of what it compels the Church and individual believer to take seriously, which is seeing the world as the arena of God's activity as much as the Church. Liturgy is the inclusive focus of the Church's worship, not its exclusive locus, because for the Church to function in the modern world she also understands herself to be the vessel of God's mission in the world heralding the Kingdom. *Liturgy and Society* reinforces that point emphatically. Hebert believes that the Church must grow and be vibrant; but that is not at the cost of patience and having a sense of time that flows from the liturgical rhythms of the year. Following the threefold argument laid out, it becomes clear that Hebert's value has been historically underplayed; that he has an affinity with contemporary writers; and that a fresh appreciation of his work is important for the contemporary Church. The dynamic outworking of this non-anxious, sustainable and sustaining liturgical and eucharistic vision as applied both to individual persons and the Church corporately is the subject of the next chapter.

Notes

1 Andrew Walker, *Telling the Story: Gospel, Mission and Culture* (London: SPCK, 1996).
2 Paul Roberts, 'Mission and Liturgy: A Case of Jacob and Esau? An Exploration of a Relationship in Church and Academy', *Anaphora*, 4/2 (2010), 1–14.
3 See also Stephen Platten, 'The Uses of Liturgy: Worship Nourishing Mission', *Worship*, 83/3 (2009): 234–49. Platten explores the presumed dichotomy between liturgy and mission, and also casts it in terms of the shaping and strengthening of Christians as instruments of mission in the wider world.
4 Arthur Gabriel Hebert, *God's Kingdom and Ours* (London: SCM Press, 1959).
5 David J. Bosch, *Transforming Mission* (New York: Orbis, 1991).
6 Jeffrey explores the roots of the variety of approaches to Mary and Martha from Gregory the Great onwards in David L. Jeffrey, *Luke* (Grand Rapids, MI: Brazos, 2012), 152–3. See also, Luke Timothy Johnson, *The Gospel of Luke* (Collegeville, MN: Liturgical Press, 1991), 176.
7 Roberts, 'Mission and Liturgy', 1.
8 Roberts, 'Mission and Liturgy', 1.
9 Roberts, 'Mission and Liturgy', 4.
10 Roberts, 'Mission and Liturgy', 4.
11 Buchanan, *Anglo-Catholic Worship*, 7.
12 Louis J. Luzbetak, *The Church and Cultures: New Perspectives in Missiological Anthropology* (Maryknoll, NY: Orbis, 1988), 103.
13 John Fenwick and Bryan Spinks, *Worship in Transition: The Liturgical Movement in the Twentieth Century* (Edinburgh: T&T Clark, 1995), 37–40, and Gray, *Earth and Altar*, 40.
14 Fenwick and Spinks, *Worship in Transition*, 42.
15 Roberts, 'Mission and Liturgy', 4.
16 Roberts, 'Mission and Liturgy', 4.
17 Roberts, 'Mission and Liturgy', 5.
18 Roberts, 'Mission and Liturgy', 5.
19 Lössl suggests other factors that have a bearing on contemporary accounts of the Church's engagement in society: 'social sciences, cultural anthropology, various approaches in psychology, computer science, cultural criticism, literary criticism and many other newly emerged disciplines'. Lössl, *The Early Church*, 40.
20 Davison and Milbank, *For the Parish*, 41–63.
21 *Common Worship* comprises a family of editions covering Holy Communion, initiation, pastoral services, the major seasons of the Church's year and material for celebrating the saints. Associated material includes *New Patterns for Worship* (see bibliography).

22 An obvious exception is Dix, who had excoriating things to say about the Book of Common Prayer. Dix, *The Shape of the Liturgy*, 660.

23 Hebert, *Liturgy and Society*, 126.

24 Roberts, 'Mission and Liturgy', 4.

25 Roberts, 'Mission and Liturgy', 5.

26 Hebert, *Liturgy and Society*, 112.

27 Hebert, *Liturgy and Society*, 234–6.

28 Hebert, *Liturgy and Society*, 112.

29 Morris, 'Building Community', 39.

30 Roberts, 'Mission and Liturgy', 5.

31 Roberts, 'Mission and Liturgy', 5.

32 Vincent Donovan, *Christianity Rediscovered: An Epistle from the Masai* (London: SCM Press, 1982).

33 Hebert, *God's Kingdom and Ours*, 15.

34 Hebert, *Liturgy and Society*, 230.

35 Hebert, *Liturgy and Society*, 163.

36 Roberts, 'Mission and Liturgy', 5.

37 Roberts, 'Mission and Liturgy', 1, 2.

38 Thomas H. Schattauer, 'Liturgical Assembly as Locus of Mission', in *Inside Out: Worship in an Age of Mission*, ed. Thomas H. Schattauer (Minneapolis: Augsburg Fortress, 1999). 1–19.

39 Schattauer, 'Liturgical Assembly as Locus of Mission', 1–19.

40 Schattauer, 'Liturgical Assembly as Locus of Mission', 2.

41 Stephen Cottrell, 'Parable and Encounter: Celebrating the Eucharist Today', in *Mass Culture: The Interface of Eucharist and Mission*, ed. Peter Ward (Abingdon: Bible Reading Fellowship, 1999, 2008), 65.

42 Schattauer, 'Liturgical Assembly as Locus of Mission', 2.

43 Schattauer, 'Liturgical Assembly as Locus of Mission', 2.

44 Sarah Coakley, *God, Sexuality and the Self: An Essay 'On the Trinity'* (Cambridge: Cambridge University Press, 2013), 87.

45 Schattauer, 'Liturgical Assembly as Locus of Mission', 2.

46 Schattauer, 'Liturgical Assembly as Locus of Mission', 3.

47 Schattauer, 'Liturgical Assembly as Locus of Mission', 3.

48 Schattauer, 'Liturgical Assembly as Locus of Mission', 3.

49 Platten, 'The Uses of Liturgy', 237.

50 Gordon W. Lathrop, 'Liturgy and Mission in the North American Context', in *Inside Out: Worship in an Age of Mission*, ed. Thomas H. Schattauer (Minneapolis: Augsburg Fortress, 1999) 207.

51 Platten, 'The Uses of Liturgy', 237.

52 Platten, 'The Uses of Liturgy', 238.

53 Michael Perham, *New Handbook of Pastoral Liturgy* (London: SPCK, 2000), 4.

54 Platten, 'The Uses of Liturgy', 249.

55 A point made by David Robinson with reference to the theology and preaching of Leo the Great, in David Robinson, 'Informed Worship and Empowered Mission: The Integration of Liturgy, Doctrine, and Praxis in Leo the Great's Sermons on Ascension and Pentecost', *Worship*, 83/6 (2009), 529.

56 Walker, *Telling the Story*, 95. That said, contemporary society is not what it was; the sands of technology shift, and some of what Walker describes as possible is now actual and really rather routine – for instance 'movie magic', the manipulative possibilities of work with images and film.

57 This should not be confused with the notion of 'post-Christendom' because Christendom practices and assumptions still prevail in the Church of England's official baptismal and marriage practice and funeral pastoral practice.

58 Walker, *Telling the Story*, 2–4.
59 Hebert, *Liturgy and Society*, 28.
60 Hebert, *Liturgy and Society*, 32.
61 Hebert, *Liturgy and Society*, 32.
62 Hebert, *Liturgy and Society*, 28.
63 Morris, 'Building Community', 39.
64 Hebert, *Liturgy and Society*, 11, his italics.
65 Walker, *Telling the Story*, 6.
66 Woodhead, 'Introduction', 13.
67 Walker, *Telling the Story*, 26.
68 Walker, *Telling the* Story, 27.
69 Walker, *Telling the* Story, 32.
70 Walker, *Telling the* Story, 51–4.
71 Walker, *Telling the* Story, 56.
72 Walker, *Telling the* Story, 56–7.
73 Hebert, *Liturgy and Society*, 254.
74 Walker, *Telling the* Story, 64.
75 Walker, *Telling the* Story, 74.
76 Hebert, *Liturgy and Society*, 13.
77 Walker, *Telling the Story*, 89.
78 Hebert, *Liturgy and Society*, 75.
79 Walker, *Telling the* Story, 91 and Hebert, *Liturgy and Society*, 11.
80 Walker, *Telling the* Story, 188–201.
81 Hebert, *Liturgy and Society*, 167.
82 Wendelin Köster, 'Recovering Collective Memory in the Context of Postmodern-ism', in *Liturgy in a Postmodern World*, ed. Keith Pecklers (London: Continuum. 2003), 32.
83 He suggests this following the work of Lesslie Newbigin. Walker, *Telling the Story*, 189.
84 See also Stanley Hauerwas and William H. Willimon, *Resident Aliens: Life in the Christian Colony* (Nashville: Abingdon Press, 1989), especially 30–48.
85 Walker, *Telling the Story*, 99, my italics.
86 Walker, *Telling the Story*, 99.
87 See 1 Corinthians 11.2 and, more liturgically, 1 Corinthians 11.23–32.
88 Walker, *Telling the Story*, 189.
89 Walker, *Telling the Story*, 190.
90 See Bayes and Sledge, *Mission-shaped Parish*. This also raises the issue of the parish as a convenient unit of organisation or a celebration of place and the social life that exist within it.
91 Walker, *Telling the Story*, 196.
92 Walker, *Telling the Story*, 195.
93 Walker, *Telling the Story*, 195.
94 Walker, *Telling the Story*, 196.
95 Walker, *Telling the Story*, 197.
96 Walker, *Telling the Story*, 198.
97 Roberts, 'Mission and Liturgy', 5.
98 Hebert, *Liturgy and Society*, 65.
99 Hebert, *Liturgy and Society*, 163.
100 Roberts, 'Mission and Liturgy', 5.
101 He devotes two chapters of *Liturgy and Society* to 'The Expression of the Spirit' and 'Symbolic Art'. Hebert, *Liturgy and Society*, 237–42 and 242–50.
102 Hebert, *Liturgy and Society*, 251–5.
103 Hebert, *Liturgy and Society*, 241.

104 Hebert, *Liturgy and Society*, 241.

105 Irvine, *Worship, Church and Society*, 115.

106 Guiver, *Vision upon Vision*, 32

107 Guiver, *Vision upon Vision*, 32.

108 Guiver, *Vision upon Vision*, 195.

109 Guiver, *Vision upon Vision*, 33.

110 Hebert, *Liturgy and Society*, 246.

111 Hebert, *Liturgy and Society*, 242.

112 Hebert, *Liturgy and Society*, 241.

113 Hebert, *Liturgy and Society*, 241.

114 Hebert, *Liturgy and Society*, 244.

115 Eliot *The Complete Poems and Plays*, 186, and Hebert, *Liturgy and Society*, 246.

116 Roberts, 'Mission and Liturgy', 1.

117 Hutton describes the origin of these festivals, and notes that rogation is an older cel-
     ebration than harvest. Ronald Hutton, *The Rise and Fall of Merry England: The Rural
     Year 1400–1700* (Oxford: Oxford University Press, 1994).

118 Often the two get muddled. For instance, a classic harvest hymn is actually about
     rogation: 'We plough the fields / and scatter the good seed on the land / but it is fed
     and watered by God's almighty hand.' Matthias Claudius, trans. Jane Montgomery
     Campbell in *Complete Anglican: Hymns Old and New*, ed. Kevin Mayhew (Stowmarket:
     Kevin Mayhew), 719.

119 Greggs, 'The Eschatological Tension of Theological Method', 341.

120 Martyn Percy, *The Ecclesial Canopy: Faith, Hope, Charity* (Farnham: Ashgate, 2012),
     143.

121 This also has biblical resonance especially in the gospels but it is set within the context
     of God's harvest. See also John 4.37; 1 Corinthians 3.6; 2 Corinthians 9.6.

122 October is a key month in the gathering of church statistics. It usually includes Har-
     vest Festival, when churches can reasonably assume a spike in numbers.

123 Intriguingly, it is with the advent of *Common Worship: Times and Seasons* (2006) that
     the Church of England has comprehensive provision for rogation; indeed it gives
     extensive provision for the agricultural year, including, rogation, Plough Sunday,
     Lammas and harvest. See the Archbishops' Council, *Common Worship: Times and
     Seasons* (London: Church House, 2006), 594–633.

124 Church Growth Research Programme, *From Anecdote to Evidence: Findings from the
     Church Growth Research Programme 2011–2013*, http://www.churchgrowthresearch.
     org.uk/UserFiles/File/Reports/FromAnecdoteToEvidence1.0.pdf [accessed 12 June
     2015].

125 *From Anecdote to Evidence*.

126 Jeffrey, *Luke*, 151–3.

127 George B. Caird, *St Luke* (London: Penguin, 1963). 149.

128 Johnson, *The Gospel of Luke*, 174.

129 Hebert, *Liturgy and Society*, 260.

130 Eliot, *The Complete Poems and Plays*, 148.

131 Croft, *The Future of the Parish System*, viii.

6   *Liturgy and Society*

Eucharist Shaping

This chapter will identify the foundations of Hebert's 'liturgical anthropology'. His insights and prescience are laudable and of value in exploring the significance of ecclesiology and missiology. However if his intention is to describe the function of the Church in the modern world, which it is, then this must have some purchase both within the life of the Church corporately and in the individual believer. Hebert's understanding of what constitutes being human needs exploration to begin to set it within a liturgical framework. In *Liturgy and Society* Hebert enunciates the importance of the individual worshipper: conceiving the human being as one who worships and is shaped and formed within the Church. As previously stated, this is not a coercive or totalitarian notion. Paradoxically it is part of Hebert's critique of individualism, that the individual finds meaning and purpose in the corporate. It is in that context, and in the notion of active participation, that the question of the self in liturgy is raised. This will be explored with particular reference to the work of the contemporary theologian James Smith.[1] Hebert's quest to understand the function of the Church in the modern world demands that some account be given of the person who acts in the world shaped by liturgy. That association will be explored through the lens of offertory and the relationship between work and fruits received and offered. The ethical and political dimensions of the function of the Church in the modern world are unavoidable.

The trajectory of the first four chapters leads us to an exploration of the place of the eucharistic shaping of persons and the Church to function in the modern world. Thus far these threads have been approached in a necessarily dismembered way, considering ecclesiology and mission separately: this chapter draws together those threads of the reflection on Hebert's treatment of Church and mission. This is not an isolated enquiry. Samuel Wells in *God's Companions* makes a similar undertaking.[2] Wells describes the life of a worshipping community in a parish, and weaves that into a liturgical framework. Wells' work is ethnographic in character and relates ecclesiology, mission and liturgy in the ways in which the three interrelate and are lived out by individuals and a community. In the same way *Liturgy and Society* is an intricate ecology, and Hebert's whole project collapses if those three areas cannot relate, not simply to each other, which is theologically imperative, but also to society. The question is about impact. The influence of *Liturgy and Society* has to be measured in its theological coherence and in the wider issues it raises, including how far it moved and moves the Church to function at all in the modern world. Interest in liturgy and ecclesiology *potentially* disables that function: ecclesiology can be paralysing if introspective; liturgy as well, if too aesthetically restrictive. Even mission, which properly is the moving of the Church's arena of activity away from herself and fulfilling her mission in the world for the sake of God's Kingdom, can be ill-conceived and 'churchy' and not relate to society.[3] It raises the question of the 'shape' of the Church: Christ-shaped, mission-shaped, Eucharist-shaped. It is noteworthy that Hebert's robust defence and deployment of the necessity of dogma does not fit the contemporary *zeitgeist*; nevertheless it grounds his reflections in a wider hinterland of Anglican theological reflection, not least in its incarnational theology. Hebert is undogmatic in his deployment of dogma, except that the Eucharist represents a Christ-shaped Church in word and sacrament.

Who Am I in Liturgy?

Questions of human identity, both corporate and individual, pervade the Bible. Liturgy has to wrestle with the consequences of the tension of the personal and corporate. Each person stands distinct before God, and yet ever in relationship to God and fellow human beings. Trinitarian theology allows for distinction and differentiation before God, undergirded by the uniquely precious place that each person has in relation to God. Hebert explores this tension and concludes that human beings are not autonomous, but are acting persons-in-relationship who find meaning in the Body of Christ and contribute to the corporate nature of society. The prism through which this is both viewed and lived is the Eucharist, which is simultaneously a personal and corporate action. Alexander Schmemann captures something of this in saying, 'everything pertaining to the Eucharist pertains to the church, and everything pertaining to the church pertains to the Eucharist and is *tested* by interdependence'.[4] That can be developed further to say that everything pertaining to the Church and the Eucharist is shaped and formed in relation to the world for the sake of the Kingdom. The doctrines of the Resurrection of the Body and the Body of Christ, the Church, act in a pragmatic sense as correctives against narcissistic individualism and overbearing corporatism in which individuality is lost.

Liturgy and Society has the capacity to engage fruitfully with current eccle-siological, liturgical and missiological concerns. Its reach touches public and ecclesiastical architecture, art, ethics, politics, the relationship between offer-ing and work; it demands reflection upon the nature of human meaning, and challenges the current transactional language of social capital and human resources. Essentially it offers a *liturgical anthropology*: a way of accounting for human being and acting that is drawn from, and shaped by, a liturgi-cal source. It identifies liturgy as the primary source of reflective Christian action in the world, and continues the ongoing reflection on the function of the Church in the modern world. So *Liturgy and Society* is not a relic of the past or significantly time limited; rather Hebert's reflections on individualism and the nature of the Body of Christ in its social outworking are pressing and urgent in the contemporary Church. It further demands reconsideration of the place of liturgy so that it is not viewed simply as either a 'shop window' or 'battery recharger' for mission, but a place where mission is enacted and embodied and a holy people comes to be shaped and be more fully what it already is.

The notion of liturgical anthropology requires a conceptual framework, and James Smith's work enables such a construction.[5] Smith writes princi-pally with a view to a theology of education that values formation. Integral to his vision is the place of liturgy. Whilst Hebert's primary purpose is not educational in the sense of the academy, the placing of his work alongside that of Smith helps frame the connection between dogma and life, and then the way in which the liturgical person acts in the world.

Fundamental to Smith's approach is the idea that the relationship between worship and the concept of the worldview needs to be re-thought, and the approach he outlines is through connecting liturgy, learning and forma-tion.[6] This is based on the conviction that educational strategies based solely on the transmission of ideas will fail to educate because they fail to *form* people. Smith articulates a deeply significant insight in this study of Hebert: 'behind every pedagogy is a philosophical anthropology, a model or picture of the human person'.[7] The root of Hebert's anthropological philosophy is accounted for in our first chapter; it is then worked out in ecclesiology and missiology.

Smith's contention is that human beings are liturgical animals because they are *desiring* creatures.[8] This has the danger of collapsing everything, including the pursuit of wisdom and truth, into a liturgical framework; nevertheless it is what Hebert does in *Liturgy and Society*. Smith's conception of desire is open to questioning too. He rejects a polarised distinction between *agape* and *eros*, something that Hebert does not treat so lightly. Throughout *Liturgy and Society* Hebert rejects an individualistic notion of self and sets it corporately;

liturgy is formative and a social vision flows from it. Smith's account of the liturgical person is to see the human person as lover.

This entails a move from the Cartesian understanding of personhood to a quite different one – one that predates it, but one that is recast post-Descartes. Smith rejects the notion that the ability to think is the sum of what makes a human being. The simple faith response to that is to say that 'I *believe* therefore I am'. Positively this acknowledges that there is more to the human being than thought. Moreover humans do not just think; they think about *things*, as Heidegger demonstrates, which has consequences on how persons act in the world. So to say 'I believe' moves the proposition further from Descartes and creates distance from his assertion. Hebert's emphasis on dogma might give the impression that he posits an assertion of being human that is not based on thinking but on believing, as if the two are different. However Smith points out that the move from 'I *think*' to 'I *believe*' does little more than organise discussion around a clash of worldviews, but does not move the debate from a 'cognitivist anthropology . . . that is fixated on the mind'.[9] He sees both as a 'reductionist picture of the human person' in which different ideas are set in the same intellectual framework.[10] The challenge for Hebert's anthropology is to go beyond such a reductionist picture of thinking, or even believing, but to a more capacious vision in which desire and meaning feature.

Hebert moves beyond a reductionist picture of both the Cartesian position and its faith-based response in three ways that are of value to the contemporary discourse. First, Hebert does not objectify reason because his dogmatic language is not an appeal to a body of thought that is remote from acting in Church and society. Secondly, he does not assume that in place of a clash of ideas there is a clash of beliefs; he posits a different way of being human, since he maintains the embodied character of being human that the person-as-believer, rather than thinker, perpetuates. Finally, his insistence on the corporate nature of the Church means that he conceives being human as shaped by the mediation of the Church, not personal preference or opinion.

The roots of Hebert's philosophical position are Augustinian. This is something that Smith explores. This is not to claim that Hebert consciously draws from this tradition, but it is to suggest that in some way he is formed by it. It thus places *desire* centrally in Hebert's thought. As translator of Anders Nygren's classic work *Agape and Eros* (in two volumes, 1930 and 1936) Hebert was fully apprised of Nygren's portrayal of desire. Sarah Coakley describes this as a presentation 'in which selfless Christian *agapē* draws one upwards, and selfish Greek *erōs* draws one downwards'.[11] Coakley, like Smith, rejects Nygren's 'sharp dichotomy' along with current scholarship. As Smith notes, Augustine distinguishes the two cities in *City of God* not by ideas or belief but by love, hence his comment that 'our primordial orientation to the world is not knowledge, or even belief, but *love*.[12] Smith's notion of desire and his collapsing of *agape* and *eros* into one and the same thing does not undermine Hebert's treatment of it; it is more that Smith wants to locate all desire and love in the impulse to worship as our 'ultimate love'.[13]

This is then a 'non-reductionist approach' that sees human persons as 'embodied agents of desire or love'.[14] Drawing on Heidegger, Smith sees that it is *involvement* in the world that is essential, and this is only to be achieved by desiring persons. As intentional, non-cognitive beings the liturgy is not something to be observed but to be participated in. Liturgy, for Smith, has an educative value, but it has to be acted upon by persons as desiring, liturgical and teleological creatures; that is to say, 'what we love is a specific vision of the good life, an implicit picture of what we think human flourishing looks like'.[15] Such a statement has to be tempered with the theological reflection that a specific vision of anything is not the object of worship; indeed it is not an object or thing that is worshipped by Christians. Christians worship no *thing*; they worship God, since, as Hebert says, 'Christian worship is in the first place and above all the worship of God, the acknowledgement by the rational creature of the sovereignty of the Creator to whom he belongs and for whose glory he exists.'[16] This is the liberating contribution of rootedness in dogma. It should be seen in connection with Smith's comment that the good life gives a destination to the liturgical person beyond the sanctuary. It can be seen further in relation to Hebert's contemporary, Evelyn Underhill, who writes:

> It is possible to regard worship as one of the greatest of humanity's mistakes; a form taken by the fantasy-life, the desperate effort of bewildered creatures to come to terms with the surrounding mystery. Or it may be accepted as the most profound of man's responses to reality; and more than this, the organ of his divine knowledge and the earnest of eternal life.[17]

Worship then is about meaning and purpose grounded in response, to God and 'man's responses to reality'. This resonates with Hebert's point about the function of the Church in the modern world that is reinforced by Wells.[18] This further situates the positive value of Hebert's voice today. The pursuit of the good life and the habits and practices that shape it are as integral to Smith's educational vision as they are to Hebert's vision of liturgy. This vision has many components coalescing around what good relationships look like; what a just economy and distribution of resources looks like; and the built and natural environment and what sorts of works count as good work. Smith also states, echoing Hebert's impulse, 'this is a *social* vision'.[19]

Hebert's emphasis is not simply to establish a social vision that is somehow reified into an object of worship. It is not the creation of utopia. It flows from a social vision of God, not the other way round. Drawing on the work of Charles Taylor, Smith describes the shift from worldview to 'social imaginary': this is useful insofar as it helps trace the implications rather than the sources of Hebert's work. His appeal to dogma could imply that it is simply another thought system to compete with a secular or theologically liberal one. However he moves decisively beyond dogma as holding an opinion.[20] Hebert confidently declares orthodoxy to be an authority under which men and women are free from the domination of the opinions of others and become free to obey their own conscience.[21] So the Creed is not a statement of doctrine but 'an act of personal allegiance'; and it is a prompt to worship, not a thing of itself to be worshipped.[22]

Creeds and dogma are a mapping exercise of the landscape of Christian belief and norms. Smith draws from Taylor the analogy of a map to describe his social imaginary, which is essentially how we *imagine* the world rather than how we *think* of it.[23] Taylor points out that the person who has grown up somewhere has no need of a map. So the Creed can be understood as a map of a social imaginary. That social imaginary is many layered and, whilst mapped within dogma, the paths are not always well worn. Hebert's point, to push the analogy, is that eucharistic living is an area of the social imaginary of the Church of England that was not as well trodden as it should be. Dogma is the cartographical guarantee of the historic teaching of the Church which the Christian comes to inhabit. Smith's description echoes Hebert:'Discipleship and formation are less about erecting an edifice of Christian knowledge than they are a matter of developing a Christian know-how that intuitively "understands" the world in the light of the fullness of the gospel.'[24]

The writer Robert Macfarlane in his description of the history of cartography enables a rich understanding of the map analogy and its role of *poesis*.[25] He also gives an account of cartography from the time of the Enlightenment – when cartography helped define two nations, the United States and France – 'before it was a field science, cartography was an art'.[26] This echoes the scholastic misidentification, as Hebert sees it, of seeing faith as *correct beliefs*, thus ossifying dogma. The distinction Macfarlane makes is between grid maps and story maps:

> The power of grid maps is that they make it possible for any individual or object to be located within an abstract totality of space. But their virtue is also their danger: that they reduce the world only to data, that they record space independent of being.[27]

Hebert is attuned to the story map view of dogma rather than the grid map. The story map is essentially participative, which is how the liturgical connection can be made. Liturgy as the study and definition of rubrics and authorised texts is the grid map; liturgy understood as the place of *poesis*, a making sense of the world in which we are set, inhabited by the worshipper, is the story map. As Macfarlane suggests, the story map is sensuous, whilst the grid map is undoubtedly accurate.[28] *Liturgy and Society* presents dogma as a story map in which the Eucharist is the defining topographical feature.

The story map image is suggestive of how the Eucharist is intrinsic to the identity of the Church. It also raises the question of how far *Liturgy and Society* takes us in the forming of the *homo eucharisticus*.[29] This situates Hebert within contemporary theology. For example, David Ford notes that the Eucharist is a corporate practice before it is an ethical code or set of doctrines.[30] This is consistent with Hebert's approach, as is the concept of *habitus* derived from Bourdieu and deployed by Ford to describe the dispositions which structure and generate practices and representations. He specifically focuses on the ' "art" of the *necessary improvisation*' which defines 'excellence' in living in a culture.[31] Ford states the need for eucharistic theology to be immersed in *habitus*. Furthermore, in delineating the nature of this *habitus*, Ford suggests that:

> often it is neither the words nor the confessed theological understanding that are most helpful in appreciating the dynamics of the celebration. Rather, one needs to follow the patterns of architecture and decoration; how and why these particular people gather in these ways; practices of welcoming or excluding; habits of presiding; forms of attentiveness and inattentiveness; the distribution of roles; dress, body language, music and other non-verbal symbols.[32]

The concept of following patterns and expression fits with Macfarlane's description of the story map, rather than the more rigid approach to words and rubrics.

Engagement with Smith further enables the mapping of Hebert's thought, and defines him outside the narrow confines of a grid map understanding of liturgy. In this respect Hebert is someone who has a clear sense that liturgy in general, and the Eucharist in particular, shapes the Body of Christ and individuals within it. It accounts for Hebert's rejection of corporatist totalitarianism, individualism and anxious missiology. Primarily the Eucharist shapes the Body of Christ, and secondarily is shaped by the Body of Christ. The shaping the Church gives to the Eucharist is only ever, Hebert contends, in fidelity both to the gospel and the understanding of the Church as eucharistically assembled. From that Hebert promotes the primacy of practices within the

Church. So the Church exists first as a liturgical proposition from which ethical action flows. Smith comments that 'from most expositions of "the Christian worldview", you would never guess that Christians worship!'[33] This suggests that Hebert's vision remains relevant and the (re)appropriation of it of deep value to the Church as a whole. This positioning of the argument enables exploration of some of the leads set by Hebert.

The principle of the 'active participation' of all the faithful, coined by Pope Pius X and amplified by another of Hebert's influences, Lambert Beauduin, undergirds *Liturgy and Society*. Lathrop reflects on participation and the pressures on it in contemporary society. Seekers' services, he suggests, see membership of an audience of participation which is not, by definition, participatory. Problematic issues of participation are not only related to the treatment of a congregation as an audience, because, as Lathrop describes, the exclusivity that active participation can engender is problematic for those seeking to participate. Nevertheless, there is a need for self-definition, and identity is expressed in participation.[34] The question of participation is not 'are you doing something?'; it is rather questions such as, 'how are you present?', 'how are you attentive?' and 'how do you identify?' that are more decisive. Outward forms of participation do not necessarily equate to actual participation, and participation in worship is also defined by acting in the world outside the formal liturgy.

Liturgy and the World

Hebert asks what it means for worldly persons to engage with the Church, with all that they bring from the modern world. Contemporary society is largely suspicious of public expressions of faith, devotion and conspicuous piety unless there is a visible outcome that does not impinge on the sensibilities or rights of others. Generally, personal and corporate faith is tolerable insofar as it is discreet.[35] This suggests two pressure points on the liturgical person.

First, and most obviously, a liturgical anthropology demands reflection on the choices made at the end of the liturgy: this is expressed in a question posed by Wells as he reflects on the final part of the eucharistic liturgy, 'The Dismissal' or 'Sending Out': '[the congregation] have been given everything they need. What will they now be asked to do? That is the perennial question of ethics, and that is the burden of the final part of the liturgy.'[36] That question gives an ethical dimension to the interface between liturgy and society. It would be misplaced, however, solely to locate the question of action in the world and in society simply in 'The Dismissal', as sometimes happens.[37] If that is done then liturgy and mission are divorced and the language of an 'interface' of Eucharist and mission suggests binary opposites, as if there is no implicit link between the two: Hebert rejects that dichotomy. To identify the act of dismissal as being the sole locus of engagement with the world diminishes the liturgical action which engages worship with the whole of life and not a fragmented aspect of it for those people who choose to engage in it. This takes seriously the embedded nature of the Church, through its members in the life of society and the multiplicity of roles lived out: 'Everyone is engaged in other practices as well as the eucharist, and the interpenetrations of these constantly changes the overall ecology.'[38]

Secondly, the liturgical action of 'The Gathering' is significant. Wells' question – 'what will they now be asked to do?' – places the direct application and ethical dimension of eucharistic living in the world to the moment before leaving the assembly. 'The Gathering' is equally ethically demanding, since it is not a neutral act; but neither is it a *conscious* act of engagement with the world.[39] To gather at the Eucharist demands a conscious association with the value of the action being undertaken and the awareness of its implications. John Milbank casts 'The Gathering' as the moment when unity is revealed, in a Pauline manner, as the 'harmonious blending of differences'.[40] That reinforces his point that gathering is a key act in making Church. He excoriates the notion that the Church 'should "plant" itself in various sordid and airless interstices of our contemporary world, instead of calling people to "come to Church"'. This is because, he argues, 'the refusal to come out of oneself and *go to* church is simply the refusal of church *per se*'.[41] Ninna Edgardh is less polemical in tone, noting that in The Gathering 'we constitute ourselves as a "we"'.[42] In common with Milbank, she sees gathering as actualising basic ecclesiological issues. Both entering and leaving the eucharistic assembly are actions that situate liturgy in the world for the sake of something bigger.

Hebert shows that no part of the eucharistic liturgy is purely introspective or extrospective; all is missional in that none of the eucharistic action can be removed from the meeting of liturgy and society. Hardy helpfully takes this notion further as he describes the eucharistic liturgy as a gathered interval in the scattered life of the Church in which 'all the "spread-out-ness" of social meaning is "processed" and enacted as the common meaning of the people together before God'.[43] Without this, 'the "outer side" of the Church does not meet the "inner side", and – bit by bit – people begin to think that the "inner side" is all that is needed, or that the "outer side" can be free from the "inner side"'.[44] Thus, as I have argued, the very act of gathering at the beginning of the Eucharist is not a neutral or antipathetic act that somehow removes the worshipper from the world, but properly is a conscious act of stepping more deeply into the reality of the world rather than an act of stepping out of the world and its concerns. Williams illustrates the decisive nature of the act of assembling:

> Standing in this place, I am also challenged to examine every action or policy in my life in the light of what I am; and I am, through the common life of the 'Assembly', made able to change and to be healed, to feed and be fed in relations with others in the human city. [45]

The Eucharist enacts precisely that engagement with the world, and drives the dynamic sense that the liturgical person brings the world to worship and worship to the world. The Rite of Penitence within the liturgy enables this connection further. Drawing on the work of Herbert McCabe, John Berkman notes 'both the dramatic character of reconciliation and its relation to the Eucharist' in the context of describing penance as a 'sacrament of return'.[46] Engagement with the world and its sinfulness drawn into the eucharistic assembly frames the priestly character of the People of God. The consequence of this is not simply about individual sin but about the 'we' constituted in the Gathering. In this way the penitential rite, which in contemporary liturgy is situated within the Gathering, unlike what Hebert would have known in the Book of Common Prayer, is part of the constitution of the identity of the Body. The act of penitence enables both contrition for the sinfulness of the world and the acknowledgement of personal culpability within that, a reality which is then transformed through the declaration of God's forgiveness of the individual and the corporate Body. The liturgical person becomes a vessel of God's forgiveness in the world for the sake of the Kingdom.

In the interface between liturgy and society the prayers of intercession have a pivotal role. They enable the connection between the needs and concerns of society which are then placed within the context of the *missio Dei* unfolding in the liturgical gathering. Wells describes the intercessions and the way in which 'they not only educate the church's desire and humble offering. They also shape the congregation in particular virtues'.[47] Kelly Johnson is keen to emphasise the way in which the Prayer of the Faithful forms the identity of the Body.[48] The danger of intercession only being about habit forming within the Body is that the liturgy loses its context of serving the world. Intercession necessarily embraces the world just as each worshipper gathers out of the context of the world. Wells relates the story of the woman who leads intercessions for the first time who realised that, 'this was a moment when she was like Jesus, standing before the Father bringing the people with her'.[49] The priestly act of intercession, engaging the whole eucharistic assembly, draws the world and human society more obviously into the eucharistic assembly.

Indeed *Common Worship* makes this explicit in suggesting that prayer is offered for 'creation, human society, the Sovereign and those in authority'.[50] In Wells' terms it is the moment when God would ask, ' "where are all the others?" – and she could reply, "Here, in my prayers." '[51]

The world and human society are quite literally named in intercession. In Hebert's terms this is not to suggest that there is a disparity or chasm between worship and world. It is very much more nuanced. More than dragging the world into worship, intercession places the believer with Christ in intercession to the Father in the power of the Spirit. Therefore the worshipper is drawn, sometimes painfully Coakley suggests, 'into the newly expanded life of "Sonship" '.[52] St Paul recurrently uses body imagery and language in accounting for the nature of the Church, and 1 Corinthians 11 relates ethical action to a liturgical setting and the breaking of bread. The liturgy has a cardiac role; the heart has a constant flow of taking in and sending out of blood, and giving a transformed quality to what is of essence the same before it enters the heart as when it leaves.[53] Intercession locates worship within the needs and yearnings of the world as the arena, with the Church, of God's redemptive and re-creative work.

This is the priestly character of the People of God. So, for instance, the act of sharing peace is an act of liturgy and society. It is a social act that is denuded of meaning if left in the place of worship and not carried away from that place. The Peace is an enactment of the peace of Christ and not a deliberate act of the making of peace as if none existed before. William H. Willimon describes a Church 'sticking with' the Peace. It began with the perfunctory exchange of the Peace until it became a joyful manifestation of peace and unity. However there is some caution to be attached to Willimon's description as he describes the Peace as a 'resource' which implies a utilitarian understanding of it as community building rather than pressing it to its more profound meaning as an intensification of what is already present, whether offered exuberantly or not.[54] The Peace anticipates the fulfilled and fulfilling peace of Christ in the world, and not the false peace, or truce, that human society most generally both seeks and accepts.[55]

Psalms, Scriptures and Preaching

Liturgy is the colour painted into the pencil sketches of ecclesiology; or, to appropriate a biblical image, it is the sinews and ligaments on the dry bones that animate the body. One of Hebert's key insights and insistent convictions is that liturgy, ecclesiology and mission are not only related but also generative of each other. This applies to Hebert's treatment of scripture, in which his sense of ecclesiology informs how it is treated and handled.

For a man best known in his day as a biblical scholar the place of scripture cannot be underestimated.[56] Hebert's account of the value of scripture fits very clearly within his conceptual framework of the significance of that which roots Christians within Church tradition. It is very distinctly an ecclesial reading of scripture: scripture is interpreted not simply as an individual interaction with a text but within an interpretive community. This catholic understanding of the place of scripture does not preclude a reformed concern with its significance for the individual.[57] Hebert's point is not to diminish scripture but to situate it away from the interpretation of an individual in the first instance: '[The scriptures] belong to the Church before they belong to us.'[58] The psalms are a particular example of this. Hebert particularly commends the common recitation of the psalms as being of value in speaking and in hearing: 'we do well if we listen, in spirit, to other people saying them, and hear in them the voice of Him who speaks to all the members of His Body'.[59] Thus the interpretation of scripture is a corporate undertaking, flowing from Hebert's ecclesiological sensibility.

It is in his consideration of psalms, scriptures and preaching that Hebert most frequently uses the language of the Body of Christ. It is in that context that he connects the Daily Office and the Eucharist to the lived life of the Christian. This is entirely consistent with his rejection of the assertion of individualism: 'the prayer of the individual member of the Body is not something separate from the prayer of the Body, but a part of it'.[60] In this process preaching is indispensable. The art of enabling the individual Christian to remain part of the Body in daily life is a task that exercises many today; it relates back to Wells' question, 'what will they be asked to do now?' Hebert can only answer that question in this context with an appeal to the 'common life of faith and love by which the Body lives'.[61] In other words, scripture is discerned by the Church, the Word of God in the Body of Christ.

So, the sermon 'gives expression to the common faith of Christians, their common approach to God as children in their Father's House, as members of the Body'.[62] To that end the sermon is not conceived of as being 'theological' – in terms of a scholastic or doctrinally based style – or 'devotional' in terms of dealing with individual spiritual lives and ways of individual prayer.[63] The sermon is a piece of celebratory theology delivered to and with the gathered congregation. Frances Young sees preaching as 'the primary genre of theological discourse'.[64] Hebert sees the sermon relating to liturgy in two key ways. First, the sermon is part of the liturgical continuum and not an insertion to it; it is not a foreign body that the liturgy should try and expel, but a natural expression of the gospel, the reading of which directly precedes it. Young echoes this, suggesting that 'theological affirmation [through preaching] in the context of liturgy is surely performative, and not merely descriptive, reflective or second order'.[65] Secondly, for Hebert liturgy shapes and forms thinking and action, a process which the sermon aids. This sense is picked up by Richard Giles, who excoriates preachers who preach with a view to compiling an anthology of sermons.[66] Hebert sees the sermon in the same way:

> It will connect the liturgy with private prayer, by bringing the unchanging forms of the service into relation with the 'here' and 'now'. For every sermon that is a good sermon is, so to speak, dated and addressed.[67]

Hebert understands the sermon as making a connection between the liturgical proclamation of the word and the lived experience of Christians.[68] How that might be done effectively, in different contexts, is the challenge laid down.[69] Wells' consideration of the sermon also envisages the liturgical context of the sermon 'to ensure that the congregation discover that through the Scripture and reflection on its experience they have come face to face with God'.[70]

Offertory: Work and Fruit

The liturgical action of the offertory, embodied in the offertory procession, exemplifies issues at stake in the eucharistic shaping of the individual and community. This will engage current writers, as well as Hebert's contemporary, Michael Ramsey. It is not the most heavily emphasised area of *Liturgy and Society*, but I will argue that it demonstrates the interaction of the sociality of the Church and her relationship with the world and creation.[71] The argument that a reappraisal of Hebert can be of benefit to the contemporary Church is encapsulated in this because the offertory is the point liturgically where liturgy and society, in terms of the everyday life of the individual worshipper, come together. The offertory is also heavily associated with the Parish Communion Movement, and intriguingly was not seen as a 'party' (High or Low) matter.[72]

Julie Gittoes identifies the anxiety that has surrounded the use of the language of offering; but she also identifies the crucial place of giving and receiving: 'we offer the elements of bread and wine so that they may be returned to us by Christ in such a way that we receive life from him'.[73] This is integral to understanding how the liturgical person may be shaped in acting in the world, and will be explored further below.

It is first important to acknowledge Ramsey's critique of the offertory because, as Gittoes alludes, the offertory procession, and what it expresses, has been contentious. Ramsey articulates this.[74] He mocks superficial expressions of the offertory that display a 'most alarming lopsidedness':[75]

> [T]he offering to Almighty God of the bread and wine as the token of the giving to him of the people's common life. Appropriate ceremonial brings out this moment in the rite: layfolk carry the elements in procession from the back of the Church, and lumps of coal and other objects may be brought to Church to reinforce the point.[76]

Ramsey's challenge suggests that the offertory is a liturgical action that is not integral to the liturgy, but incidental and functional and open to misinterpretation. Thus for him the connection of self-offering and the offertory is 'a shallow and romantic sort of Pelagianism'.[77] He continues: 'For we cannot, and dare not, offer aught of our own apart from the sacrifice of the Lamb of God, "Look, Father, look on his anointed face; And only look on us as found in him."'[78] Ramsey suggests that any offering can be made 'only in so far as we abase ourselves before the all-sufficiency of the "Lamb of God that takest away the sins of the world"'.[79] The critical act of offering is that of the Son to the Father expressed in the eucharistic prayer itself.

In *Liturgy and Society* Hebert is not responding directly to Ramsey's treatment of offertory. Indeed his handling of offertory does not start in a polemical or adversarial manner. He does not seek to make offertory routine or functional but expressive of something more. A decisive influence on Hebert's own approach to offertory and sacrifice is seen in his warm preface as translator of *Christus Victor*. In that preface Hebert is irenic and conciliatory, while also expressing the dissatisfaction of many, 'both with the satisfaction-theory and the exemplarist explanation'. For him, and for many, Aulén's 'classic' idea of the Atonement was a refreshing recapitulation of a key strand of Christian theology.[80] Ford's foreword to the 2010 edition highlights this, in that Aulén's work shows 'implications for the whole way Christian salvation is understood and lived today'.[81] Furthermore Ford draws attention to the impact of *Christus Victor* on both Hans Urs von Balthasar and Karl Barth, and suggests that Aulén's approach, liturgically articulated by his fellow Swede Brilioth, has been vindicated. Ford also comments on its 'utterly incarnational' character – something which, not surprisingly, Hebert draws attention to as well. The appeal for Hebert of an account such as Aulén's lay clearly in its ecumenical potential as well as how offertory might be construed.

Wells presupposes that the Eucharist and the eucharistic assembly are social. This is a direct inheritance of *Liturgy and Society*. As he describes the offertory, the congregation is taken to act as one whilst being differentiated only by the scale of gift that one or other might offer. 'The offering', for Wells, 'initiates not only a reordering of society but also a reassembly of creation'.[82] Furthermore the Anglican squeamishness about the language of offering is diffused by Wells' noting of the inadequacy of language of stewardship in relationship to creation.[83] Engaging with *Liturgy and Society* demands a rich understanding of offertory, where the Eucharist 'becomes a defining moment between goodness and glory, source and end, creation and eschaton'.[84] Wells summarises this as, '[t]he relationship of humanity to creation is not just to ensure its flourishing, still less simply to prevent its extinction, and even less again to assert dominance over it: instead it is to bring creation into the relationship of praise and thanksgiving toward God epitomized by the Eucharist'.[85] Hebert's description of an offertory procession at a Mass in Liège approaches the whole question differently.[86] For all his concern about dogma, or normative theology, he does not approach the offertory from the doctrinal route. He begins by being descriptive – 'we sketch the picture' – in a recognisably ethnographic approach, and then offers an ecclesio-theological interpretation. There are traces of Aulén's method in that whilst not jettisoning doctrine, he uses it imaginatively. Hebert identifies his attraction to the offertory procession, that in it 'the congregation is engaged in offering the holy sacrifice'.[87] And he continues, 'The people mean to unite themselves with the sacrifice of Christ; therefore they go up behind the altar, and deposit their offertory gifts.'[88]

The culmination of the Mass he observes is associated with the reading of Galatians (5.24) – 'They that are Christ's have crucified the flesh with the affections and lusts' – from which he reflects, '[t]his happens in the Mass, for in it we do not merely represent the death on the cross, but we ourselves hang with Christ on the cross, we unite ourselves with his sacrifice'.[89] Offertory is about identification: identification with Christ and his self-offering to the Father; and mystically being identifiable as part of his Body. Perhaps unwittingly, but certainly carelessly, Hebert implies that in the Eucharist *we join ourselves* to Christ, contrary to Augustine who insists that in Communion it is Christ *who joins us to himself* in his self-offering to the Father.[90] Offertory is about participation and not passivity; participation in liturgy demands participation in society. Nevertheless it is the initiative of Christ to join the Church to himself in offering and in his mission in the world. Offertory is also about a two-way recognition: recognition of what of daily life – actual interests, home, hobbies, work – can be offered to God as what is 'to be laid on God's altar and redeemed'; and recognition that the act of offertory 'might show him the value of his little daily job'.[91] In Hardy's terms this is the *outer side* of the Church impinging on its *inner side*. It is not about appropriating Christ in our mission, but us in his.

Hebert and Ramsey are as one in seeking to move beyond a stark Catholic and Protestant/Evangelical divide in approaches to offertory. It is Hebert who, following Brilioth, explicitly links offertory and an account of Atonement in this context. Brilioth is clear that 'the deepest religious meaning of the oblation of material gifts is seen in their symbolical significance, as representing the oblation of self which is a necessary part of all living faith'.[92] This does not fully address Ramsey's critique of the offertory, and it to this that I will now turn. For Hebert the liturgy is an action that expresses the way in which common prayer functions, and 'the individual drops into his place as a member of the worshipping Body'.[93] It is within this mystical Body that the whole of life, including that of labour and work, is 're-orientated towards God as its centre, and is transformed, sanctified and glorified'.[94] Returning to Hebert's description of Liège, it becomes clear that Kenneth Stevenson's concept of 'soft points' in liturgy becomes significant in responding theologically to Ramsey. Hebert is emphatic that:

> The offering of the gifts must always have been the speaking symbol of the people's will to offer up themselves to God; and here the self-oblation of the Church, the *Corpus Christi*, is set forth as a matter of the sacramental *Corpus Christi*. Here, as in St Paul, the two senses of 'the Body of Christ' are allowed to run together: the offering up of the Body of Jesus Christ in the Sacrament is one with the offering-up of His Body which is the Church.[95]

So, as he continues, the 'offertory-act . . . is consummated in the Communion'.[96] Hebert has a grounded theological and liturgical rationale for his understanding of offertory and the associated procession.

What Ramsey is alert to is the danger of the offertory being understood as more than it is. Ramsey is uncomfortable with this 'soft point' in the liturgy.[97] The soft point is essentially a moment in the liturgy when something functionally needs to happen, in preparation, and the action involved has been rendered either to misinterpretation or over-elaboration leading to ossification. Stevenson suggests that 'these soft points are not to be derided'.[98] Hebert knows the procession is not the summation of the offering of Christ to the Father, but to the outside observer what is expressed in the offertory procession could be the contrary. With Stevenson these soft points have a theology, but it can be elusive. In what follows I will endeavour to identify that theology in such a way that addresses Ramsey's anxieties about Pelagianism but that also values human labour and work, in the spirit of Hebert.

This suggests a liturgical connection to work, society and fruitfulness. Offertory engages the 'secular' world of work and daily labour with that of the 'sacred'. R.R. Reno states that 'work demands social interaction'.[99] This social interaction is not necessarily to be confused with becoming friendly with colleagues, but, as it were, draws coalitions of people together working in a common purpose. Reno makes the link to worship, saying:

> The intrinsically social nature of worship intensifies this pattern, calling individuals to a common altar. However important are the moments of solitude, the center [sic] of Christian worship, the eucharist, cannot be celebrated in isolation. Even the Tridentine practice of the private mass presupposed a spiritually present congregation of the heavenly hosts. Thus, in worship, the respect for others that secular work can inculcate is pressed toward the divine commandment of love, and the figure for cooperation in pursuit of worldly ends is fulfilled in a common prayer that seeks the heavenly goal of glorifying God.[100]

Hebert would emphatically not concede the Tridentine point, but nevertheless the sentiment is the same.[101] Reno sees work as setting patterns of discipline that can be replicated in worship and the creativity of work which also share the social ethic so evident in Hebert.

Hebert's conception of offertory also draws on his understanding of the nature of work. This is where Ramsey's critique becomes live. Is the offertory really about human self-congratulation being placed before God? I will explore more about the offertory and creation below, but first I will consider Hebert's emphasis on work. Work, for Hebert, relates first to how he sees Incarnation and social life.[102] Whilst notions of secular and sacred are broken down, Hebert notes that to take the Kingdom seriously (*'not* of this world, but very much *in* the world') then the nature of the relationship between the two must be understood in the light of the Incarnation: 'Christianity is deeply concerned with "secular" activities of every kind: not so that the sacred becomes secularized, but so that the secular activities are redeemed to God.'[103] The church in a community does not stand in contrast to other buildings such as factories, shops and public houses, but shows that 'these others are claimed for Him'.[104] This is the social idealism that Hebert acknowledges for himself. This is predicated on Hebert's thesis that society has become atomised and the way to counter this is through the life of the Body, the Church. As noted above, Hebert is open to the accusation of romanticism in his understanding of post-industrial society. However, for him the liturgy values both the individual and the social. The offertory is expressive of this – that the individual, not individualism, is central. He proposes this against totalitarianism, both communist and fascist. So work enables 'God's meaning for human life' because it takes the life of the individual and places him or her meaningfully within society.[105] Individuals are persons, 'not in the abstract, not in terms of statistics, but in terms of the life which men, children of God, are living'.[106] Hebert's theology of work and working people is also reflected in Eliot's *The Rock*. His reference to 'take no thought of the sowing' is situated in the first chorus, which concludes, '*in the semi-darkness the voices of WORKMEN are heard chanting*'.[107] Amongst those lines is a vision of the individual working for the common good: 'There is work together / A Church for all / And a job for each / Every man to his work.' This line is repeated, but beginning, 'We build the meaning'.[108]

This study of *Liturgy and Society* leads us to similar questions being explored in contemporary writers. Reno's conclusion is like Hebert's thesis, and links offertory (liturgy) and work (society):

> Social outreach is important; educational programs are necessary; budgets must be balanced and buildings repaired. All this work is quite real and contributes to the flourishing of the church. Nonetheless, it is the work of worship that makes the church a church rather than a benevolent association. The act of worship makes the community into the people of God. Of course, it is God's work.[109]

Hebert never describes the offertory procession in Ramsey's rather carica-tured terms (lumps of coal etc.).[110] Ramsey's allegation of Pelagianism seems at worst misplaced and at best ungenerous. In his preface to *Christus Victor* Hebert is impatient with Anglican theologians of the late nineteenth and early twentieth centuries (with the 'one exception' of Maurice) in their failure to establish a sufficient theology of the Atonement because of their 'semi-Arian' theology of Incarnation.[111]

Ben Quash redresses the balance of offering and Incarnation by stating that in the offertory, 'there is a display of what it was that Christ assumed in the Incarnation – the things of earth in their real earthliness'.[112] So references to 'gifts' at the offertory are not gifts offered to God, but gifts already given by God for humanity; and the act of offertory acknowledges that *giftedness*. Offertory has a place within the doctrine of creation as well as redemption. Quash casts the offertory within a framework of the treasuring of creation and acknowledgement of the creator. This means that the response, 'Blessed be God for ever', is the place where formation and ethical awareness is aroused:[113]

> In these liturgical exchanges the congregation learns to think about the whole creation (in connection with these specific gifts of the creation) as belonging to God ('Lord of all creation'). It learns in appropriate

humility (without what Clark would call 'delusions of grandeur') to acknowledge that it 'has' these gifts only because of life-giving forces wholly in excess of its own control ('through your goodness'; 'which earth has given').[114]

This means that the offering is not exclusively located in the gifts of bread and wine, or even in the body of the believer. Rather it becomes the inclusive focus of the transformation of what the person believes to be in his or her control – his or her material resources – and becomes properly seen as derived from God. The act of handing over, of offering, allows the gifts to be what God wants them to be, 'rather than what human beings wish to make them'.[115] So, for Quash, the canticle *Benedicite, Omnia Opera* takes the social dimension of creation further, arguing that '[non-human creatures] are shown to be known and loved by God in a way that does not always need to make reference to human beings, though we *are* encouraged to see ourselves as in relationship (in *fellowship*) with them'.[116] Bread and wine, with the whole creation, become oriented 'to the disclosure of God'.[117] Echoing Hebert, Quash writes:

> if there is to be a serious recognition that the *lex orandi* should be allowed to shape the *lex credendi* then the liturgy ought to teach Christians that they should not seek to shape and direct the ends of other creatures unless there is first a recognition that they are fellows in relationship to God (even, potentially, friends).[118]

Quash sketches out Christian practice standing in sharp contrast to an immanentist position in which only particular interests, and not the absolute value of things, are prized. The *lex orandi* understands all things as gifted, and not as things in themselves. The consequence of this is eschatological because of the Christological ordering of things, in which Christ is the one in and for whom all things exist.

Offertory is part of the liturgical formation of the Christian within the Body and the world. Framed in such terms it is profoundly social, and not limited to human society but to the global *oikoumene*. It is far more missional, incarnational and world engaging than it might seem at first. Offertory values the fruit of society, including work, and places that within liturgy – which in turn points to God, the source of all gifts. From that transformative capacity of offertory the worshipper is prompted to consider how that giftedness is deployed back in society. In response to Ramsey's critique of the offertory, I have identified it, with Stevenson, as a 'soft point' and set out a theological response to him, in proposing the way in which the offertory sweeps up human social life in work and industry into the primary offering of Christ to the Father. It is in that action in the eucharistic prayer that Hebert says, amongst other things, the Church is enabled, and therefore her members, 'to be a reasonable, holy and living sacrifice, and *to live a sacrificial life in the world*'.[119] This directly leads me to the ethical-political dimension of eucharistic life and the arena of the function of the Church in the modern world.

Conclusion

This chapter has explored both Hebert's understanding of Church and Eucharist through the key themes of *Liturgy and Society*, and that of other writers, from which the foundations of a 'liturgical anthropology' have been further developed. This has been necessarily wide-ranging, just as Hebert is. There are connections between Hebert and Smith because *Liturgy and Society* moves from seeing the person in Cartesian terms to understanding the self as one who desires. For Hebert, as for Smith, the fulfilment of this desire is in worship. Hebert develops this so that worship feeds and shapes the person, always in company with others. Active participation in the liturgy involves the time of worship, but also life that is lived outside the confines of an ecclesiastical building, hence the connection between work and liturgy. Work and offertory offer a means of clarifying the consequences of Hebert's thinking in a contemporary setting. This reinforces a key point of this thesis: that Hebert's contribution, in keeping with the Parish Communion trajectory, helps reframe contemporary debate because he highlights the need to see worship and human existence in society as a whole. Consistently Hebert is seen to be both a man of his time and also one who offers a robust but irenic contribution to current ecclesiological and liturgical debate. Crucially, *Liturgy and Society* is demonstrably tuned to propel the worshipper into the public arena of ethical and political living.

Notes

1 James K.A. Smith, *Desiring the Kingdom: Worship, Formation and Cultural Worldview* (Grand Rapids, MI: Baker Academic, 2009).
2 Samuel Wells, *God's Companions: Reimagining Christian Ethics* (Oxford: Blackwell, 2006).
3 Martyn Percy explores this temptation in relation to Mission Action Plans and programmatic mission. See Percy, *The Ecclesial Canopy*, 20, 142–3.
4 Alexander Schmemann, *The Eucharist: Sacrament of the Kingdom* (Crestwood NY: St Vladimir's Seminary Press, 1987), 215, his italics.
5 Smith, *Desiring the Kingdom*.
6 Smith, *Desiring the Kingdom*, 39.

7 Smith, *Desiring the Kingdom*, 40.

8 Smith's account of desire is not to be confused with a Girardian treatment of *mimetic* desire because that focuses on desire as covetousness. Smith's account of desire could also be expressed as *yearning*. See René Girard, *I See Satan Fall like Lightning* (Maryknoll, NY: Orbis, 2001), 10–11 and Michael Kirwan, *Discovering Girard* (London: DLT, 2004), 14–37.

9 Smith, *Desiring the Kingdom*, 43.

10 Smith, *Desiring the Kingdom*, 43.

11 Sarah Coakley, *God, Sexuality and the Self: An Essay 'On the Trinity'* (Cambridge: Cambridge University Press, 2013), 30.

12 Smith, *Desiring the Kingdom*, 46.

13 Smith, *Desiring the Kingdom*, 51.

14 Smith, *Desiring the Kingdom*, 47.

15 Smith, *Desiring the Kingdom*, 52.

16 Hebert, *Liturgy and Society*, 183.

17 Underhill, *Worship*, 4.

18 Wells, *God's Companions*.

19 Smith, *Desiring the Kingdom*, 53.

20 Hebert, *Liturgy and Society*, 87, 100–2.

21 Hebert, *Liturgy and Society*, 111.

22 Hebert, *Liturgy and Society*, 109.

23 Smith, *Desiring the Kingdom*, 66.

24 Smith, *Desiring the* Kingdom. 68.

25 Robert Macfarlane, *The Wild Places* (London: Granta, 2007).

26 Macfarlane, *The Wild Places*, 140.

27 Macfarlane, *The Wild Places*, 141.

28 Macfarlane, *The Wild Places*, 142–3.

29 David Ford, *Self and Salvation: Being Transformed* (Cambridge: Cambridge University Press, 1999), 162–5.

30 Ford, *Self and Salvation*, 140.

31 Ford, *Self and Salvation*, 140, original italics.

32 Ford, *Self and Salvation*, 140.

33 Smith, *Desiring the Kingdom*, 64.

34 Gordon W. Lathrop, *Holy People: A Liturgical Ecclesiology* (Minneapolis: Augsburg Fortress, 1999), 94.

35 Woodhead, 'Introduction', 23. For example, Woodhead details *causes celebres* around the wearing of faith symbols which are seen as an imposition of personal or private faith upon public sensibilities.

36 Wells, *God's Companions*, 214.

37 See previous chapter.

38 Ford, *Self and Salvation*, 143.

39 Wells, *God's Companions*, 214.

40 John Milbank, 'Stale Expressions: The Management-Shaped Church', *Studies in Christian Ethics* 21/1 (2008), 124.

41 Milbank, 'Stale Expressions', 124.

42 Nina Edgardh, 'Towards a Theology of Gathering and Sending', *Worship*, 82/6 (2008), 509.

43 Hardy, *Finding the Church*, 255.

44 Hardy, *Finding the Church*, 255.

45 Rowan D. Williams, *Faith in the Public Square* (London: Continuum, 2012), 93.

46 John Berkman, 'Being Reconciled: Penitence, Punishment and Worship', in *The Blackwell Companion to Christian Ethics*, eds Stanley Hauerwas and Samuel Wells (Oxford: Blackwell, 2004), 101.

47 Wells, *God's Companions*, 182.

48 Kelly S. Johnson, 'Praying: Poverty', in *The Blackwell Companion to Christian Ethics*, eds Stanley Hauerwas and Samuel Wells (Oxford: Blackwell, 2004), 228–36.

49 Wells, *God's Companions*, 183.

50 Archbishops' Council, *Common Worship 2000, 174.*

51 Wells, *God's Companions*, 183.

52 Coakley, *God, Sexuality and the Self*, 55–6.

53 'Nairobi Statement on Worship and Culture: Contemporary Challenges and Opportunities' 1.1, http://www.elca.org/Growing-In-Faith/Worship/Learning-Center/LWF-Nairobi-Statement.aspx [accessed 22 March 2013].

54 William H. Willimon, *Worship as Pastoral Care* (Nashville: Abingdon Press, 1979), 180. It also recalls the children's song, 'Let there be peace on earth, and let it begin with me.'

55 The work of René Girard draws attention to the point that scripture exposes a false truce in texts such as Jeremiah 6.14, 8.11 and Ezekiel 13.10, 13.16.

56 For instance, *The Throne of David* 1941; *Scripture and Faith* 1947; *The Authority of the Old Testament* 1947; *The Bible from Within* 1951; *Fundamentalism and the Church of God* 1957; *When Israel Came Out of Egypt* 1961; *The Christ of Faith and the Jesus of History* 1962; *The Old Testament from Within* 1962.

57 See Scott Hahn, *Covenant and Communion: The Biblical Theology of Pope Benedict XV* (London: Darton, Longman, Todd), 2009 and Joseph Ratzinger, *Verbum Domini: The Word of God in the Life and Mission of the Church* (Vatican City: Libreria Editrice Vaticana, 2010).

58 Hebert, *Liturgy and Society*, 219.

59 Hebert, *Liturgy and Society*, 219.

60 Hebert, *Liturgy and Society*, 222.

61 Hebert, *Liturgy and Society*, 222.

62 Hebert, *Liturgy and Society*, 223.

63 Fenwick terms this the Liturgical Sermon, which he dismisses on grounds of its typical length, equating the length of a sermon with its quality. He also neglects the liturgical context: the sermon is not the sole locus of catechesis. Fenwick, 'These Holy Mysteries', 14.

64 Frances Young, *God's Presence: A Contemporary Recapitulation of Early Christianity* (Cambridge: Cambridge University Press, 2013), 4.

65 Young, *God's Presence*, 4.

66 Richard Giles, *Creating Uncommon Worship: Transforming the Liturgy of the Eucharist* (Norwich: Canterbury Press, 2004), 122–3.

67 Hebert, *Liturgy and Society*, 223.

68 This is echoed in Robinson's description of the preaching of Leo the Great, in Robinson, 'Informed Worship and Empowered Mission', 527.

69 For a treatment of ways of engaging the congregation in the sermon see Wells, *God's Companions*, 170–71.

70 Wells, *God's Companions*, 168.

71 One of the often commented upon aspects of the Parish Communion Movement was that of the restored offertory procession.

72 Michael Ramsey, *Durham Essays and Addresses* (London: SPCK, 1957), 16.

73 Julie Gittoes, *Anamnesis and the Eucharist: Contemporary Anglican Approaches* (Aldershot: Ashgate, 2008),118.

74 Ramsey, *Durham Essays and Addresses.*

75 Ramsey, *Durham Essays and Addresses.* 18.

76 Ramsey, *Durham Essays and Addresses.* 18.

77 Ramsey, *Durham Essays and Addresses*, 18.

78 Ramsey, *Durham Essays and Addresses*, 18. Ramsey is citing the hymn 'And now, O Father, mindful of the love' by William Bright, in Mayhew *Complete Anglican Hymns*, 34.

79 Ramsey, *Durham Essays and Addresses*, 18.

80 Arthur Gabriel Hebert, Translator's Preface to *Christus Victor: An historical Study Of three Main Types of the Idea of the Atonement*, by Gustav Aulén, trans. Arthur Gabriel Hebert (London: SPCK, 2010), xvi.

81 David Ford, foreword to *Christus Victor: An Historical Study of Three Main Types of the Idea of the Atonement*, by Gustav Aulén, trans. Arthur Gabriel Hebert (London: SPCK, 2010), ix.

82 Wells, *God's Companions*, 193.

83 This is borne out in *Common Worship* where the word 'offer' is replaced by 'set before you' in the *berekah* prayers, which are described as 'Prayers at the Preparation of the Table'. Archbishops' Council, *Common Worship*, 291.

84 Wells, *God's Companions*, 193.

85 Wells, *God's Companions*, 193.

86 Hebert, *Liturgy and Society*, 136.

87 In Guiver's phrase all are 'co-actors with God in the liturgical action'. Guiver, *Vision upon Vision*, 33.

88 Hebert, *Liturgy and Society*, 136.

89 Hebert, *Liturgy and Society*, 138.

90 Hebert appears to be drawing from Augustine's words, 'we too were represented there [at Calvary]. What hung upon the cross, if it was not that humanity that He had taken from us? Christ nailed our weakness to the cross where, as the Apostle says, our old self was crucified with him.' For Augustine see, for example, Eamon Duffy, 'On Not Quite Starting Again', in *Walking to Emmaus* (London: Burns & Oates, 2006), 71.

91 Hebert, *Liturgy and Society*, 194–5.

92 Brilioth, *Eucharistic Faith and Practice*, 283.

93 Hebert, *Liturgy and Society*, 64.

94 Hebert, *Liturgy and Society*, 65.

95 Hebert, *Liturgy and Society*, 77.

96 Hebert, *Liturgy and Society*, 78.

97 Kenneth Stevenson, *Do This: The Shape, Style and Meaning of the Eucharist* (Norwich: Canterbury Press, 2002), 33–40.

98 Stevenson, *Do This*, 37.

99 R.R. Reno, 'Participation: Working Toward Worship', in *The Blackwell Companion to Christian Ethics*, eds Stanley Hauerwas and Samuel Wells (Oxford: Blackwell, 2004), 327.

100 Reno, 'Participation', 327.

101 Hebert, *Liturgy and Society*, 82–3.

102 Hebert, *Liturgy and Society*, 191–5.

103 Hebert, *Liturgy and Society*, 191.

104 Hebert, *Liturgy and Society*, 192.

105 Hebert, *Liturgy and Society*, 197.

106 Hebert, *Liturgy and Society*, 198.

107 Eliot, *Complete Poems and Plays*, 149–50, original italics from stage direction.

108 Eliot, *Complete Poems and Plays*, 149–50.

109 Reno, 'Participation', 329.

110 Ramsey, *Durham Essays and Addresses*, 18.

111 Hebert, Translator's Preface, xvii.

112 Ben Quash, 'Treasuring the Creation', in *The Blackwell Companion to Christian Ethics*, eds Stanley Hauerwas and Samuel Wells (Oxford: Blackwell, 2004), 313.

113 Archbishops' Council, *Common Worship*, 291.
114 Quash, 'Treasuring the Creation', 311.
115 Quash, 'Treasuring the Creation', 312.
116 Quash, 'Treasuring the Creation', 312.
117 Quash, 'Treasuring the Creation', 312.
118 Quash, 'Treasuring the Creation', 312.
119 Hebert, *Liturgy and Society*, 208, my italics.

7   Acting in Society
The Ethical–Political Dimension

Liturgy and Society invites the Church to the consideration of the public arena of ethical and political living informed by liturgical practice. In *Liturgy and Society* Hebert ends his chapter 'The Church Service' – in which he considers the Church, the Parish Eucharist, scripture and homiletics, and liturgical traditions – with a call to 'Common Action'. Hebert sees the Church as 'the actualization of the organic life of the Body'.[1] This actualisation provokes the Church's capacity to offer a re-imagined politics through its concept of the nature of the Church as *Body*. Hebert's abhorrence of totalitarianism, stated elsewhere in *Liturgy and Society*, reinforces his critique of democracy. He is drawn inexorably back to the liturgical shaping of the Church through the primary Pauline image of the Church as a body. He asks: 'Can anything but this common faith and this organic life re-create our secular politics?'[2] This final chapter is a response to that question.

The society into which Hebert spoke is dramatically different from today. This is not simply in technological innovation but in the heightened awareness of the diversity of human lifestyles, outlooks and beliefs in the local and global.[3] To attempt to survey the full breadth of societal issues with which the Church engages is beyond the scope of this enquiry. The challenge when using Hebert's method and conclusions in *Liturgy and Society* in the contemporary setting is that the assumptions he makes and supposes to be commonly held are self-evidently not commonly held: for example, his implicit hierarchical assumptions about family, Church and nation in 'What I Learnt in the House of the Lord'. Christianity has lost its monopoly. The broadly secularising character of Western society has not eradicated the religious sensibility, but it has changed and fragmented it further. Many common assumptions are formed not by liturgy but by other forces; Christians are as likely to share as many opinions as wider society, even on issues of personal ethical choice and morality.[4] The way in which societal currents shape and affect Christian thinking and acting, and how liturgy holds the Christian narrative in such a way that the disciple is equipped, within the Body, to negotiate faithful living in that context, is the focus of this chapter since it locates Hebert's priorities in contemporary society.

'Common action' spilling out from the formative action of liturgy is at the heart of *Liturgy and Society*. James K.A. Smith and William Cavanaugh represent two current theological voices that address that question from different perspectives. The voice of Ian McEwan in his novel *Saturday* diverges from the account that a theistically based account of being human offers. Common action in his account is not an imperative from the common body, but the action of individuals in coalition. This is a fundamentally different approach from Hebert as well as Smith and Cavanaugh.

Desiring the Kingdom: Formation in Community

Smith's interest is primarily in the way in which individuals within the life of the Church are shaped and formed. Smith speaks to a very different situation. In *Desiring the Kingdom* he describes the impact of the consumerism of the late twentieth and early twenty-first centuries. Hebert's critique of consumerism is very similar. Both he and Smith, albeit separated by over half a century, see that consumerism comes out as an anti-liturgy. Smith's description of the features of the North American (and North Atlanticist) shopping mall leads him to conclude that it is a 'religious institution' because it is a *liturgical* institution, and that it is a pedagogical institution because it is a *formative* institution.[5] This connects cultural liturgy (the more generous term) and formation, as surely as Christian liturgical worship is formative. It is because of this connection that his stated task is 'to raise the stakes of Christian education, which will also mean raising the stakes of Christian worship'.[6] This connects with the *Liturgy and Society* project in that his goal, and Hebert's, is 'nothing less than the formation of radical disciples who desire the kingdom of God'.[7]

Having set out his proposition through critiquing 'secular liturgies', Smith undertakes a similar exercise to Wells in *God's Companions* by going through the order of the Eucharist and reflecting on its component parts. This is not a reductionist or fragmentary approach but, rather, seeing liturgy more akin to the refracted light of a prism. Smith sees liturgy as 'Practicing (for) the Kingdom'.[8] Part of what Smith alerts us to is the apparent familiarity of the liturgies of consumerism (after all we all exist within that culture) that mask their strangeness from Christian liturgical practice.

A legitimate question to ask of Smith is to what extent his critique of a cultural worldview of contemporary culture actually removes the disciple from engagement in society. Is his approach, if not world-hating, then world-sneering, as if Christian liturgy should be overlaid on culture? Is Smith's approach simply to counter culture as thoroughly suspect? This is something

Smith rejects, seeing Christian worship as training to the worshipper in 'all aspects of life: social, political, economic, and so on'.[9] In this he sees worship as a vision not simply for spiritual flourishing (which, as we will suggest below, is potentially narcissistic) but also for human flourishing, 'training for temporal, embodied human community'.[10] Hebert asks us to see the Church's liturgy as world-affirming whilst at the same time a call to repentance and amendment of life and the injustices of society, as his references to Eliot's *The Rock* illustrate. Smith himself is clear that he does not counsel 'abstention "from culture" *as such*, which would amount to pietist withdrawal from the goodness of creation'.[11]

So what of life in the world according to Smith? This life he refers to as 'practices beyond Sunday'.[12] As he notes, eucharistic worship typically lasts an hour or so for the vast majority of Christians, and 'this is not much time to enact counter-measures to the secular liturgies in which we are immersed the rest of the week!'[13] So it is possible to surmise that liturgical worship, and not all Christians will participate in that week by week, might be ineffectual purely on time grounds. However in the face of secular liturgies, Smith sees even a small amount of liturgical worship as 'both dense and charged', and 'we ought not to underestimate the power of even a relatively brief encounter with the transforming triune God'.[14] What he also says is that the very act of naming consumerist cultural practices as *liturgies* exposes them for what they are, 'formative liturgies bent on shaping and aiming our desire'.[15] The antidote is the cultivation of patterns formed by liturgy. This includes monasticism, a notion informed by his vision of the context peculiar to the United States of Christian colleges; and education, in which a college can have a quasi-monastic character. Even more than that, 'families and friendships can be powerful incubators of desire for the kingdom'.[16] This is persuasive stuff, and yet leaves the question of political and ethical acting outside the ecclesial fold. Such a reservation is proper, but in reflecting on the dismissal element of the Eucharist Smith addresses it by saying that 'Christian worship is an affective school, a pedagogy of desire in which we learn not how to be spiritual or religious, but how to be *human*, how to take up the vocation given to us at creation'.[17] The way in which we act in the world is as human, not spiritual or religious. Otherwise spirituality or religion becomes another marketable comestible. Smith seeks to redirect human desire and longing away from that which can be purchased and towards desire for the kingdom. His fundamental emphasis is on the fundamental place of liturgy within this. Liturgy is the place of encounter with the living God, not exclusively, but a focal point to inform practices of hospitality, service and delight throughout the week, whilst not being a mere practice itself, but sacramentally charged with power from on high.

Spirituality and religiosity can be sold as merchandise in contemporary society. Smith describes the pernicious formative influence of consumerism, a notion reflected in Spinks' *The Worship Mall*.[18] In that Spinks quotes John Clammer, who observed that 'shopping is not merely the acquisition of things: it is the buying of identity'.[19] Liturgy helps form identity within the Body of Christ and lived out as the Body of Christ in the world.

The legacy of the Parish Communion Movement in general and *Liturgy and Society* in particular continues to be generative in ecclesiology and liturgy. *Liturgy and Society* has at its heart the imperative for the Church to function in modern society, echoing the connection between liturgy and praxis.[20] The link between liturgy and society is eucharistically shaped persons who move between the Church and the world, both embraced by the Kingdom of God.

How the Christian acts within the Church and society is mission in its widest sense. A caricature of mission is to see it as an ideological pursuit of a self-conscious promotion of values, doctrine and lifestyle. This is not tenable as an understanding of mission because it fails to serve the world and need not function in the world. Indeed it could be entirely distinct from it. We have seen that *Liturgy and Society* propels Christians into the 'modern world'. Williams highlights this as he engages faith 'in the public square', and he notes:

> If we who adhere to revealed faith don't want to be simply at the mercy of this culture, to be absorbed into its own uncritical stories about the autonomous self and its choices, then we need to examine the degree to which our practice *looks* like a new world.[21]

Visibility in the Public Square

Smith focuses primarily on the inner life of the Church to enable her to look outwards. Another radical expression of eucharistically shaped ethical living is powerfully described by Cavanaugh. This approach looks at the outer life of the Church which enables attention to her inner life. He recounts the initial silence of the Church in Chile in the face of the Pinochet regime. This was more than caution on the part of bishops and the institutional Church. Cavanaugh attributes this fissure between in the Church in Chile and wider society and politics to an over-spiritualised ecclesiology following the establishment of *Catholic Action* in Chile. This move had paradoxical consequences since its aim was to engage Chileans socially after withdrawing them from political parties. What prompted the move away from political engagement was, ironically, the desire to build 'social Catholicism', a tradition which championed social justice and human rights for the disadvantaged. The 'melancholy side' of this was that the Church first identified all 'politics' with party politics; and secondly, by creating a sphere it called 'social', enabled the 'political' sphere to be occupied by malign statist interests.[22] It was, in Hardy's terms, the 'inner side' of the Church only relating to itself and not to its 'outer side'. In Hebert's terms, Cavanaugh highlights the consequences, in a particularly acute way, of the failure to connect liturgy and society to such an extent that the Church does not function in that society. For Cavanaugh it is the Eucharist that holds the Church to her embodied presence in society even, or especially, in a society like Chile in the 1970s and 80s.[23]

Cavanaugh's account of the withdrawal into interiorised faith renders the Church invisible and as a consequence in which the Body of Christ begins to disappear, as surely as tortured bodies began to disappear. The turning point came, he suggests, as the Church became faithful again to the embodied nature of the Eucharist; an embodied Church shaped by eucharistic practice challenged the Church itself in its inability to resist the disciplines of the state. Cavanaugh posits that as the Church, the Body of Christ, reappeared, the disappeared bodies of those tortured and killed were named and made visible again: the Body of Christ was constituted and made visible in the Eucharist. It was a eucharistic sensibility derived from practice that enabled the Church to be again the fullness of the Body of Christ in witness and engagement in society and crucially in politics. In Chile it mattered that the Church moved from what he calls the 'ecclesiology of a disappearing church'.[24] The overbearing preoccupation with the inner meaning of the Church led to any sense of the common action urged by Hebert. And yet, crucially, within the Church's own narrative the notion of the 'ecclesiology of a disappearing Church' is tautologous and therefore unsustainable.

Liturgy and Society places the Church clearly in the social sphere rather than the explicitly political. To that extent it can be associated with the 'mystical body' theology of the inter-war period that derives from Jacques Maritain. More specifically, the influence of Herwegen is evident as Hebert captures a flavour of his thought: 'the celebration of the Christian Mysteries is a social act, by which the worshippers are brought out of their isolation into fellowship with one another in the Church, which is Christ's mystical Body'.[25] Cavanaugh's critique of a mystical body theology focuses on 'the imagination of a disincarnate church which hovers above the temporal, uniting Christians in soul while the body does its dirty work'.[26] Hebert's project is to move the Church from seeing its liturgy as 'hovering above' to an engagement with society; however, he cannot be said to move the body towards really dirty work, hence his emphasis on incarnation that we have already identified. There are, on Hebert's part, echoes of Pope Pius XII's encyclical *Mystici Corporis Christi* (1943), which post-dates *Liturgy and Society*, and that suggests that a well-ordered Church will be a source of hope to which the bloodied nations of Europe will command admiration and emulation. That sentiment arose, like Hebert's disillusionment with liberal theology, from the wreckage of post-First World War Europe. Rather than retreat from the colossal disappointment of the First World War we see Hebert's themes of ecclesiology, dogma and incarnation and societal engagement through properly oriented mission, the engagement of liturgy and society.

Liturgy and Society articulates an engagement with human society that neither demeans nor sacralises. In the terms of Stanley Hauerwas and William Willimon, *Liturgy and Society* rejects an accommodationist approach that sees human society as 'tweakable'. Hauerwas exemplifies that by rejecting an *activist* model of Church which is concerned only with building a better society through the humanisation of social structures, which in its politics becomes 'a sort of religiously glorified liberalism'.[27] Conversely, as Hauerwas suggests, the *'conversionist* church' retreats from societal engagement to the individual soul. The *'confessing* church' becomes a radical alternative to the other two approaches; thus, 'the confessing church finds its main political task to lie, not in the personal transformation of individual hearts or the modification of society, but rather in the congregation's determination to worship Christ in all things'.[28] This sounds very Hebertian; and, lest it sounds like a choice between faithfulness rather than effectiveness, Hauerwas and Willimon describe the characteristics of such a Church, concluding that 'the confessing church has no interest in withdrawing from the world, but it is not surprised when its witness evokes hostility from the world'.[29] Echoing Williams, they suggest, '[t]his church knows that its most credible form of witness (and the most "effective" thing it can do for the world) is the actual creation of a living breathing, visible community of faith'.[30] *Liturgy and Society* is a call to the same sort of Church. Hebert eschews the accommodationism of the Church in Germany between the wars, and recognised that over-association with the state leads not only to compromise but also to the radical disassociation of the Church from being the community of the cross. The quality of the Church's life is a witness to the gospel. However, for Hebert the Church's integrity is not equated to purity because the Church exists for the sake of the kingdom which is expressed in its contribution to the Common Good. As I have shown, Hebert locates the impulse and source of that manner of life in the Eucharist. Williams develops this, but by citing Dix as the inspiration (not Hebert) and his notion of *homo eucharisticus*: 'a humanity defined in its eucharistic practice'.[31]

Chile in the 1970s is an extreme but salutary case. Cavanaugh's description of the failure of the Church to be incarnate, having forgotten both her dogma and sense of necessity to engage robustly in society – however understandable that is in the face of state-sponsored violence and oppression – powerfully recalls the Church to the need to function in the modern world and not retreat. For Cavanaugh that functioning is liturgically shaped and inextricably bound to eucharistic practice.

A Dissonant Voice

The novelist Ian McEwan is acknowledged as one of the 'New Atheist' school, whose texts are united by 'the conviction that religious belief is not simply irrational but immoral and dangerous'.[32] McEwan's treatment of narrative and personhood is outside a religious framework, as is the way he treats the connection of the individual to society. This is directly at odds with Hebert, Smith and Cavanaugh, yet McEwan's work demands consideration by theologians for the themes it opens up and areas it explores. Donna Lazenby calls such a consideration a 'diagnostic space', a diagnostic space that opens up.[33] Hebert's work appears to be everything that McEwan's is not: dogmatic, bound to form and convention, religious outlook and practice, and not totalitarian. Smith proposes that the consumer culture of late modernity constitutes its own liturgy that is deeply implicated in the cultural formation of our times: passionately concerned with issues around formation, we might say he critiques *society shaping*. He points to the corporate, societal liturgy of consumerism. Cavanaugh describes an ecclesial failure which is reversed, he suggests, through liturgical practice and becomes the starting point for engagement in the politics of a particularly brutal totalitarian environment. Cavanaugh's treatment of identity and narrative is from an explicitly eucharistic position. There is more to McEwan's use of 'everything – free speech, individuality, rationality and even a secular experience of the transcendental – that religion seeks to overthrow'.[34] The measure of *Liturgy and Society*'s enduring value is how it can be used to suggest a vision that is more expansive about being human, human society and flourishing than McEwan.

McEwan sits within a contemporary genre of writing that captures something of the *zeitgeist* of the late modernity of the early twenty-first century. Considering McEwan opens up concerns that manifest themselves in contemporary society. For McEwan and other 'New Atheist' authors literature *replaces* religion; but, as Lazenby argues, it could be said that 'things that are claimed to be especially precious and redemptive about literature are actually recycled *religious* ideas'.[35] McEwan articulates the sense of a lack of purpose and hope that characterises post-Christendom. He also seeks to articulate something that points to mystery and purpose outside the religious sphere. If it is a recycling, then ideas that he uses will be found to be similar to those of religion, albeit mutated. Therefore as we read Hebert alongside McEwan there are recognisable concerns that emerge, yet are handled quite differently.

McEwan and others 'identify religion with a failure of moral imagination'; and, we shall see, religious people are implicated in such failures. Nevertheless, what our treatment of Hebert recalls us to is the sense that within the 'moral imagination' of Christianity the narrative is of recovery from such failures, implicit and explicit, in eucharistic practice.[36] This embodied eucharistic narrative is, as Lazenby puts it, of other Christian practices, '[a] powerful invitation to people to locate themselves within the situations of others, precisely in order to realize the moral landscapes of their life, so that they may develop their spiritual, empathetic and imaginative view of reality'.[37] As noted above, McEwan's work demands consideration by theologians for the themes it opens up and areas it explores. Indeed, Rowan Williams notes that McEwan's work, notably *Atonement*, 'remind[s] us that our narratives of ourselves and others are impossible to reduce to a single line, a single point of view'.[38] The Eucharist layers the narratives of those worshipping upon the narrative of Jesus Christ so much so that his narrative is appropriated by the believer, thus effecting his or her incorporation into the self-offering of Christ to the Father.

The critique of failure of moral imagination from New Atheist authors is one that people of faith are already alert to. In this chapter we will explore two instances of failure to respond and the way in which a eucharistic sensibility redirects that failure. In the previous chapter, the eucharistic liturgy served to exemplify the connection between the daily life of the Christian in society and the sphere of liturgical worship. Having laid the foundations of a liturgical anthropology that informs the way in which liturgically shaped Christians act, our move now is from the liturgical arena into the societal one. Bound up in this move is the necessary understanding of ethics as embracing the purpose and nature of Christian decision making within Church and society. Politics is the engagement of the ethical citizen within society. This is not about party politics, but more specifically the way in which the Christian acts within the *polis*, in other words faith in the public square.

Ian McEwan: *Saturday*

In *Saturday* McEwan blends themes of 'militant atheism, evolutionary biology, neuroscience and political Neo-Conservatism'.[39] As in other of his novels McEwan task is to reawaken moral imagination. Yet, it is never clear from where that awakening comes. Lazenby suggests that 'the transformative power of redemptive events which [New Atheist authors] claim can take place through literature lacks the necessary metaphysical grounding which a religious context provides'.[40] For writers such as Martin Amis, independence of mind is as important as atheism, and this implies a decisive rejection of the religious mind which closes down thought and is not independent precisely because of the language used, typified by Hebert, of dogma, tradition and community. This raises the question of how sustainable notions of community are within the New Atheist framework, and also what spirituality becomes outside the supposed irrationality of faith.

Saturday raises questions of identity and purpose which are couched in a spiritual or mystical sounding language. It is language that hints at liturgical anthropology; whilst the 'liturgy' is formative it is not Christian liturgy. McEwan describes the central character of the book, Henry Perowne – a neurosurgeon who is operating on a young man, Baxter. Baxter had held Perowne and his family at knifepoint during a bungled break-in. Perowne had earlier identified Baxter as having a neurological condition that needed urgent attention. Later Baxter has fallen down some stairs and had head injuries. Following Baxter's accident Perowne is called to operate on him. So Perowne operates on the man who had violently threatened his family – an incident during which he also learnt that his daughter was pregnant. So this follows a traumatic experience earlier in the day:

> For the past two hours he's been in a dream of absorption that has dissolved all sense of time, and all awareness of the other parts of his life. Even his awareness of his own existence has vanished. He's been delivered into a pure present, free of weight of the past or any anxieties about the future. In retrospect, though never at the time, it feels like profound happiness. It's a little like sex, in that he feels himself in another medium, but it's less obviously pleasurable, and clearly not sensual. This state of mind brings a contentment he never finds with any passive form of entertainment. Books, cinema, even music can't bring him to this. Working with others is part of it, but it's not all. This benevolent dissociation seems to require difficulty, prolonged demands on concentration and skills, pressure, problems to be solved, even danger. He feels calm, and spacious, fully qualified to exist. It's a feeling of clarified emptiness, of deep, muted joy.[41]

It is a beguiling account of meaning construed by compressed moments into an experience of *ekstasis*, that is, a standing outside of the self.[42] It might be said to be an almost mystical experience. There is a sense of liberation conveyed by it. So what is going on here? And why might it be a legitimate way in to exploring Hebert's anthropology further? This passage represents the process of individuation out of the whole. In that respect it is entirely contrary to Hebert's liturgical anthropology. Nevertheless it is so enticingly close to mystical or religious experience that it needs to be treated carefully. On one hand it is akin to a secular, egocentric confession of faith, a seeking of 'what makes me *me*' – just as Hebert sought to do in 'What I Learnt in the House of the Lord'; on the other it is measured only by sensory stimulation.

Hebert's liturgical anthropology in the Eucharist demands a journey *into* oneself in which the Spirit shapes and configures the believer so that the same Spirit prompts and enables a journey *out of* oneself in such a way that shapes and forms the individual in relation to the Body of Christ acting – that is, functioning – in the world. It is the journey out of oneself that defines Hebert's liturgical anthropology, since it is *meaning-in-relationship* that is primary. That is the whole point of the relational character, albeit in now dated language, of 'What I Learnt in God's House', as we saw above.

So, to draw phrases from McEwan, the dissolution both of a sense of time and of the cognisance of 'the other parts of life' implies something holistic and focused in the experience undergone in which the world is no longer viewed as fragmentary, something against which Hebert warns. Liturgical anthropology is comfortable with the awareness of one's own existence vanishing and being subsumed in the life of Christ – 'it is no longer I who live, but it is Christ who lives in me' (Galatians 2.20) – and also the experience of *kairos* in which the worshipper is not bound by a chronological time, but enters into a new sense of time that is God's presence and eternity. However it is not about the atomisation of life. Williams, considering speech and time, notes that to set the self firmly in a temporal context is to initiate a 'venture of understanding' that is located in 'processes of linguistic *exchange*'.[43] This is significant because, as Williams continues, 'to be a time-conditioned self is also to be a *social* self, a self-formed in interaction'.[44] Williams asks, 'how do you "let yourself matter" to another human subject?'[45] This is something Perowne fails to do throughout the novel. His account of himself is self-consumed as well as being egocentric: as Hebert would note, an account motivated by *eros* not *agape*.[46] Interaction with others shapes who I am, says Williams, and sociality is one of Hebert's key emphases as we have seen. McEwan's account of Perowne reveals a selfhood formed without need of social interaction. Williams notes:

> If my selfhood is determined from outside, if . . . it simply plays out a determined script, I am not in fact 'uttering' at all: I am performing an operation whose outcomes are principle predictable. Either of these perspectives would be an avoidance of risk, of the moment of self-abandoning uncertainty involved in actually saying who I am – allowing myself to be comprehended, in Cavell's phrase, and owning my expression as mine.[47]

The use of the word 'operation' aside, this diagnoses Perowne's issue of identity and his fragmentary perception of himself, as if the only validation of himself is in his work, albeit highly skilled.

McEwan suggests that the surgeon at work is working as an artist who is at one with his medium. For a liturgical anthropology this suggests a profoundly incarnational sense that not only is the Incarnate Word the potter with the clay, but at the same time is the clay. Indeed the clay is so profoundly associated with the potter that the audacious claim of *theosis* may be made, and that Sonship is shared with Christ. This is not in any sense a passive relationship. The inadequacy of worship that has lost the vision of active participation is for Hebert an empty exercise which both diminishes the social and corporate identity of the Body of Christ and strips away the priestly character of the People of God: the priest then becomes the exclusive locus, not inclusive focus, of the priestly action of Christ in the Eucharist, and the sacrament itself a parody of the Body of Christ.

McEwan's description of working with others echoes that sense of Hebert's corporately generated liturgical anthropology, although the sense of 'benevolent dissociation' echoes a dangerously interiorising tendency that over-spiritualises. What can emerge is a totalitarianism in which the individual is lost within the Body, with a consequent and concomitant loss of identity without the individual imposing his or her identity to the detriment of the corporate character of the body. The apparent passivity of much worship – whether in an overformal distant form of worship or an over-familiar comfortable style of worship – strips away the sense of liturgy being engaged with, and any sense of the difficulty, demands and danger involved. Active participation, of the sort envisaged by Hebert, shapes a liturgical anthropology that is anything but passive or dissociated, and is demanding and potentially harrowing both within the time of worship and in the acting in society that precedes and follows: this is integral to that liturgy. An image of this is described by Hebert in his description of the way in the Liturgical Movement sought to restore to the laity their participation in the prayer of the Church.[48]

McEwan's narrative gives expression to the effect of liturgy on the worshipper, yet does not fully account for it. The language of feelings can be a distraction in that it potentially subjectifies the experience undergone. Yet, just as with beauty – something which postmodernism has great difficulty in acknowledging, let alone identifying – 'calmness', 'spaciousness' and 'qualification to exist' are evocative and generative, rather than restrictive, words and phrases. McEwan's narrative evokes a sensuality that is integral to communion, the embodiment necessary for the act of communion, in which feelings and the senses are engaged. McEwan appears to engage an embodied sensibility in his reference to sex and the implication of physicality; however, he describes

Perowne's experience as 'clearly not sensual'. This is curious, since operating on a human body is a sensual experience, even if it is not an erotic one. Liturgical anthropology is necessarily embodied, sensual and filled with desire. This embodiment is also integral to the living out of liturgy post-dismissal.

The term *spaciousness* is one that prompts consideration for a liturgical anthropology. It would seem to originate in, or at least be deeply associated with, Buddhist meditation practices.[49] It is certainly an evocative term. However, spaciousness is not neutral and can be disorientating. Sara Maitland alerts us to 'confusions about time and/or spatial location', but that there is also is a 'more common and profound' phenomenon in which 'the self/other (or the I/thou) boundary becomes unclear'.[50] Maitland affirms the mystical dimension to this experience of spaciousness. This makes it hard to set alongside a liturgical setting.

Liturgy often seems to rule out mysticism, in the sense that liturgy has prescribed forms and patterns that appear to put a constraint on mysticism. However, Hebert's near contemporary Evelyn Underhill in *The Essentials of Mysticism* notes that 'the Christian mystic . . . grows up from the Christian society'.[51] Therefore the mystic is not cut off from the Body. Indeed, she sees the mystic as rooted in liturgical action and language and the liturgy, 'bear[ing] the stamp of mystical feeling'.[52] Spaciousness can be appropriated if it implies engagement with the physical space in which liturgy is performed and informs how the built environment interacts with the liturgical spaciousness created in word, gesture and encounter. This is not a given in spaces dedicated to the performance of liturgy:[53] this applies as much, if not more, to buildings that are notionally 'functional' or 'flexible'. Indeed to describe a building as 'functional' or 'flexible' potentially overdefines what might be expected in the building and proscribes the possibility of unexpected delight or spaciousness into which space God might lead or guide.

Despite its spatial implications, spaciousness is not simply a concept that has to relate to the physical environment of a building; but neither is it liturgically a vacuum into which anything might enter, but rather what emerges when the self is engaged in worship so as to allow space for God to dwell. The ways in which such space for the indwelling of God is created moves us, as Underhill sees it, between habit that is potentially ritualist and attention that is potentially pietist.[54]

Further exploration of the liturgical dimension of spaciousness is the resting in Sabbath, which itself is a 'Saturday'. Sabbath points to a different form of spaciousness, one that is captured both liturgically and theologically in both Judaism and Christianity. In Christian theology Hans Urs von Balthasar asserts the Trinitarian aspects of Holy Saturday and links it to the doctrine of *kenosis*,[55] whilst Williams picks up on the spaciousness created by the Sabbath of Holy

Saturday: 'The empty tomb *is* . . . an absence, in the sense that the Risen One is
not there for the legitimation of any particular programme.'[56] He develops this
further by suggesting that the emptiness, or spaciousness, of the empty tomb
tradition, especially in Mark, precludes the Church controlling the outcome of
her own life. Sabbath spaciousness is not a clearing of mental space, creation of
a vacuum or the dismissal of distraction. Rather, it is an active sense resting in
the spaciousness of God; it is profoundly un-egocentric and kenotic.

Williams asserts the necessity of understanding that Jesus is neither the
dead founder of the Church nor the heavenly Lord 'whose power and identity
is untrammelled by any record of historical acts and sufferings'.[57] Liturgy that
forms the Body of Christ demands spaciousness. The impulse of the religious
mind is to fill the space 'between the cherubim' and to exalt its own mores
to the empty throne. Dogma or liturgical forms are often given that exalted
place. However spaciousness demands that, as Williams suggests, the temptation is either to fill the space by casting Jesus as either a dead founder who
needs to be remembered, as if a mental act of will guarantees fidelity to a
once preached message, or by casting him as a Heavenly Lord who is radically
removed from materiality. It is easy to want to place liturgy or sacraments into
the space to claim of it that it uniquely straddles the space holding both the
story and giving the materiality to it, but that runs the grave risk of suggesting that the space is to be filled other than with 'the aniconic and paradoxical
"presence" of the God of the covenant'.[58]

The practical, pastoral, ethical outcome of this reflection on spaciousness
is to reject the presumption, *contra* McEwan, that in engagement with society the Church brings a pre-packaged set of truth claims. Williams suggest
that the theologian's task is often 'less the speaking of the truth . . . than the
patient diagnosis of untruths, and the reminding of the community where its
attention belongs'.[59] In *Liturgy and Society* Hebert does precisely that, so that
both dogma and liturgy are not simply seen as answers given to silence critics,
within or without the Church, but rather the given framework – supremely
the Eucharist – which generates the reminder to the community of where its
attention belongs, that attention to her inner life is always for the sake of the
kingdom. This further necessitates the rejection of consumerism, individualism and totalitarian corporatism, all of which deflect the Church's gaze from
the point of her existence.

Finally, spaciousness implies an unhurried and eschatological understanding of the liturgical formation of the person: taking 'no thought of the
harvest'. Essentially this is identification through baptism with the *mysterium
paschale*, of the grain that has fallen into the earth. The paschal character of
baptism and Eucharist is primarily in confronting the spaciousness of death
in the hope of resurrection. Hebert speaks of Easter Eve and the blessing of

the font which takes place within the liturgy, drawing on the language of the font as a womb.[60] The Sabbath (Holy Saturday) within the Triduum Sacram is regenerative. It is a space from which life springs forth. The character of Perowne offers a diagnostic space. Diagnosis of a medical condition leads to the surgery he is undertaking, so he becomes a diagnosing figure. The diagnosis that can be made of him is that he finds his meaning and existence not in the reality of the familial relationships that surround him, but in the skill of his work. It is in a fractured doctor/patient relationship that he finds his fulfilment and meaning in existence. Theologically this is an inadequate and impoverished account of the human condition. Perowne's relationships echo Hebert's account of the dehumanisation of the working man as expressed in Eliot's *The Rock*.[61] Furthermore Perowne's reaction to the man he is operating on is a facing of mortality, both the patient's and his own. As Hebert notes, death is 'the one thing common to all mankind, amid all diversities of character, temperament, race, and education; even the pitiful sub-human beings in the *Brave New World* have got to die'.[62] Perowne finds his patient, Baxter, abhorrent not only because of his moral choices and action; he also has a visceral loathing of his attitudes and appearance. Yet Perowne shares with Baxter the fact of mortality. Ultimately Perowne's relationship with Baxter is wordless and is less *with* and more *for*. Operating and saving his life is *for* him and not *with* him, which is the heart of redemption as understood theologically: the saving death is both *for* us and *with* us in our humanity.[63]

Perowne finds meaning in a wordless operation. The meaning of language and language of meaning in worship is problematic and complex. In *The Edge of Words*, Rowan Williams explores the habits of language and its capacity to open out possibilities rather than close them down. Language for him is not a simple matter of cause and effect, or even of descriptive accuracy. So, reference to the divine in liturgy is also multi-layered. Graham Hughes' exploration of 'worship as meaning' reveals such complexity and the strategies with which it might be tackled: is it the ethnographic or impressionistic approach; is it gauging what might be called 'worshipful'; is it the separation or interface of the official or public meaning or the private or normative readings?[64] The search for personal or individual meaning has a magnetic pull away from the social and political to the individual.

Different theological voices give another bearing on how meaning is understood in worship. Hebert resides primarily in normative theology (what he would call the dogmatic approach). For him the meaning found in worship is to be seen through the theological lens of what is understood to be authoritative. What is paramount to him is the theology which determines the way in which churches worship and form disciples, since what is done is the outcome and meaning of what ought to be done and what is said to be done. It is the embodied and enacted theology that is most significant as the way in which the ecclesiological character of a community is defined. That becomes the connection between liturgy and society. Therefore liturgical meaning is not simply in the experience or feeling engendered by it, but by the extent to which it can be said to exist for the sake of the kingdom and to what extent it is practised within the community. Hardy encapsulates Hebert's tendency in describing 'the *intensity of participation* in the new life of Christ and in the *extension of its benefit*'.[65] Whilst operating Perowne has a social function, one that is deeply beneficial to society and the individual concerned; it sees no further than its end and function. It is sociality and not *sociopoiesis*, as Hardy describes it.

Yet Perowne feels 'fully qualified to exist'. On a simple level this is the reflection of a man who feels that his work has given him a way into a deeper level of existence that is validating and affirming. It is also a theologically pregnant and evocative phrase. First, fullness and abundance are rich New Testament themes: the call to fullness of life; the 'taking hold of the life that really is life'; the overflowing nature of *pleroma*.[66] Irenaeus speaks of the glory of God being the human person 'fully alive'.[67] Secondly, qualification evokes both completion *and* provisionality. In the first sense someone who has qualified is someone who is authorised, authenticated – as, for instance, a doctor or graduate. Following a course and sitting examinations, they are now fully qualified. There is both a giveness to this sort of qualification and an associated reward for something completed. Qualification gives authority to act in the name of something, most often an institution, greater than one's own self. The second sense of qualification implies provisionality: qualifications can be attached to a statement or dispensation. If something, or someone, has a qualification attached to it/them then it is restricted or limited in some way.

This dual meaning of qualification holds in tension the sense of accomplishment in worship, and also the way in which worship cannot be said to accomplish anything: the worshipping community, and the worshipper, does not of itself *achieve* anything in worship; it can only be said to offer. Williams notes something of the provisionality of qualification, speaking of it as a way of 'shifting the entire set of expectations within a scheme of discourse'.[68] The qualification of the Church to worship is that in worship offering of praise and thanksgiving is made to God, and that the act of corporate worship itself is a qualification *to* and a qualification *on* mission and engagement with society. That is to say, the Church is fully qualified to be commissioned to engagement with the world, but it goes with the qualification that the mission engaged in is God's already.

The call to existence is God's call. Creation is the naming into existence of all things animate and inanimate.[69] There is an echo too of Paul's insistence at the Areopagus that the unknown God is not one whom we as human beings call into existence, 'formed by the art and imagination of mortals', but the one who calls us into existence, 'in whom we live and move and have our being' (Acts of the Apostles 17.16–34). It is not about an individual or corporate therapeutic experience, or even a point on a journey. Worship, and its meaning, is located in the forming and forming again of the people of God in engagement with society, by acting as the society of witnesses to the change already effected in Jesus Christ. Hebert does not see worship in terms of an individual or even a group therapeutic experience or destination on a spiritual journey. His account of worship is profoundly ecclesial, rejecting any sense that worship might be self-indulgent: Christ makes the Church 'fully qualified to exist', expressed by St Paul in Colossians (1.15–20).

One approach to understanding what the function of the Church is in the modern world might be to look at its liturgy and to say, 'this is what it looks like'. The danger is that the Church's worship is reduced to being seen as containing certain components that seek to build a fellowship or group, to inspire to good action and to give a sense of comfort, assurance and fulfilment. This involves corporate singing, inspirational reading and refreshments. This distillation of liturgy in this way can be seen in the 'atheist Church' 'Sunday Assembly', which understands itself as a movement for 'wonder and good'. Its website speaks of its gatherings in this way:

> Hearing talks, singing as one, listening to readings and even playing games helps us to connect with each other and the awesome world we live in . . . we aim to provide inspiring, thought-provoking and practical ideas that help people to live the lives they want to lead and be the people they want to be.[70]

The implication is that the Church has something worth replicating if the dogmatic elements are stripped out. That is liturgy without ecclesiology, dogma or a sense of *sociopoiesis*. Worship is always qualified in that it looks beyond itself to God and the coming kingdom. Worship is anticipatory: the witnessing character of the Church and the formation and configuration of the Church as the Body of Christ is for the sake of the kingdom in the world.

The Liturgical Response

Worship engaged in truthfully is worship that acknowledges the relational quality of existence and the often fractured nature of relationship. To be part of the Body of Christ is not to be satisfied with the fractured body, but to respond to the imperative for the unity of the Church, 'that the world may believe that you sent me' (John 17.21). Hence Hebert's concern for worship and the function of the Church in the modern world turns outward: just as he is impatient with the consumerism of the quiet making of '*my* communion', he is equally so of a Church that makes its communion with no reference to the world.[71] Worship that only is about self or ecclesial affirmation and meaning cannot typically account for, or engage with, barrenness or bewilderment. Liturgy has an objective character about it so that it does not become an end in itself. Hebert never argues for an unchanging liturgy, quite the contrary; but asks fundamental questions of the nature of the Church and her worship in order that she might become more fully what she is called to be. This also feeds the imperative for unity which is of such significance for Hebert; unity is fundamentally a relational priority.

Liturgy should not remove the believer from the world as if the two are unconnected. Engagement in liturgy does however heighten the awareness of the daily lived experience of discipleship. The liturgical being, such as envisaged by Hebert, is a person who responds to the call of the Church to worship and is therefore gathered in, but who also responds to the commission of the Church to live and work to God's glory in the world. Hebert's insistence on the significance of dogma is a claim to having the norms and standards of Christian living understood and applied to everyday life. In this sense Hebert claims an ethical dimension to the function of the Church in the modern world. His work, *contra* individualism, brings an ethic that is rooted in community, a community that is a liturgical community seeking to be and become more fully the Body of Christ.

Hebert conceives of human beings and being human in a very clear way – 'There are only two things in the universe that man can ultimately live for: God or himself.'[72] His anthropology is totally bound up in his conception of worship. The dominant theme of Hebert's conception of worship is that it is never private, atomised or individualistic, since such worship is idolatrous because it directs adoration to the self and not outwards (to God). This has a social dimension in the economy of the Common Good. The individual finds his or her place within corporate worship, but it is not a corporatism in which personality is subsumed and identity lost; quite the contrary, the individual finds his or her identity within the corporate sphere. Thus 'self-fulfilment' as a concept is alien to Hebert's way of thinking: fulfilment of self can only take place through God in company with others. In that sense he has a Johannine sensibility that love of God has to be made real in love for others (1 John 4.20).

Worship is the deflection of the self from the Ego. For Hebert the redemptive work of Christ is that 'Christ died on the Cross and rose again to save man from himself and redeem him to God.'[73] As Hebert develops this theme he draws upon Anders Nygren's conception of *agape* and *eros*, and does not merge them as we saw with Smith. This is not surprising on one level, as Hebert translated the work from the Swedish; but more fundamentally it frames his notion of a life turned out towards God and his creation, including human society, and not a life turned in on itself. This he develops in part to counter the 'characteristic limitations of Liberal theology with regard to belief in God' as he states:'In the faith of the Bible and the Church, God is the living God; He is creative and spontaneous Agape. But to the whole liberal and humanistic tradition god is not the Seeker but the Sought, not Agape but the object of Eros.'[74] Hebert is constantly alert to any sign of individualism within the life and practice of the Church. He sees mysticism in this context:

> Mysticism, the typical expression of the Way of Eros, is manifestly for an *elite*, for the religiously gifted, for the few choice souls. It is a solitary path; the mystic pursues his way alone, and is not thereby united with his fellows. It does not involve any redemption of the body, since it proceeds by the exercise of the faculties of the mind and spirit, and in its pagan forms it desires above all to escape from the body. And in so far as it proposes to attain to the end of union with God by mystical experience, it stands in no particular need of the Incarnation or of the sacraments.[75]

Mysticism represents fracture as far as Hebert is concerned and is associated with *eros*, which he sees as human activity.[76] The issue is the distance that mysticism might put between knowledge of God and the incarnation and sacraments. Hebert may have had in mind the sort of example, given by Kenneth Kirk, of the early hermits avoiding the reception of Holy Communion: 'I do not need the communion for I have seen Christ Himself to-day.'[77] Kirk illustrates this further in suggesting the link between the ascetic denial of the good things of life and the Eucharist is a good thing, therefore to be denied. And in a similar spirit, 'the Church is a family, and as with the natural family all participation in its life is to be given up by the monk for Christ's sake'.[78] All this contrasts with Kirk's account of mysticism as a 'the greatest of human accidents' which comes to all daily:'What Christianity offers with its fellowship and sacraments . . . its preaching of the Incarnate Son of God, is the same vision of increasing plenitude'.[79]

Hebert is emphatic that:

> [W]orship or adoration is the *collective act of the Church*, and is the confession of the *common faith* with regard to the foundation on which the universe and human society rests: it is also the personal act of each individual, the charter of his freedom as a child of God.[80]

Hebert's project is encapsulated in this liturgical anthropology that has a truly societal impact as the person is shaped, renewed and liberated by participation in liturgy. McEwan's description of spaciousness, meaning and existence complements Hebert's anthropology and does not threaten it, because, as Lazenby argues, the New Atheist approach takes and recycles religious language. Hebert, then, can be appropriated today not simply in enriching reflection on the nature of the Church, or of mission, or in the function of the Church in the modern world, but in being a creature of God.[81] As a creature of God the liturgically shaped person acting in society also becomes equipped in Christian apologetic.

What Might the Liturgically Shaped Person Look Like in this Context?

McEwan's approach to personhood is profoundly remote and atomising and ultimately lonely. Politics is necessarily social and involves negotiation. To miss the dimension of society and sociality in politics misses something fundamental to humanity. It is this fundamental that liturgy picks up. The New Atheist stable of authors draws attention to the failure of moral imagination. For Hebert the liturgy is the place in which that coherent framework is given, which equips the worshipper for mission and to function in society, drawing from a deep moral imagination. Liturgy is the expression of the Church's dogma that keeps it faithful to the gospel. Nevertheless the statement made at the beginning of this book was that the person is at stake in this (the task of the functioning of the Church in the modern world) as much as the Church herself.

The challenges of the diagnostic space opened up by McEwan come to the Church in how she envisages the person acting in contemporary society and what reference points distinguish the Christian believer from the description of Perowne and Sunday Assembly. The liturgical response offered above suggests that Hebert's sees liturgy involving the formation of those who live beyond a Sunday encounter but who are shaped and formed by it in such a way that their discipleship informs their decision making and actions, in George Herbert's words, 'seven whole days, not one in seven'.[82] This is a patient process, as Hebert knows well but as Smith describes too. The long-term, patient forming of communities of wisdom that then form others runs counter to the atomising and egocentric tendencies of a character such as Perowne. This pursuit of wisdom begs the question of how those who are essentially introspective can fully engage in the delight and wonder of creation if not relationally implicated in it. Cavanaugh's work also illustrates that a body of people that do not have a public presence become anonymous and untrue to that which holds them to account; in Walker's phrase 'gospel amnesiacs'. This finally comes down to the understanding of being human beyond the intellect and into an expansive vision of humanity that lives beyond itself.

Conclusion

The subtitle of *Liturgy and Society* is 'The Function of the Church in the Modern World'. In this final chapter different theological ways in which the Church can function in the modern world and the challenges that it faces have been explored. This has been with the underlying conviction that Hebert has that worship spills out into the world and informs what is made of that world by those who worship. McEwan's work gives a sense of the de-Christianised narrative of contemporary society into which the Church speaks and acts. A positive response to McEwan is that in its conception of being human Christianity offers a larger vision through its liturgy which draws from deeper sources than sociability or *esprit de corps*. The ecclesiological values of the Church – her corporate nature, dogma and sense of truth – come under more sustained pressure today than in Hebert's time, yet are enduring and capable of flourishing. The fostering of worshipping communities pursuing wisdom, as described by Smith, echoes Hebert's vision in many ways because it is rooted in the virtues and practices that shape disciples to act and witness. Cavanaugh demonstrates that anonymity serves Church and society poorly when the Church neglects the priority to function, visibly, in the modern world. The Eucharist and eucharistic practice generate, for him, a causal relationship between the theology of the Eucharist and societal change.

Hebert asks, '[c]an anything but this common faith and this organic life re-create our secular politics?'[83] This is a rhetorical question that has been explored in this chapter. If it is a question that closes down the debate then Hebert is misread; rather, he opens up a question to the Church:

> Are we demonstrating to our own satisfaction, after the manner of apologetic, that Christianity is true? Does this claim stand in view of the seeming fact that Christianity has failed, and that a civilisation which grew up under the aegis of the Church is in the process of collapse? Any one who wishes may point out the Church's failure, and criticize her shortcomings. Only let him beware lest his criticism of the Church's sins be, in fact, a psychological self-defence to save him from confessing his own; lest, in picking holes in the Church's doctrines, he should be seeking to hide from himself his own unpreparedness to respond to Truth.[84]

Hebert is not content for the Church to rest secure in any past 'achievement', but always to live in future hope. This is the answer to the New Atheists, and also those Christians who want their liturgy to serve a sense of group wellbeing, their mission to be about their own purpose and not God's or see ecclesiology as their Church existing only for her own sake. This is the common faith that re-creates secular politics, which is why ongoing reflection on her worship, liturgy and ways of forming disciples is fundamental. It is this vision of the kingdom that is sustaining: 'For us also, present imperfection and conflict are shot through with the triumph that is still future.'[85]

Notes

1 Hebert, *Liturgy and Society*, 234.
2 Hebert, *Liturgy and Society*, 234.
3 Matthew Guest, Elizabeth Olsen and John Wolffe, 'Christianity: The Loss of Monopoly', in *Religion and Change in Modern Britain*, eds Linda Woodhead and Rebecca Catto (London: Routledge, 2012), 57–78.
4 This is particularly true of the young; see Matthew Guest et al., *Christianity and the University Experience: Understanding Student Faith* (London: Bloomsbury, 2013).
5 Smith, *Desiring the Kingdom*, 23, see also 19–23.
6 Smith, *Desiring the Kingdom*, 19.
7 Smith, *Desiring the Kingdom*, 19.
8 Smith, *Desiring the Kingdom*, 155.
9 Smith, *Desiring the Kingdom*, 173–4.
10 Smith, *Desiring the Kingdom*, 174.
11 Smith, *Desiring the Kingdom*, 209, his italics.
12 Smith, *Desiring the Kingdom*, 207.
13 Smith, *Desiring the Kingdom*, 207.
14 Smith, *Desiring the Kingdom*, 208.
15 Smith, *Desiring the Kingdom*, 208–9.
16 Smith, *Desiring the Kingdom*, 212.
17 Smith, *Desiring the Kingdom*, 205.
18 Bryan D. Spinks, *The Worship Mall: Contemporary Responses to Contemporary Culture* (London: SPCK, 2010).
19 Spinks, *The Worship Mall*, xvi.
20 'Leo [the Great] frequently links mystery (*sacramentum*) and example (*exemplum*) in his sermons, and, thus, makes an explicit connection between the liturgical celebration of the divine mysteries and fidelity to the divine pattern in Christian praxis'; in Robinson, 'Informed Worship and Empowered Mission', 530.
21 Williams, *Faith in the Public Square*, 96.
22 William Cavanaugh, *Torture and Eucharist: Theology, Politics and the Body of Christ* (Oxford: Blackwell, 1998), 137.
23 It is important to note that Cavanaugh's assertion of the change in Chile has not gone unchallenged. Without dismissing it, Cavanaugh's work should be read in a wider context of what was happening in Chilean society and politics. Other forces were also at work. See David Martin, *Forbidden Revolutions: Pentecostalism in Latin America, Catholicism in Eastern Europe* (London: SPCK, 1996).
24 Cavanaugh, *Torture and Eucharist*, 123–50.
25 Hebert, *Liturgy and Society*, 65.

26 Cavanaugh, *Torture and Eucharist*, 207.

27 Hauerwas and Willimon, *Resident Aliens*, 45.

28 Hauerwas and Willimon, *Resident Aliens*, 45.

29 Hauerwas and Willimon, *Resident Aliens*, 47.

30 Hauerwas and Willimon, *Resident Aliens*, 47.

31 Williams, *Faith in the Public Square*, 96.

32 Donna J. Lazenby, 'Apologetics, Literature and Worldview', in *Imaginative Apologetics*, ed. Andrew Davison (London: SCM Press, 2011), 49. Lazenby draws on the work of Arthur Bradley and Andrew Tate, *The New Atheist Novel: Fiction, Philosophy and Polemic after 9/11* (London: Continuum, 2010).

33 Lazenby, 'Apologetics, Literature and Worldview', 47.

34 Lazenby, 'Apologetics, Literature and Worldview', 50.

35 Lazenby, 'Apologetics, Literature and Worldview', 49.

36 Lazenby, 'Apologetics, Literature and Worldview', 50.

37 Lazenby, 'Apologetics, Literature and Worldview', 50.

38 Rowan D. Williams, *The Edge of Words: God and the Habits of Language* (London: Bloomsbury, 2014), 137.

39 Lazenby, 'Apologetics, Literature and Worldview', 49.

40 Lazenby, 'Apologetics, Literature and Worldview', 51.

41 Ian McEwan, *Saturday* (London: Vintage, 2006), 258.

42 Mark A. McIntosh, *Mystical Theology: The Integrity of Spirituality and Theology* (Oxford: Blackwell, 1998), 49.

43 Williams, *The Edge of Words*, 81, original italics.

44 Williams, *The Edge of Words*, 81.

45 Williams, *The Edge of Words*, 82.

46 Hebert, *Liturgy and Society*, 140–41.

47 Williams, *The Edge of Words*, 83.

48 Hebert, *Liturgy and Society*, 125–38.

49 Buddhist Dharma Education Association, 'Advice on Meditation', http://www.bud-dhanet.net/e-learning/advicemed.html [accessed 3 May 2013].

50 Sara Maitland, *A Book of Silence: A Journey in Search of the Pleasures and Powers of Silence* (London: Granta, 2008), 71–2.

51 Evelyn Underhill, *The Essentials of Mysticism and Other Essays* (London: Dent, 1920), 29.

52 Underhill, *The Essentials of Mysticism*, 41.

53 Richard Giles, *Re-Pitching the Tent: Re-Ordering the Church Building for Worship and Mission in the New Millennium* (Norwich: Canterbury Press, 1996), 113.

54 Underhill, *Worship*, 27.

55 Hans Urs von Balthasar, *Mysterium Paschale: The Mystery of Easter*, trans. Aidan Nichols (Edinburgh: T&T Clark, 1990).

56 Williams, *On Christian Theology*, 192.

57 Williams, *On Christian Theology*, 194.

58 Williams, *On Christian Theology*, 195.

59 Williams, *On Christian Theology*, 196.

60 Hebert, *Liturgy and Society*, 59–60.

61 Hebert, *Liturgy and Society*, 200.

62 Hebert, *Liturgy and Society,* 57.

63 Samuel Wells, 'Taking Care of Neighbours' (paper presented at the Guildford Diocesan Triennial Conference 2015, Swanwick, Derbyshire, 4 June 2015), http://www.cofeguildford.org.uk/whats-on/news/detail/2015/06/11/audio-clergy-conference-2015—-taking-care-(talks) [accessed 17 June 2015].

64 Graham Hughes, *Worship as Meaning: A Liturgical Theology for Late Modernity* (Cambridge: Cambridge University Press, 2003), 115–19.

65 Hardy, *Finding the Church*, 135–6.

66 John 10.10b; 1 Timothy 6.19; Luke 6.38; cf. also Ford, *Self and Salvation*, 107–36.

67 New Advent, 'Irenaeus of Lyons *Adversus Haereses*', 4. 34. 5–7, http://www.newadvent.org/fathers/0103434.htm [accessed 20 May 2013].

68 Williams, *The Edge of Words*, 174.

69 Rowan D. Williams, *Open to Judgement: Sermons and Addresses* (London: Darton, Longman, Todd, 1994), 173.

70 Sunday Assembly, https://sundayassembly.com [accessed 9 June 2015].

71 Hebert, *Liturgy and Society*, 210.

72 Hebert, *Liturgy and Society*, 184.

73 Hebert, *Liturgy and Society*, 184.

74 Hebert, *Liturgy and Society*, 185.

75 Hebert, *Liturgy and Society*, 142.

76 Hebert, *Liturgy and Society*, 141.

77 Kenneth K. Kirk, *The Vision of God: The Christian Doctrine of the Summum Bonum* (Cambridge: James Clarke, 1934; abridged edition), 85.

78 Kirk, *The Vision of God*, 86.

79 Kirk, *The Vision of God*, 194.

80 Hebert, *Liturgy and Society*, 183, my italics.

81 Hebert, *Liturgy and Society*, 101.

82 George Herbert, 'King of Glory, King of Peace', in *Complete Anglican: Hymns Old and New*, ed. Kevin Mayhew (Stowmarket: Kevin Mayhew, 2000), 375.

83 Hebert, *Liturgy and Society*, 234.

84 Hebert, *Liturgy and Society*, 258.

85 Hebert, *Liturgy and Society*, 259.

Postscript

Three key points underlie this book. First, that the origins of the Parish Communion Movement and its influence are understated in contemporary Anglican ecclesiology and missiology – and that this is a significant deficiency. Secondly, and more importantly, that in *Liturgy and Society* Gabriel Hebert articulates an essential voice which helps to reframe current debate about the nature of the Church and mission because of his approach to Church, mission and personhood. Thirdly, in reappraising Hebert there are resonant contemporary voices that show affinity with his work whilst not having a specific link to the Parish Communion Movement. Hebert has credibility in offering a robust but irenic challenge to contemporary theological discourse. More than that the questions he raises and the method he uses give an opening into engaging with how faith is situated in the public square of contemporary society. *Liturgy and Society* is a book of its time, but one that repays careful attention today: reading it today is not a nostalgic pursuit because the issues that Hebert addresses are perennial.

In this thorough reappraisal of *Liturgy and Society* an anonymous and muted voice has been named and rearticulated. That voice is theologically *celebratory* in timbre. It is a voice that delights in the Church and her dogma and has a doxological tenor. A Church that is unaware of *Liturgy and Society* is impoverished in her reflection on her intrinsic nature and her function in the modern world. It is not that the assumptions and premises of *Liturgy and Society* are wholly absent today, but that their origin is little known. This is to the detriment of ecclesiological discourse, because the Church has always benefited from a wide range of voices and Hebert contributes to a multi-vocal theology. Those who claim a 'traditional' approach can fail to hear the robust but irenic voice of Hebert that is imaginative, ungrudging and generous. Those who see 'inherited Church' as overbearingly traditional and bound up in empty forms lose the perspective of the radicalism of Hebert in his own day.

Hebert's ability to reframe the debate about the nature of Church, mission and personhood manifests itself in the way in which he approaches the issues; by avoiding the sterility of polarisation and making the connection between the Church and the world. Both *Mission-shaped Church* and *For the Parish* are fundamentally introspective in their thinking about the Church. Hebert is extrospective. The Church is not removed from the world but is integral to the shaping of it through the shaping of individual lives, in relationship, who engage with society around them. As Hebert asks, 'it is thus that the Church has the power to create a social life, not through mere organisation but through the actualisation of the organic life of the Body. Can anything but this common faith and this organic life re-create our secular politics?'[1] His understanding, as has been shown, is very much more organic – that the Eucharist shapes persons, and the Church, by osmosis undergirded by dogma. As he insists, 'Christian worship is in the first place a confession of faith in God, and a communication of God's work of salvation; *and then* an expression of the application of that salvation to the whole of human life.'[2] The value of Hebert in contemporary discourse is to provide a necessary reminder of the contribution of the Church to the whole of human life and society. It is about faith in the public square made visible by a worshipping presence. Hebert's work accords to the 'Five Marks of Mission' of the Anglican Communion, which includes the teaching and nurturing of new believers as well as responding 'to human need by loving service' and '[transformation] of unjust structures of society'. Mission is not simply a numerical target.

Situating Hebert with contemporary writers is generative and fruitful, but the challenge inevitably is in how he can be deployed today. Williams poses a challenge for the contemporary Church, and it is one that *Liturgy and Society* has to answer too:

> Faced with the claims of non-dogmatic spirituality, the believer should not be insisting anxiously on the need for compliance with a set of definite propositions; he or she should be asking whether what happens when the Assembly meets to adore God and lay itself open to his action looks at all like a new and transforming environment, in which human beings are radically changed.[3]

The test of this argument is in Hebert's ability to respond to that challenge. If Hebert's is a retroactive proposition and is read simply as an appeal to a dogmatic, ossified Christianity, then his point is missed: orthodoxy, yes; anxious compliance, no. Rather he moves in the way Williams does when he suggests that the Christian faith is not about the acquisition of new ideas or even emotions; rather, 'it *is* moving into a set of renewed relationships with God and the world, moving into the New Creation and so understanding that the ambient world is not what we thought it was'.[4] What matters for Hebert is what liturgy is saying about the 'new humanity within the new creation'; hence his emphasis on the Church, the human person and the transformation and shaping action of liturgy, most supremely the Eucharist.[5] Hebert's is a non–utilitarian, non-anxious ecclesiology and missiology rooted in God through worship in which 'doctrine, morals and the liturgy coalesce'.[6]

Liturgy and Society develops a clear vision of a *Eucharist-shaped Church*. That vision feeds Hebert's ecclesiology, missiology and liturgical anthropology. The value Hebert places on the Eucharist is not about *how* it is done – what is worn, what style of music is used – but it is about *why* it is done and that there is active participation. Hebert does not see the Eucharist as a battleground in Anglican polity, but as a place where the relationship of individual person to one another and to God within the Church is properly expressed. That is the context of his remark that, 'the Holy Eucharist is not one service among many, but the centre of all'.[7] Therefore it cannot be a badge of a particular style of churchmanship or reduced to being an 'expression'. A functionalist approach to liturgy, in which liturgy is a 'toolkit' or solely a generator of mission, is alien to him.[8]

Hebert is not a liturgical elitist – on the contrary, he wants to open the Eucharist up to enable the recovery of the missional and formational lifegiving and enriching possibilities it offers to the world. Stephen Platten, clearly influenced by the legacy of the Parish Communion Movement, captures the spirit of Hebert as he describes liturgy as 'the air we breathe', and distils much of *Liturgy and Society* in saying that 'liturgy has a direct impact upon our *knowledge* of the faith, our *confidence* in the faith, and our *living* of the faith'.[9] That triad captures Hebert's dogmatic, celebratory and anthropological character.

Through the pastoral-prophetic character of *Liturgy and Society* Hebert has a constant eye to the function of the Church in the modern world. This ensures that his thinking compels the Church to act and engage in the world. The Church is therefore not a self-contained system that is closed to interrogation and development. Hebert does not claim this of the Church, but says, 'therefore the Church in this world does not stand as something complete, perfect and finished. When the Church seeks to present herself as if she had already attained, she is deeply false to herself.'[10]

Hebert's ecclesiology is generous about the Church and her purpose as the Body of Christ. His missiology is generous for the sake of the world. His anthropology is generous in its vision of the capacity of human beings to order their lives in such a way that they can live in hope for the future. Such a hope means that even if society is made perfect the Church is still called to exist and offer its worship. Fundamentally for Hebert, the Church lives by hope and expectation in the future, sustained by the grace of God:

> I say unto you: *Make perfect your will.*
> I say: take no thought of the harvest,
> But only of the proper sowing.[11]

Notes

1   Hebert, *Liturgy and Society*, 234.
2   Hebert, *Liturgy and Society*, p. 207, my italics.
3   Williams, *Faith in the Public Square*, 93.
4   Rowan D. Williams, 'An address by the Archbishop of Canterbury Given to a Meeting of the Alcuin Club at Lambeth Palace', http://www.archbishopofcanterbury.org/2449 [accessed 15 November 2010].
5   'An address by the Archbishop of Canterbury'.
6   Platten, 'The Uses of Liturgy', 248.
7   Hebert, *Liturgy and Society*, 207.
8   For example Gilly Myers speaks of *Common Worship* and the Book of Common Prayer as comprising 'the basic tool box of the worship leader'. In this view the tool box seems only accessible to the 'leader' and disenfranchises the congregation who no longer have ready access to texts and sources. Gilly Myers, 'Liturgical Future', in *God's Transforming Work: Celebrating Ten Years of Common Worship*, ed. Nicholas Papadopulus (London: SPCK. 2011), 149–50.
9   Platten, 'The Uses of Liturgy', 238.
10 Hebert, *Liturgy and Society*, 259.
11 Hebert, *Liturgy and Society*, 260.

Bibliography

Books and Articles

Anglican Communion News. 'Indigenous and Culture Found in Lambeth Indaba Reflections'. Accessed 22 January 2013. http://www.anglicannews.org/news/2008/08/indigenous-and-culture-found-in-lambeth-indaba-reflections.aspx.

Assmann, Jan. *Religion and Cultural Memory*, translated by Rodney Livingstone. Stanford, CA: Stanford University Press, 2006.

Aulén, Gustav. *Christus Victor: An Historical Study of Three Main Types of the Idea of the Atonement*, translated by Arthur Gabriel Hebert. London: SPCK, 2010. Originally published in 1931.

Bailey, Simon. *A Tactful God: Gregory Dix Priest, Monk and Scholar*. Leominster: Gracewing, 1995.

Balthasar, Hans Urs von. *Credo: Meditations on the Apostles' Creed*, translated by David Kipp. Edinburgh: T&T Clark, 1990.

———. *The von Balthasar Reader*, edited by Medard Kelh and Werner Löser. Edinburgh: T&T Clark, 1982.

———. *Mysterium Paschale: The Mystery of Easter*, translated by Aidan Nichols. Edinburgh: T&T Clark, 1990.

Bayes, Paul and Tim Sledge. *Mission-shaped Parish: Traditional Church in a Changing Context*. London: Church House, 2006.

Berkman, John. 'Being Reconciled: Penitence, Punishment and Worship'. In *The Blackwell Companion to Christian Ethics*, edited by Stanley Hauerwas and Samuel Wells, 95–109, Oxford: Blackwell, 2004.

Bethge, Eberhard. *Dietrich Bonhoeffer: A Biography*. London: Collins, 1970.

Bishop, Edmund. *Liturgia Historica: Papers on the Liturgy and Religious Life of the Western Church*. Oxford: Clarendon, 1918.

Bosch, David J. *Transforming Mission*. New York: Orbis. 1991.

Bradley, Arthur and Andrew Tate. *The New Atheist Novel: Fiction, Philosophy and Polemic after 9/11*. London: Continuum. 2010.

Brilioth, Yngve. *Eucharistic Faith and Practice: Evangelical and Catholic*, translated by Hebert, Arthur Gabriel. London: SPCK, 1930.

Buchanan, Colin, ed. *Anglo-Catholic Worship: An Evangelical Appreciation after 150 Years*. Bramcote: Grove, 1983.

Bunting, Ian. *Celebrating the Anglican Way*. London: Grove, 1996.

Buddhist Dharma Education Association. 'Advice on Meditation'. Accessed 3 May 2013. http://www.buddhanet.net/e-learning/advicemed.html.

Burrows, William R. 'The Importance of Liturgy in Ecclesial Mission Animation'. *Missiology: An International Review*, 38/1 (2010): 37–49.

Caird, George B. *St Luke*. London: Penguin, 1963.

Cameron, Helen, Philip Richter, Douglas Davies and Frances Ward, eds. *Studying Local Churches: A Handbook*. London: SCM Press, 2005.

Cavanaugh, William. *Torture and Eucharist: Theology, Politics and the Body of Christ*. Oxford: Blackwell, 1998.

Chadwick, Henry, trans. *St Augustine: Confessions*. Oxford: Oxford University Press, 1991.

Church Growth Research Programme. 'From Anecdote to Evidence: Findings from the Church Growth Research Programme 2011–2013'. Accessed 12 June 2015. http://www.churchgrowthresearch.org.uk/UserFiles/File/Reports/FromAnecdoteToEvidence1.0.pdf.

Clarahan, Mary A. 'Mystagogy and Mystery'. *Worship*, 83/6 (2009): 502–23.

Coakley, Sarah. *God, Sexuality and the Self: An Essay 'On the Trinity'*. Cambridge: Cambridge University Press, 2013.

Cocksworth, Christopher. *Evangelical Eucharistic Thought in the Church of England*. Cambridge: Cambridge University Press, 1993.

Cottrell, Stephen. 'Parable and Encounter: Celebrating the Eucharist Today'. In *Mass Culture: The Interface of Eucharist and Mission*, edited by Peter Ward. Abingdon: Bible Reading Fellowship, 1999, 2008.

Cray, Graham. 'Focusing Church Life on a Theology of Mission'. In *The Future of the Parish System: Shaping the Church of England for the Twenty-First Century*, edited by Steven Croft, 61–74. London: Church House, 2006.

Critchton, J.D. *Lights in the Darkness: Fore-Runners of the Liturgical Movement*. Dublin: Columba Press, 1996.

Croft, Steven, ed. *The Future of the Parish System: Shaping the Church of England for the 21st Century*. London: Church House, 2006.

————— and Ian Mobsby, eds. *Fresh Expressions in the Sacramental Tradition*. Norwich: Canterbury Press, 2009.

Cumming, G.J. *A History of Anglican Liturgy*. London: Macmillan, 1969.

Davison, Andrew and Alison Milbank. *For the Parish: A Critique of Fresh Expressions*. London: SCM Press, 2010.

Dix, Gregory. 'The Idea of "The Church" in the Primitive Liturgies'. In *The Parish Communion*, edited by Arthur Gabriel Hebert, 97–143. London: SPCK, 1937.

—————. *The Shape of the Liturgy*. London: Continuum, 1945, 2005.

Donovan, Vincent. *Christianity Rediscovered: An Epistle from the Masai*. London: SCM Press, 1982.

Edgardh, Nina. 'Towards a Theology of Gathering and Sending'. *Worship*, 82/6 (2008): 505–18.

Eliot T.S. *The Complete Poems and Plays of T.S. Eliot*. London: Faber, 1969.

Fenwick, John. 'These Holy Mysteries'. In *Anglo-Catholic Worship: An Evangelical Appreciation after 150 Years*, edited by Colin Buchanan, 9–16. Bramcote: Grove, 1983.

————— and Bryan Spinks. *Worship in Transition: The Liturgical Movement in the Twentieth Century*. Edinburgh: T&T Clark, 1995.

Ford, David. *Self and Salvation: Being Transformed*. Cambridge: Cambridge University Press, 1999.

————. Foreword to *Christus Victor: An Historical Study of Three Main Types of the Idea of the Atonement*, by Gustav Aulén, translated by Arthur Gabriel Hebert, ix–xi. London: SPCK, 2010.

————. *The Future of Christian Theology*. Oxford: Wiley-Blackwell, 2011.

———— and Daniel Hardy. *Living in Praise: Worshipping and Knowing God*. London: Darton, Longman, Todd, 2005.

Giles, Richard. *Re-Pitching the Tent: Re-Ordering the Church Building for Worship and Mission in the New Millennium*. Norwich: Canterbury Press, 1996.

————. *Creating Uncommon Worship: Transforming the Liturgy of the Eucharist*. Norwich: Canterbury Press, 2004.

————. *Times and Seasons: Creating Transformative Worship throughout the Year*. Norwich: Canterbury Press, 2008.

Girard, René. *I See Satan Fall Like Lightning*. Maryknoll, NY: Orbis, 2001.

Gittoes, Julie. *Anamnesis and the Eucharist: Contemporary Anglican Approaches*. Aldershot: Ashgate, 2008.

————, Brutus Green and James Heard, eds. *Generous Ecclesiology: Church, World and the Kingdom of God*. London: SCM Press, 2013.

Gray, Donald. *Earth and Altar: The Evolution of the Parish Communion in the Church of England to 1945* Norwich: Alcuin Club Canterbury Press, 1986.

Greggs, Thomas. 'The Eschatological Tension of Theological Method: Some Reflections after Reading Daniel W. Hardy's "Creation and Eschatology"'. *Theology*, 113/875 (2010): 339–47.

Guardini, Romano. *The Spirit of the Liturgy*. New York: Herder, 1930.

Guest, Matthew, Elizabeth Olsen and John Wolffe. 'Christianity: The Loss of Monopoly'. In *Religion and Change in Modern Britain*, edited by Linda Woodhead and Rebecca Catto, 57–78. London: Routledge, 2012.

————, Kristin Aune, Sonya Sharma and Rob Warner. *Christianity and the University Experience: Understanding Student Faith*. London: Bloomsbury, 2013.

Guiver, George. *Vision upon Vision: Processes of Change and Renewal in Christian Worship*. Norwich: Canterbury Press, 2009.

Hahn, Scott. *Covenant and Communion: The Biblical Theology of Pope Benedict XV*. London: Darton, Longman, Todd, 2009.

Hardy, Daniel. *Finding the Church*. London: SCM Press, 2001.

————. *Wording a Radiance: Parting Conversations on God and the Church*. London: SCM Press, 2010.

Hauerwas, Stanley and William H. Willimon. *Resident Aliens: Life in the Christian Colony*. Nashville: Abingdon Press, 1989.

Healy, Nicholas. *Church, World and the Christian Life: Practical-Prophetic Ecclesiology*. Cambridge: Cambridge University Press, 2000.

Hebert, Arthur Gabriel. *Intercommunion: A Theological Study of Christian Unity*. London: SPCK, 1932.

————. *Liturgy and Society: The Function of the Church in the Modern World*. London: Faber, 1935.

————. *The Form of the Church*. London: Faber, 1944.

————. *An Essay in Baptismal Regeneration*. Westminster: Dacre, 1947.

————. *Fundamentalism and the Church of God*. London: SCM Press, 1957.

————. *God's Kingdom and Ours*. London: SCM Press, 1959.

————. *Apostle and Bishop: A Study of the Gospel, Ministry and the Church Community* London: Faber, 1963.

————. Translator's Preface to *Christus Victor: An Historical Study of Three Main Types of the Idea of the Atonement*, by Gustav Aulén, translated by Arthur Gabriel Hebert, xv–xxi. London: SPCK, 2010.

————, ed. *The Parish Communion*. London: SPCK, 1937.

Higton, Mike. *Difficult Gospel: The Theology of Rowan Williams*. London: SCM Press, 2004.

House of Bishops. *Issues in Human Sexuality: A Statement by the House of Bishops of the General Synod of the Church of England, December 1991*. London: Church House, 1991.

Hughes, Graham. *Worship as Meaning: A Liturgical Theology for Late Modernity*. Cambridge: Cambridge University Press, 2003.

Hutton, Ronald. *The Rise and Fall of Merry England: The Rural Year 1400–1700*. Oxford: Oxford University Press, 1994.

Hylson-Smith, Kenneth. *The Churches in England from Elizabeth I to Elizabeth II (Volume III) 1833–1998*. London: SCM Press, 1998.

Inge, John. *A Christian Theology of Place*. Aldershot: Ashgate, 2003.

Irvine, Christopher. *Worship, Church and Society: An Exposition of the Work of Arthur Gabriel Hebert to Mark the Centenary of the Society of the Sacred Mission of Which He Was a Member*. Norwich: Canterbury Press, 1993.

————. *The Art of God: The Making of Christians and the Meaning of Worship*. London: SPCK, 2005.

————, ed. *They Shaped our Worship: Essays on Anglican Liturgists*. London: SPCK, 1998.

Jasper, Ronald C.D. *The Development of the Anglican Liturgy 1662–1980*. London: SPCK, 1989.

Jeffrey, David L. *Luke*. Grand Rapids, MI: Brazos, 2012.

Johnson, Kelly S. 'Praying: Poverty'. In *The Blackwell Companion to Christian Ethics*, edited by Stanley Hauerwas and Samuel Wells, 225–36. Oxford: Blackwell, 2004.

Johnson, Luke Timothy. *The Gospel of Luke*. Collegeville, MN: Liturgical Press, 1991.

Jones, Simon. Introduction to *The Shape of the Liturgy* by Gregory Dix, x–xxviii. London: Continuum, 1945, 2005.

Kirk, Kenneth E. *The Vision of God*. Cambridge: James Clarke, 1931.

————. *The Vision of God: The Christian Doctrine of the Summum Bonum*. Cambridge: James Clarke, 1934 (abridged edition).

Kirwan, Michael. *Discovering Girard*. London: DLT, 2004.

Köster, Wendelin, 'Recovering Collective Memory in the Context of Postmodernism'. In *Liturgy in a Postmodern World*, edited by Keith Pecklers, 32–5. London: Continuum, 2003.

Lathrop, Gordon W. *Holy Things: A Liturgical Theology*. Minneapolis: Augsburg Fortress, 1993.

————. 'Liturgy and Mission in the North American Context'. In *Inside Out: Worship in an Age of Mission*, edited by Thomas H. Schattauer, 201–12. Minneapolis: Augsburg Fortress, 1999.

————. *Holy People: A Liturgical Ecclesiology*. Minneapolis: Augsburg Fortress, 1999.

Lazenby, Donna J. 'Apologetics, Literature and Worldview'. In *Imaginative Apologetics*, edited by Andrew Davison, 46–58. London: SCM Press, 2011.

Lewis-Anthony, Justin. *If You Meet George Herbert on the Road, Kill Him: Radically Re-Thinking Priestly Ministry*. London: Mowbray, 2009.

Lössl, Josef. *The Early Church: History and Memory*. London: T&T Clark, 2010.

Lutheran World Federation. 'Nairobi Statement on Worship and Culture: Contemporary Challenges and Opportunities' 1.1. Accessed 22 March 2013. http://www.elca.org/Growing-In-Faith/Worship/Learning-Center/LWF-Nairobi-Statement.aspx.

Luzbetak, Louis J. *The Church and Cultures: New Perspectives in Missiological Anthropology.* Maryknoll, NY: Orbis, 1988.

McEwan, Ian. *Saturday.* London: Vintage, 2006.

Macfarlane, Robert. *The Wild Places.* London: Granta, 2007.

McIntosh, Mark A. *Mystical Theology: The Integrity of Spirituality and Theology.* Oxford: Blackwell, 1998.

McPartlan, Paul. *The Eucharist Makes the Church: Henri de Lubac and John Zizioulas in Dialogue.* Edinburgh: T&T Clark, 1993.

Maitland, Sarah. *A Book of Silence: A Journey in Search of the Pleasures and Powers of Silence.* London: Granta, 2008.

Marshall, Michael. *Free to Worship: Creating Transcendent Worship Today.* London: Marshall Pickering, 1996.

Martin, David. *Forbidden Revolutions: Pentecostalism in Latin America, Catholicism in Eastern Europe.* London: SPCK, 1996.

Mascall, Eric L. *Christ, the Christian and the Church: A Study of the Incarnation and its Consequences.* London: Longmans, Green, 1946.

———. *Saraband: The Memoirs of E.L. Mascall.* Leominster: Gracewing, 1992.

Mayhew, Kevin, ed. *Complete Anglican: Hymns Old and New.* Stowmarket: Kevin Mayhew, 2000.

Middleton, Arthur. *Fathers and Anglicans: The Limits of Orthodoxy.* Leominster: Gracewing, 2001.

Milbank, John. *The Suspended Middle: Henri de Lubac and the Debate Concerning the Supernatural.* London: SCM Press, 2005.

———. 'Stale Expressions: The Management-Shaped Church'. *Studies in Christian Ethics*, 21/1 (2008): 117–28.

Miyamoto, Ken. 'Mission, Liturgy and Transformation of Identity'. *Mission Studies*, 27/1 (2010) 56–70.

Mobsby, Ian. *Emerging and Fresh Expressions of Church: How Are They Authentically Church and Anglican?* Westminster: Moot Community Publishing, 2007.

Morris, Jeremy. *F.D. Maurice and the Crisis of Christian Authority.* Oxford: Oxford University Press, 2005.

———. 'Building Community: Anglo-Catholicism and Social Action'. In *Generous Ecclesiology: Church, World and the Kingdom of God*, edited by Julie Gittoes, Brutus Green and James Heard, 34–60. London: SCM Press, 2013.

Morris, Jeremy, ed. *To Build Christ's Kingdom: F.D. Maurice and His Writings.* Norwich: Canterbury Press, 2007.

Myers, Gilly. 'Liturgical Future'. In *God's Transforming Work: Celebrating Ten Years of Common Worship*, edited by Nicholas Papadopulus, 146–60. London: SPCK, 2011.

New Advent, 'Irenaeus of Lyons *Adversus Haereses*, 4. 34. 5–7'. Accessed 20 May 2013. http://www.newadvent.org/fathers/0103434.htm.

North, Philip and John North. *Sacred Space: House of God, Gate of Heaven.* London: Continuum, 2007.

Nygren, Anders. *Agape and Eros*, translated by P.S. Watson. London: SPCK, 1957.

Percy, Martyn. *Shaping the Church: The Promise of Implicit Theology.* Farnham: Ashgate, 2010.

———. *The Ecclesial Canopy: Faith, Hope, Charity.* Farnham: Ashgate, 2012.

Perham, Michael. *New Handbook of Pastoral Liturgy.* London: SPCK, 2000.

Platten, Stephen. 'The Uses of Liturgy: Worship Nourishing Mission'. *Worship*, 83/3 (2009), 234–49.

Pickard, Stephen. *Seeking the Church: An Introduction to Ecclesiology.* London: SCM Press, 2012.

Quash, Ben. 'The Anglican Church as a Polity of Presence'. In *Anglicanism: The Answer to Modernity*, edited by Duncan Dormer, Jack McDonald and Jeremy Caddick, 38–57. London: Continuum, 2003.

———. 'Treasuring the Creation'. In *The Blackwell Companion to Christian Ethics*, edited by Stanley Hauerwas and Samuel Wells, 305–18. Oxford: Blackwell, 2004.

——— and Michael Ward, eds. *Heresies and How to Avoid Them: Why It Matters What Christians Believe.* London: SPCK, 2007.

Ramsey, Michael. *Durham Essays and Addresses.* London: SPCK, 1957.

———. *The Gospel and the Catholic Church.* London: SPCK, 1990.

Ratzinger, Joseph. *The Spirit of the Liturgy*, translated by John Saward. San Francisco: Ignatius Press, 2000.

———. *Verbum Domini: The Word of God in the Life and Mission of the Church.* Vatican City: Libreria Editrice Vaticana, 2010.

Rees, F.D. 'Three Ways of Being Church'. *International Journal for the Study of the Christian Church*, 5/1 (2005): 41–57.

Reno, R.R. 'Participation: Working Toward Worship'. In *The Blackwell Companion to Christian Ethics*, edited by Stanley Hauerwas and Samuel Wells, 319–31. Oxford: Blackwell, 2004.

Richards, Sam. 'Doing the Story: Narrative, Mission and the Eucharist'. In *Mass Culture: The Interface of Eucharist and Mission*, edited by Peter Ward. Abingdon: Bible Reading Fellowship, 1999, 2008.

Rilke, Rainer Maria. *Selected Poems with Parallel German Text*, translated by Susan Ranson and Marielle Sutherland; edited by Robert Vilain. Oxford: Oxford University Press, 2011.

Roberts, Paul. 'Mission and Liturgy: A Case of Jacob and Esau? An Exploration of a Relationship in Church and Academy'. *Anaphora*, 4/2 (2010): 1–14.

Robinson, David C. 'Informed Worship and Empowered Mission: The Integration of Liturgy, Doctrine, and Praxis in Leo the Great's Sermons on Ascension and Pentecost'. *Worship*, 83/6 (2009): 524–40.

Rouwhorst, Gerard. 'In Search of Vital Liturgical Communities: The Liturgical Movement Considered from a Social Anthropological Perspective'. *Worship*, 84/2 (2010): 137–53.

Rowell, Geoffrey. Foreword to *The Gospel and the Catholic Church* by Michael Ramsey, i–v. London: SPCK, 1990.

Schattauer, Thomas H. 'Liturgical Assembly as Locus of Mission'. In *Inside Out: Worship in an Age of Mission*, edited by Thomas H. Schattauer, 1–19, Minneapolis: Augsburg Fortress, 1999.

Schmemann, Alexander. *The Eucharist: Sacrament of the Kingdom.* Crestwood, NY: St Vladimir's Seminary Press, 1987.

Sheldrake, Philip. *Spaces for the Sacred.* London: SCM Press, 2001.

Skidelsky, Robert and Edward Skidelsky. *How Much Is Enough? Money and the Good Life.* London: Penguin, 2012.

Smith, James K.A. *Desiring the Kingdom: Worship, Formation and Cultural Worldview.* Grand Rapids, MI: Baker Academic, 2009.

Spinks, Bryan. D. *The Worship Mall: Contemporary Responses to Contemporary Culture.* London: SPCK, 2010.

Stevenson, Kenneth. *Do This: The Shape, Style and Meaning of the Eucharist.* Norwich: Canterbury Press, 2002.

Stringer, Martin D. *A Sociological History of Christian Worship.* Cambridge: Cambridge University Press, 2005.

Talley, Thomas J, ed. *A Kingdom of Priests: Liturgical Formation of the People of God.* Nottingham: Grove, 1988.

Taylor, Charles. *A Secular Age.* Cambridge, MA: Belknap Press of Harvard University Press, 2007.

Temple, William. *Personal Religion and the Life of Fellowship.* London: Longman, Green, 1926.

―――, ed. *Doctrine in the Church of England: The Report of the Commission on Christian Doctrine Appointed by the Archbishops of Canterbury and York in 1922.* London: SPCK, 1938.

Thornton, Lionel. *The Common Life in the Body of Christ.* London: Dacre, 1941.

Underhill, Evelyn. *The Essentials of Mysticism and Other Essays.* London and Toronto: Dent, 1920.

―――. *Worship.* London: Nisbet, 1936.

Vaughan Williams, R., ed. *The English Hymnal.* Oxford: Oxford University Press, 1933.

Vogel, Dwight W. *Primary Sources of Liturgical Theology: A Reader.* Collegeville, MN: Liturgical Press, 2000.

Walker, Andrew. *Telling the Story: Gospel, Mission and Culture.* London: SPCK, 1996.

Ward, Peter. *Perspectives on Ecclesiology and Ethnography.* Grand Rapids, MI: Eerdmans, 2012.

―――, ed. *Mass Culture: The Interface of Eucharist And Mission.* Abingdon: Bible Reading Fellowship, 1999, 2008.

Ware, Kallistos. *The Inner Kingdom: Volume 1 of the Collected Works.* New York: St Vladimir's Seminary Press, 2000.

Wells, Samuel. *God's Companions: Reimagining Christian Ethics.* Oxford: Blackwell, 2006.

Whitson Floyd, W. 'Bonhoeffer's Literacy Legacy'. In *The Cambridge Companion to Dietrich Bonhoeffer,* edited by John W. de Gruchy, 71–92. Cambridge: Cambridge University Press, 1999.

Wilkinson, Alan. *The Church of England and the First World War.* London: SCM Press, 1978, 1996.

Williams, Rowan D. *Teresa of Avila.* London: Continuum, 1991.

―――. *Open to Judgement: Sermons and Addresses.* London: Darton, Longman, Todd, 1994.

―――. *On Christian Theology.* Oxford: Blackwell Publishing Ltd, 2000.

―――. 'Theological Resources for Re-Examining Church'. In *The Future of the Parish System: Shaping the Church of England for the 21st Century,* edited by Steven Croft, 49–60. London: Church House, 2006.

―――. 'An Address by the Archbishop of Canterbury Given to a Meeting of the Alcuin Club at Lambeth Palace'. Accessed 15 November 2010. http://www.archbishopofcanterbury.org/2449.

―――. 'Archbishop's Address at 50th Anniversary of PCPCU', Vatican City, 17 November 2010. Accessed 29 November 2010, http//www.archbishopofcanterbury.org/3078#top.

―――. 'Common Worship, Common Life: Defining Liturgy for Today'. In *God's Transforming Work: Celebrating Ten Years of Common Worship,* edited by Nicholas Papadopulus, 1–16. London: SPCK, 2011.

―――. *Faith in the Public Square.* London: Continuum, 2012.

―――. *The Edge of Words: God and the Habits of Language.* London: Bloomsbury, 2014.

Willimon, William H. *Worship as Pastoral Care.* Nashville: Abingdon Press, 1979.

Woodhead, Linda. 'Introduction'. In *Religion and Change in Modern Britain,* edited by Linda Woodhead and Rebecca Catto. London: Routledge, 2012.

Young, Frances. *God's Presence: A Contemporary Recapitulation of Early Christianity*. Cambridge: Cambridge University Press, 2013.

Liturgical Texts

Archbishops' Council, The. *Common Worship: Services and Prayers for the Church of England*. London: Church House, 2000.

Archbishops' Council, The. *New Patterns for Worship*. London: Church House, 2002.

Archbishops' Council, The. *Mission-shaped Church: Church Planting and Fresh Expressions of Church in a Changing Context*. London: Church House, 2004.

Archbishops' Council, The. *Common Worship: Times and Seasons*. London: Church House, 2006.

Archbishops' Council, The. *Common Worship: Christian Initiation*. London: Church House, 2006.

The Book of Common Prayer. Cambridge: Cambridge University Press, 1662.

Church of England. *The Alternative Service Book 1980: Services Authorized for Use in the Church Of England in Conjunction with the Book of Common Prayer, Together with the Liturgical Psalter*. Cambridge: Cambridge University Press, 1980.

Scriptural references are taken from *The New Revised Standard Version*.

Index

Printed in Great Britain
by Amazon